W9-ACU-679

A NEW AMERICAN TEA PARTY

The Counterrevolution Against Bailouts, Handouts, Reckless Spending, and More Taxes

JOHN M. O'HARA

WILEY

John Wiley & Sons, Inc.

Published by John Wiley & Sons, Inc., Hoboken, New Jersey.
Published simultaneously in Canada.

No part of this publication may be reproduced, stored in a retrieval system, or transmitted in any form or by any means, electronic, mechanical, photocopying, recording, scanning, or otherwise, except as permitted under Section 107 or 108 of the 1976 United States Copyright Act, without either the prior written permission of the Publisher, or authorization through payment of the appropriate per-copy fee to the Copyright Clearance Center, Inc., 222 Rosewood Drive, Danvers, MA 01923, (978) 750-8400, fax (978) 646-8600, or on the web at www.copyright.com. Requests to the Publisher for permission should be addressed to the Permissions Department, John Wiley & Sons, Inc., 111 River Street, Hoboken, NJ 07030, (201) 748-6011, fax (201) 748-6008, or online at www.wiley.com/go/permissions.

Limit of Liability/Disclaimer of Warranty: While the publisher and author have used their best efforts in preparing this book, they make no representations or warranties with respect to the accuracy or completeness of the contents of this book and specifically disclaim any implied warranties of merchantability or fitness for a particular purpose. No warranty may be created or extended by sales representatives or written sales materials. The advice and strategies contained herein may not be suitable for your situation. You should consult with a professional where appropriate. Neither the publisher nor author shall be liable for any loss of profit or any other commercial damages, including but not limited to special, incidental, consequential, or other damages.

For general information on our other products and services or for technical support, please contact our Customer Care Department within the United States at (800) 762-2974, outside the United States at (317) 572-3993 or fax (317) 572-4002.

Wiley also publishes its books in a variety of electronic formats. Some content that appears in print may not be available in electronic books. For more information about Wiley products, visit our web site at www.wiley.com.

Library of Congress Cataloging-in-Publication Data:

O'Hara, John M., 1984–
    A new American tea party : the counterrevolution against bailouts, handouts, reckless spending, and more taxes / John M. O'Hara.
        p. cm.
    Includes bibliographical references and index.
    ISBN 978-0-470-56798-2 (cloth)
  1. Government spending policy–United States.   2. Fiscal policy–United States.
  3. United States–Economic policy–2009–   I. Title.
    HJ7537.O43 2010
    336.73–dc22

                                                2009043715

Printed in the United States of America

10 9 8 7 6 5 4 3 2 1

To my mother and father,
Jane and John O'Hara.

CONTENTS

Bailout Nation: A Spending Timeline   xi
Foreword   xxi
Preface   xxv

Chapter 1   The Tea Parties   1
    Unorganized Organizers   2
    From Stewing to Brewing   4
    The Planning   6
    Game Day   11
    We're All Community Organizers Now   12
    The Tax Day Tea Parties   13
    Institutional Organization   13
    Striking a Balance   15
    Internal Complications   16
    No, Really, We're Nonpartisan   16
    Bureaucrats and Permits   17
    April 15, 2009: The Million-Taxpayer March 18

**Chapter 2   How We Got Here: Abandoning Principles
        and the People   21**
    Touting versus Learning from Reagan   22
    1994: The Revolution That Wasn't   28

The Quasi-Conservative Presidency of George
    W. Bush   33
How to Pretend You Are Something You Aren't   35
Meltdown   35
2008 Election   36
Hope and Change We *Can* Believe In   38
A Center-Right Nation   38

Chapter 3   **The Whistling Teapot: The Financial
                Crisis and the Bailout Nation**   **41**
                The Original Sin: The CRA   42
                The Tax Code   43
                Easy Money   43
                Take a Loan off Fannie   44
                Crisis   46
                Bailouts, Handouts, and Corporate Welfare   47
                Baby You Can Buy My Car   48
                Newspapers Bailouts   48
                Balance Sheet   49
                Account Overdrawn   49

Chapter 4   **The Political Class Reacts**   **51**
                Memo from the White House: You Just Don't
                    Get It   52
                From the Department of Homeland Security:
                    A Preemptive Strike   54
                Congress Claims We're All Astroturf 62
                Straight from the Economist-in-Chief Himself   64
                The Response from the Right   68
                Others Show a Healthy Respect   70
                Out of the Loop   71

Chapter 5   **The Media Strikes Back**   **73**
                Media Blackout   74
                Mr. Obama, Are You Watching?   75
                Propaganda and Disinformation   79

Sexual Slurs 82
Bad Comedy, Worse Commentary 85
The Racism Straw Man 88
By the Numbers 94
The Media Market Reacts 94
So You Think You Can Politic? 97

Chapter 6 Radical Ideas 99
Part I: You Earn It, We Spend It 101
Part II: The Intrusion 117
Sliding Down the Slippery Slope 138

Chapter 7 Radical Tactics 141
The Playbook 143
The Organizers 144
The Enforcers 151
Sharp Distinctions 173

Chapter 8 The Teapot Boils Over: Health Care Takes Center Stage 175
The Health Care Policy Debate 176
The Government "Solutions" 177
Real Reform 181
Now or Never 182
Something's Fishy 184
Dems Feel the Heat 185
Overwhelming Public Response 186
Town Halls 187
What Happened to "Democracy in Action"? 188
Pay No Attention to the Doctors! 190
Don't Anger the Trial Lawyers! 191
White House Spin and Spam 192
Axelrod's Turf 194
Mobilizing Union Muscle 195
Lying to Grandma 196
Free-Range or Free-Market? 197

Fannie Med?   199
A Civics Lesson for Congressmen   200

Chapter 9   The Tea Party Manifesto   203
Not Our Turf   204
Who They Are and What They Believe   206
A New Avenue   208
Popular, Not Populist   210
Dispelling False Dichotomies   212
On the Role of Government   213
Not Anti-Tax   215
Rejection of Bailouts, Handouts, and
    Wealth Redistribution   217
Personal Responsibility   219
"The Ideology of Change"   223
A Rejection of Class Warfare:
    The Unholy Trinity   224
The Rejection of False Prophets   226
Rejection of the Entitlement Ethic   229
Common Sense over Regulation   231
Rejection of the Mediocrity Ethic   231
The Counterrevolution: From Theory
    to Practice   233

Chapter 10   Rules for Counterradicals   235
The 9/12 Taxpayer March   237
Arguing from an Imperfect Status Quo   238
Honing the Message   240
Mastering the Art of Rallies   242
Utilizing Coalitions   245
Coordination not Competition   246
Promoting Principles over Personalities   247
Keeping Your Cool in a Fiery Debate   248
Using Social Networking   249
Looking beyond the Rallies   250
Taking Consistent, Principled Action   250
Maintaining Accountability and Transparency   251

Taking It to the States   252
The Right Ideals and the Right People   256
In Conclusion   258

Notes   261
About the Author   301
Index   303

BAILOUT NATION: A SPENDING TIMELINE

T he following is a timeline of significant bailout spending prior to the publication deadline of this work.

March 14, 2008   **Fed backs sale of Bear Stearns**
The Federal Government gives JPMorgan Chase $30 billion in financing to help fund its purchase of Bear Stearns.

July 30, 2008   **Treasury gets authority to rescue Fannie and Freddie**
President Bush signs the "Housing and Economic Recovery Act of 2008," which included $300 billion in new loan authority for the government to back cheaper mortgages for troubled homeowners.

Sept. 7, 2008   **Government fully takes over Fannie and Freddie**
Fannie Mae and Freddie Mac are placed under the full conservatorship of the federal government. The Treasury commits up to $100 billion in government money to each company in order to cover any losses.

Sept. 15, 2008   **Lehman goes bankrupt**

Sept. 16, 2008   **First AIG Bailout**
With AIG collapsing, the Fed bails it out with access to an $85 billion credit line.

Sept. 16, 2008   **Fed puts another $80 billion into its bank/investment rescue package**

Sept. 19, 2008   **The Treasury adds $50 billion in bailout money in order to guarantee money market funds against up to $50 billion in losses**

Sept. 20, 2008   **Treasury Secretary Hank Paulson pitches TARP bailout proposal**
Treasury Secretary Hank Paulson releases a three-page, $700 billion proposal to purchase troubled mortgage-related assets, called the Troubled Asset Relief Program.

Sept. 25, 2008   **WaMu goes under**
Washington Mutual collapses and is acquired by JPMorgan Chase.

Sept. 29, 2008   **The House rejects TARP**
The House votes down the administration's bailout proposal, which had been prepared in concert with congressional leaders.

Sept. 29, 2008   **Federal Reserve boosts foreign banks with $300 billion**
The Federal Reserve provides $300 billion to the foreign central banks taking the total amount available up to $620 billion which is available through "credit swap arrangements."

Oct. 3, 2008   **The House passes TARP**
Congress and the president feeling pressure to "fix" the financial crisis, pass a $700 billion "Emergency Economic Stabilization Act of 2008" bailing out nearly the entire financial sector.

Oct. 8, 2008   **AIG bailout, Part Deux**
The Federal Reserve agrees to lend AIG an additional $37.8 billion.

Oct. 14, 2008	**Treasury announces it will inject $250 billion into banks**
Oct. 21, 2008	**The Fed props up money market mutual funds with half trillion dollars** The Federal Reserve announces that it will provide up to $540 billion in financing to provide liquidity for money market mutual funds.
Oct. 28, 2008	**$115B—8 bailouts today** Bank of America: $15 billion Bank of New York Mellon: $3 billion Citigroup: $25 billion Goldman Sachs: $10 billion JPMorgan Chase: $25 billion Morgan Stanley: $10 billion State Street: $2 billion Wells Fargo: $25 billion
Nov. 14, 2008	**$33.6B—21 bailouts today**
Nov. 14, 2008	**Freddie Mac asks for $13.8 billion** Freddie Mac loses $25.3 billion in the third quarter of 2008 and receives $13.8 billion more from the Treasury.
Nov. 21, 2008	**$2.9B—23 bailouts today**
Nov. 23, 2008	**Citigroup bailed out** The Treasury announces that it will invest $20 billion more in Citigroup as well as help it absorb losses from bad assets.
Nov. 25, 2008	**$40B—Third bailout for AIG** The government's second restructuring of AIG's bailout done in an effort to keep the insurance giant from collapsing. An additional $40 billion is injected into the company bringing the total up to $150 billion for AIG alone.
Nov. 25, 2008	**Fed and Treasury roll TALF program** The Term Asset-Backed Securities Loan Facility (TALF) a program that will lend up to $200 billion in an effort to spur consumer lending is announced by the Federal Reserve and Treasury.

Nov. 29, 2008   **$13.8B—Freddie Mac bailout**
Dec. 5, 2008   **$3.8B—35 bailouts today**
Dec. 12, 2008   **$2.5B—28 bailouts today**
Dec. 19, 2008   **$2.8B—49 bailouts today**
Dec. 19, 2008   **Auto bailout announced**
                   The Treasury announces that it will lend billions to
                   General Motors and Chrysler in order to prevent the
                   two auto giants from having to declare bankruptcy.
Dec. 23, 2008   **$1.9B—43 bailouts today**
Dec. 29, 2008   **$5.9B—2 bailouts today for GM and GMAC**
Dec. 31, 2008   **$48.5B—9 bailouts today**
Jan. 2, 2009   **$4B—Chrysler bailout**
Jan. 9, 2009   **$14.8B—43 bailouts today**
Jan. 15, 2009   **Senate votes to release second half of bailout
                   funds**
                   The Senate votes to allow President Obama's in-
                   coming administration to use the remaining $350
                   billion in TARP funds.
Jan. 16, 2009   **Bank of America bailed out**
                   The Treasury announces that it will invest $20 bil-
                   lion more in Bank of America in addition to the
                   $25 billion given to the bank back in October of
                   2008. The government also agrees to help Bank of
                   America absorb losses from its bad assets.
Jan. 16, 2009   **$35.5B—43 bailouts today**
Jan. 20, 2009   **Barack Obama takes office**
                   Obama is inaugurated as the 44th president.
Jan. 23, 2009   **$386M—23 bailouts today**
Jan. 30, 2009   **$1.2B—42 bailouts today**
Feb. 6, 2009   **$238.6M—28 bailouts today**
Feb. 10, 2009   **Timothy Geithner announces new bailout
                   plan**
                   New Treasury Secretary Timothy Geithner unveils
                   his Financial Stability Plan which includes "stress
                   tests" of the nation's largest banks. He also an-
                   nounces that government will form a public-private
                   partnership in order to buy troubled assets from

banks and commit an additional $100 billion to the TALF program.

Feb. 13, 2009   **$429.1M—29 bailouts today**

Feb. 17, 2009   **Stimulus bill passes**
President Obama signs the American Recovery and Reinvestment Act of 2009, costing taxpayers $787 billion. According to the Congressional Budget Office, approximately $355 billion of the stimulus package will not even be used until 2011 or later. A large chunk of this includes infrastructure improvement spending that was originally supposed to be at the center of the plan but now barely makes the end notes.

Feb. 18, 2009   **Home mortgage rescue plan**
The administration announces its broad plan to avert further foreclosures and to encourage modifications to existing home mortgage loans.

Feb. 18, 2009   **$50B—1 bailout today**

Feb. 18, 2009   **Treasury ups limit for Fannie and Freddie to $200 billion**
Geithner announces that the Treasury is increasing its funding commitment to both Fannie and Freddie from $100 billion to $200 billion. More info from www.ustreas.gov.

Feb. 20, 2009   **$365.4M—23 bailouts today**

Feb. 25, 2009   **Stress tests begin**
The stress tests of the nation's 19 largest banks begin in an attempt to help the Treasury determine how much more money the banks need.

Feb. 26, 2009   **Obama administration looks to spend $750 billion more**
The Obama administration's budget guesses it will need to set aside $750 billion in order to stabilize the financial sector.

Feb. 26, 2009   **Fannie Mae asks for $15.2 billion more**
Fannie Mae reports a $25.2 billion loss for the fourth quarter of 2008 bringing its losses up to $58.7 billion

for 2008 and receives an additional $15.2 billion from the Treasury.

Feb. 27, 2009   **$394.9M—28 bailouts today**

March 2, 2009   **AIG Bailout numero quatro**
The third government restructuring of AIG's bailout with the Treasury saying that it will pony up $30 billion more bringing the total up to $180 billion.

March 2, 2009   **$29.8B—1 bailout today AIG**

March 3, 2009   **$20B—1 bailout today**

March 3, 2009   **Federal Reserve launches TALF program**
The Fed and Treasury announce the launch the Term Asset-Backed Securities Loan Facility (TALF) program in an effort to increase lending.

March 4, 2009   **Administration launches homeowner bailout**
Under the administration's Homeowner Affordability and Stability Plan, the Treasury pledges to spend $75 billion on restructuring mortgage loans.

March 6, 2009   **$284.7M—22 bailouts today**

March 11, 2009   **Freddie Mac receives $30.8 billion more after bad quarter**
Freddie Mac reports a $23.9 billion net loss for the fourth quarter of 2008 and receives $30.8 billion from the Treasury bringing Freddie's total bailout to $44.6 billion so far.

March 13, 2009   **$1.5B—19 bailouts today**

March 16, 2009   **Treasury announces small business loan program**
The Treasury announces it will buy up to $15 billion in Small Business Administration loans in an effort to spur lending to small businesses.

March 16, 2009   **$15B—1 bailout today**

March 19, 2009   **Treasury announces auto parts suppliers bailout**
The Treasury announces it will provide up to $5 billion to auto part suppliers in an effort to save them from going under along with the auto companies.

March 20, 2009   **$80.7M—10 bailouts today**

March 27, 2009	**$193M—14 bailouts today**
March 30, 2009	**$35B—1 bailout today**
March 31, 2009	**$46B—Fannie and Freddie get more money**
April 3, 2009	**$54.8M—10 bailouts today**
April 9, 2009	**$3.5B—2 bailouts today**
April 10, 2009	**$22.8M—5 bailouts today**
April 17, 2009	**$40.9M—6 bailouts today**
April 20, 2009	**Treasury trims bailout in an effort to recoup bonuses**
	The Treasury charges fee in order to recoup bonuses paid to AIG employees while at the same time giving them up to $30 billion more in bailout money.
April 22, 2009	**$2B—GM receives $2 billion more**
April 24, 2009	**$121.8M—12 bailouts today**
April 29, 2009	**$780.1M—2 more bailouts today for Chrysler**
April 30, 2009	**Chrysler files for bankruptcy**
	Chrysler files for bankruptcy protection and receives $8 billion more from the Treasury in exchange for an 8 percent stake in the company.
May 1, 2009	**$3.1B—8 bailouts today, $3 billion of which goes to Chrysler**
May 8, 2009	**Fannie Mae asks for and receives $19 billion more**
	Fannie Mae reports a $23.2 billion loss for the first quarter of 2009 and receives an additional $19 billion from the Treasury.
May 12, 2009	**Freddie Mac gets $6.1 billion more**
	Freddie Mac reports a $9.9 billion net loss for the first quarter of 2009 and gets injected with $6.1 billion more from the Treasury bringing its total bailout up to $50.7 billion.
May 15, 2009	**$107.6M—14 bailouts today**
May 20, 2009	**$4.8B—GM gets $4 billion and Chrysler gets $756.9 million more in bailout money**
May 21, 2009	**$7.5B—1 bailout today**
May 22, 2009	**$108.3M—12 bailouts today**

May 27, 2009	**$7B—Chrysler gets $6.6 billion and GM gets $360.6 million in bailout money**
May 29, 2009	**$89.2M—8 bailouts today**
June 1, 2009	**GM Files for Chapter 11 bankruptcy protection**
	GM files for Chapter 11 bankruptcy and the U.S. government agrees to give them $30.1 billion in exchange for a 60 percent stake in the company.
June 3, 2009	**$23B—General Motors gets more bailout money**
June 5, 2009	**$40.3M—3 bailouts today**
June 10, 2009	**Chrysler finalizes deal with Fiat**
	Chrysler finalizes its union with Fiat creating a new company, which began operations immediately.
June 29, 2009	**Manufacturing resumes after months of idle operation in seven Chrysler plants**
June 19, 2009	**$86M—12 bailouts today**
June 26, 2009	**$3.6B—16 bailouts today**
July 8, 2009	**$30B—1 bailout today**
July 8, 2009	**Treasury to help buy up toxic securities**
	A program using up to $30 billion in TARP funds to be invested alongside private investors in order to buy toxic securities.
July 10, 2009	**$8B—3 bailouts today including $7.1 billion for GM**
July 10, 2009	**New GM begins operations**
July 17, 2009	**$91.6M—6 bailouts today**
July 24, 2009	**$87.7M—4 bailouts today**
July 31, 2009	**$10.7M—2 bailouts today**
Aug. 6, 2009	**$10.7B—1 bailout today: Fannie Mae**
Aug. 7, 2009	**$70.2M—2 bailouts today**
Aug. 14, 2009	**$1M—1 bailout today**
Aug. 21, 2009	**$9M—2 bailouts today**

Sources: Associated Press; Federal Reserve; ProPublica, "Bailout Timeline: Another Day, Another Bailout" (http://bailout.propublica.org/main/timeline/index); Investment Watch; "The List of Bailouts You Want to Remember" (http://investment-blog.net/the-list-of-bailouts-you-want-to-remember, 12/14/08).

As of this writing:

- The U.S. government and the Federal Reserve have collectively spent, lent, or committed **$12.8 trillion** in taxpayer dollars for bailouts.[1]
- When all is said and done, taxpayers could end up being on the hook for as much as **$23 trillion** from bailouts alone.[2]
- These taxpayer obligations have exacerbated an already ballooning national debt that is currently calculated to be **$11.9 trillion**.[3]
- Medicare unfunded liabilities—guaranteed benefits that must be paid by taxpayers—currently stand at over **$36 trillion**.[4]
- Social Security unfunded liabilities total over **$19 trillion**.[5]
- The total national debt, including unfunded liabilities, stands at over **$70 trillion**. That is a burden of over $233,000 per man, woman, and child in the United States.[6]
- If you remove individual citizens who don't currently pay federal income taxes (47 percent),[7] the burden doubles to **$466,000 per taxpayer** or **nearly $1 million per family**.

Despite these frightening numbers, Congress has yet to take action to significantly curb spending and bring solvency to these programs. In fact, it is poised to potentially further enable this reckless behavior by *raising* the legal national debt cap of **$12.1 trillion**.[8]

FOREWORD

*E*nough. In a word, that is the message of disgusted taxpayers across the United States fed up with the confiscatory policies of both parties in Washington. George W. Bush presocialized the economy with billion-dollar bailouts of the financial and auto industries. Barack Obama is pouring billions more down the government sinkhole. The camel's back isn't just broken. His neck and four legs have all snapped, too.

Enough. Millions of Americans joined the Tea Party movement in 2009 to protest reckless government spending in the pork-laden stimulus package, the earmark-clogged budget bill, the massive mortgage entitlement program, taxpayer-funded corporate rescues, the environmentally fraudulent cap-and-trade monstrosity, and the debt-exploding government health care takeover. Contrary to false left-wing blog smears that the hastily planned, impromptu Tea Party events were "Astro-turfed," the crowds were packed with first-time grassroots activists. They were people with families and day jobs whose usual definition of "community organizing" involves neighborhood yard sales or their kids' soccer matches.

They were members of the silent majority who decided to be silent no more.

Enough. These Tea Party protests spanned locations from the sunny Santa Monica pier to the icy streets of Chicago and Cleveland to rain-drenched Atlanta; overflowing grounds of the St. Louis Gateway Arch; massive crowds in Greenville, South Carolina; New York City; Washington, D.C.; and all points in between. The Tea Party participants held homemade signs that said it all: "Your mortgage is not my problem," "Liberty: All the stimulus we need," and "No taxation without deliberation."

At the first tax revolt in Seattle against the so-called porkulus bill, protesters waved Old Glory and "Don't Tread on Me" flags. Their handmade signs read: "Say No to Generational Theft," "Obama'$ Porkulu$ Wear$ Lip$tick," and "I don't want to pay for the SwindleUs! I'm only 10 years old!" In Mesa, Arizona, taxpayers demonstrated against President Obama as he unveiled a $100 billion to $200 billion program to bail out banks and beleaguered borrowers having trouble paying their mortgages. They jeered Obama's culture of entitlement with posters demanding: "Give Me Pelosi's Plane," "Annual Passes to Disneyland," "Fund Bikini Wax Now," "Stimulate the Economy: Give Me a Tummy Tuck," and "Free Beer for My Horses." And my favorite: "Give me liberty or at least a big screen TV."

At congressional health-care town hall meetings during the long, hot summer recess, taxpayers challenged their representatives to start reading bills before ramming them down our throats. Powerful refrains went unanswered: If government-run health care is good enough for us, why won't you legislate it on yourselves? Do you work for us or do we work for you? Can you hear us now?

The speed and scope with which Tea Party activists mobilized were due not to nefarious outside conspirators, but to social networking web sites such as Facebook and Twitter, blogs, talk radio—and to energetic, young grassroots activists like John O'Hara.

In this passionate and illuminating book, O'Hara chronicles the roots, rise, and future of the New American Tea Party movement. O'Hara dispels the left-wing myths of a top-down "angry mob"; eschews the vulgar and derogatory descriptions of Tea Party protesters used by everyone from cable TV smear merchants to former President Bill Clinton and current President Barack Obama; beats back attacks on these peaceful, ordinary citizens as "racists" and "terrorists"; and shows how the modern-day Tea Party patriots embody the founding spirit and principles of our great nation.

Disgraced Democratic Senator John Edwards was right about one thing: There are two Americas. One America is full of moochers, big and small, corporate and individual, trampling over themselves with their hands out demanding endless bailouts. The other America is full of disgusted, hardworking citizens getting sick of being played for chumps and punished for practicing personal responsibility.

Before the grassroots Tea Party movement took them by surprise, Beltway GOP strategists argued fervently that the party's traditional focus on taxes and spending had become outdated. The rebranders pitched their own expansive ideas to replace the anti-tax-and-spend agenda and inspire new voters. But what have resonated with Americans across the country are nonpartisan calls to roll back pork, hold the line on taxing and spending, end the endless government bailouts, and stop the congressional steamrollers who have pushed through mountains of legislation without deliberation. It's the three Ts, stupid: Too Many Taxes, Trillions in Debt, and Transparency.

The path to lasting Hope and Change lies with those who can make a credible case that they will support and defend fiscal responsibility. The Tea Party movement is calling out the pretenders—and is mobilized for 2010, 2012, and beyond. As one of the most popular Tea Party signs read: "You can't fix stupid, but you can vote it out."

John O'Hara's book is a living history and a call to arms: Now is the time for all good taxpayers to turn the tables on their free-lunching countrymen and their enablers in Washington. Community organizing helped propel Barack Obama to the White House. It can work for the Tea Party movement, too.

Michelle Malkin

November 2009

PREFACE

Few Americans haven't heard of the tea parties. Love them or hate them, they are in the news, they are constantly growing, and they are making a difference in the political arena.

Things didn't start out this way, though. In fact, early on, we could hardly get anyone in the media or otherwise to give us the time of day. *A New American Tea Party* chronicles how the tea party movement came to be and its place in the growing tension between competing visions of the roles of the individual and the state in American society.

The tea parties were in large part a *reaction*. Many liberal protests are in the vein of "do more for me!" while these were "do less *to* me!" Despite repeated claims by the media, the tea parties are not anti-tax protests. The average American understands taxes are necessary for fundamental functions of a government in a civil society. Just what those functions are is the sticking point. Where protestors—and most Americans—draw a clear, straight line is at bailouts and handouts for irresponsible corporations, government entities, and individual citizens.

Many have posed the question: Does the Boston Tea Party parallel work? Yes, it does. While the historical comparison isn't perfect to the "t," the general principles are identical. In the Boston Tea Party, American revolutionaries fought against the idea that tyrants in a far-off land (Britain) should dictate public policy affecting them, their children, their livelihood, and their general well-being. Today, American counterrevolutionaries fight to preserve the land these men gave their lives to create, combating the idea that tyrants in a different far away land (Washington, D.C.) should dictate public policy affecting them, their children, their livelihood, and their general well-being. The issue is no longer tea tariffs and imperial rule, but bailouts and handouts, stimulus in the face of deficits, cap and trade, universal health care, and the like dictated against the will and interest of the people, and at the peril of future generations and the nation as a whole.

When not being attacked as a bunch of anti-tax protesters, the tea party movement has been framed—incorrectly—as nothing more than a conservative tantrum against liberals, as a populist uprising, or as a disgruntled reaction to the Obama administration. This book will show that this movement is actually part of an inevitable blowback in a battle over America's constitutional principles.

I am not a paid activist nor a professional pundit. Through a variety of circumstances and a little luck I did, however, become a part of a movement that has involved millions of Americans in the political process like never before and has permanently changed the political landscape of our time.

While I was integrally involved in sowing the seeds of this popular uprising, I am not *the* tea party organizer nor am I the official spokesman for the movement. Such claims would be hubristic and counterproductive, akin to claiming to be *the* taxpayer spokesman or *the* organization dedicated to freedom or liberty. This is a movement, not a bureaucracy, not a political party, and not a vehicle for fortune and fame. Like our Republic, this movement's power is derived from the people and its momentum is carried by the people, by individual Americans concerned with the future of our nation.

My hope is that this book will do three things. One, that it will set the historic record straight on what is a critically important grassroots movement. My firsthand account is unfiltered by the liberal mouthpiece media and unspun by any White House communications czar. I hope that it will help individuals outside the movement see the history and principles behind it more clearly.

Second, that it will serve to define and articulate the principles of that movement. As there is no official spokesperson there can be no official platform or handbook for the tea party movement. It is with this is mind that I humbly present my account of the movement, from my perspective inside of it. I primarily focus on the radical growth in the size and scope of government and how this revolution has sparked an individualist counterrevolution grounded in sound philosophy and economics.

Finally, that it will help to fortify, inspire, and guide fellow counter-revolutionaries in the policy battles ahead. In this vein I have included what I believe are important, though not exhaustive, thoughts and suggestions on keeping the principles of the movement alive in public debate. This means competently taking the principles of the rallies from the streets and into the halls of the nation's state legislatures and that of the patch of former swampland carved out between Maryland and Virginia.

Only then can we turn the momentum of this movement into positive, lasting change in public policy.

I would like to thank my family and friends for their support and patience as I wrote this book. While working on it, my answer to nearly everything was "sorry, can't do it—working on the manuscript." My parents encouraged me to write at a young age. My sister Kelly served as my on-call researcher working tirelessly to track down information on virtually every topic, with my barely comprehensible, vague notes in the working manuscript as her only guide. Particular thanks to my fiancée Lauren for her encouragement and steadfast support during this project.

Thanks to my friend J.P. Freire for involving me in the tea party movement at its inception. His contributions to the movement and to this manuscript, in particular to the recent political history preceding the movement, were invaluable.

There are three other individuals whose expertise and contributions made this book complete. Sean Redmond, who contributed a wealth of knowledge and data on organized labor. Peter Fotos, who helped frame the convoluted health care debate in simple, concise language. John Nothdurft brought his expertise in budget and tax issues to the table and combed through the history of the financial crisis and the preceding bailouts to provide the helpful appendix on recent bailout spending. Their hard work, knowledge, and friendship enriched both the book and the process as a whole.

A number of people lent their expertise and experiences to this book and the movement as a whole including Eric Odom; Brendan Steinhauser of FreedomWorks; James Sherck and Bryan Darling of The Heritage Foundation; Ralph Seiffe of the Institute for Truth in Accounting; Phil Kerpen of Americans for Prosperity; Jeffrey Poor of the Media Research Center; Richard Lorenc, Kristina Rasmussen and John Tillman of the Illinois Policy Institute; Wendell Cox; Claire Fay; Nikki Sullivan; Kristine Esposo; Jonathan Hoenig; Megan Barth; and Brian Costin.

I would like to thank my boss, Lauren McCann, for supporting me as I moonlighted as a "community organizer" and as I wrote this book. The leeway afforded me by Lauren and The Heartland Institute's Joseph Bast and Latreece Vankinscott was critical in making this book a reality.

I extend a special thanks to Pamela van Giessen of John Wiley & Sons. Pamela and the folks at Wiley took a chance on me as a first-time author, and for that I am eternally grateful. Thorough editing and guidance from Pamela and from Emilie Herman put this final manuscript head and shoulders above my first draft. Pamela, Emilie, Stacey Fischkelta, and Kate Wood's patience with a first-time author was saintly and millions of concerned Americans owe them and their colleagues at Wiley gratitude for their efforts.

Finally, I would like to thank the millions of American counterrevolutionaries who make up this movement. I hope that this book does a small part to tell your story and advance the principles you and I hold dear. Thank you for all that you do to advance liberty.

CHAPTER 1

THE TEA PARTIES

The government is promoting bad behavior. This is America! How many of you want to pay for your neighbor's mortgage that has an extra bathroom and can't pay their bills? President Obama, are you listening?

—Rick Santelli, *CNBC Squawk Box*, February 19, 2009

F ollowing this line, the Chicago trading floor on which Santelli had been standing erupted in yelling and screaming. This typically happens because a stock is rallying or declining. Santelli's rant was interrupted by a nearby trader who quipped, "Maybe we should all stop paying our mortgages; it's a moral hazard."

Stock traders cheering at the political statements of an on-air business reporter? Talking about the pointlessness of paying a mortgage as a kind of moral hazard? It was like a scene from *Atlas Shrugged*, except, thankfully, the monologues were shorter.

These traders weren't reacting to the reallocation of wealth so much as the prospect of the United States' decline. These were not ideologues or talking heads, nor were they activists or lobbyists. They were simply working people who wanted the freedom to continue working and to enjoy the fruits of their labor in a fair way. Santelli's complaint about the unfairness of rewarding the irresponsible behavior of those who didn't play fair resonated.

If one small rant could get a trading floor on its feet, was it possible that others felt the same? What would it take to get them on their feet? Could they be mobilized?

The country was being sold an entire line of New Ideas that were really just the same, recycled Old Ideas. This isn't merely a rhetorical flourish. The specific legislation that inspired Santelli's rant was the president's Home Affordability Plan, which was unveiled just the day before. What did the plan promise? To prevent foreclosures. How? By transferring massive sums of money from taxpayers to borrowers who just might have bought houses too expensive for their own budgets.[1] (The bill gives aid to those whose mortgage payments are 43 percent of their income.[2])

Sound familiar? It should. The bill was essentially a way of pouring another $200 billion into Fannie Mae and Freddie Mac, government-sponsored entities that implemented government policy that had allowed people to get sweetheart mortgages that got them and all of us in trouble in the first place.

That people could get their hackles up over the minutiae of mortgages is pretty damning. There's no catchy cheer for ending irresponsible lending by government-sponsored enterprises (GSEs).

That's where we came in.

Unorganized Organizers

It seemed like a good idea at the time. As salespeople and politicians say, some of us saw a unique opportunity. Many individuals believed these sentiments were being felt, but not openly expressed, by millions of Americans.

Prior to President Obama taking office, there was significant skepticism regarding the very free-market capitalist system that has allowed our nation to be the most prosperous, generous, and powerful entity in the world.

At the dawn of the worldwide financial crisis, French President Nicolas Sarkozy proclaimed, "*Le laissez-faire, c'est fini.*" President Bush, renowned for sticking to his guns regardless of the changing winds of popular opinion, initiated the Troubled Asset Relief Program, or TARP. In an interview with FOX News' Bret Baier, President Bush said, "I will be known as somebody [who] saw a problem and put the chips on the table to prevent the economy from collapsing. I'm a free-market guy. But I'm not going to let this economy crater in order to preserve the free-market system."

Bush's willingness to abandon his free-market principles in a time of financial crisis belied a fair-weather dedication to capitalism all too common among Republican politicians. Too concerned with his legacy, Bush fell into the old trap of haphazard grandstanding steeped not in principle but gumption.

Gumption is not an ethos. It is not a mast one cleaves to in the squall. The lessons of history and even the Founding Fathers have given us stronger stuff than this. If the Republicans, conservatives in particular, are serious about freedom, it must be the centerpiece of any deliberation—especially in crisis.

Going this direction, the direction of bailouts, TARP, and massive government takeovers, was a signal not only of a lack of seriousness, but a grand new legitimacy. To have a sitting Republican president whose previous policies project the image of fealty to free markets suddenly abandon them was to say that those free markets were a failed experiment and that the serious thing to do was to overturn them. The big-government cavalry alone could save the day.

At a convention in the 1970s, Malcolm Muggeridge, onetime Communist and subsequent editor of *Punch* magazine, asked the crowd why, during such troubled times, Americans had abandoned their faith. "It is as though," he began, "a Salvation Army band, valiantly and patiently waiting through the long years for judgment day, should, when it comes at last, and the heavens do veritably begin to unfold like a scroll, throw away their instruments and flee in terror."

It was hard not to agree with Muggeridge's sentiments as the financial crisis unfolded. Not only did Bush toss his instruments and flee in terror, he handed them off to those forces he had pledged to keep at bay. And then he left town.

The early days of the Obama administration saw a vast expansion of government—both in size and scope. Besides the spending earmarked under TARP, there were plans on the table to have another round of bailouts for troubled financial institutions, car manufacturers, and bad mortgages on a person-by-person basis.

The sentiment continued to be reflected in the media and in popular opinion. The February 2009 *Newsweek* cover read "We Are All Socialists Now." A *New York Times*/CBS News poll, among others, indicated that the majority of Americans were comfortable with an expanded role for government.[3] Other headlines said in various forms that capitalism was dead, or, in the words of Milton Friedman, that we were "all Keynesians now."

But as government grew and inserted itself in the economy, as week upon week of huge spending programs—with money going to the losers!—passed by, a murmur began. People started to express concern; they began to openly worry about the debt burden and the unfairness of rewarding bad behavior by giving it more money. When Santelli ranted extemporaneously on-air, it was like compressed steam being released. All of a sudden, we could talk openly about our concerns, our potential opposition. If a bunch of working people on a trading floor were clearly upset, it didn't seem unreasonable to consider that a lot more people were also skeptical about the expansion of government rolling forth from Washington, D.C.

From Stewing to Brewing

My friend J. P. Freire called me late that night on February 19th. At the time, he was working at *The American Spectator*. The dialogue started: "You know what would be funny?"

As we spoke, it became clear that this wasn't really funny. We realized that our country stood on the brink of a new era that was hardly one worth hoping for. We were not opposed to Obama—or any other politician for that matter—as a person. We were opposed to vast government expansion, huge spending, entitlements, and intervention that would erode everything we believed was good about the United States.

But what to do about it? As conservatives, we were part of an opposition movement that had little experience in marching on Washington and instead prided itself on good behavior. And we aimed to misbehave.

The idea was to have a "tea party." There were already vague rumblings among the center-right grassroots and think tank communities about staging an event on the Fourth of July. But we thought it would be smarter to capitalize on the existing sentiment Santelli had unleashed. Already Facebook groups were multiplying, each carrying in its description iterations of the phrase "Rick Santelli is right," or "Tea Party!" People we did not even know contacted us simply because we had listed ourselves as conservatives on social media.

On the horizon was the Conservative Political Action Conference (CPAC), an event that would draw thousands of conservatives to Washington, D.C. Both of us had attended the event a number of times, but this year it had special significance.

This was a year of clarity. No longer would attendees be mealy-mouthed about the mixed results of the Bush administration and the desire to "stay in the game." Both ideological purists and their more opportunistic brethren could share ground.

While political defeat would certainly pervade the mood, defeatism would not. The voters' rejection of the Republican nominee was more vindication than failure. Run a moderate candidate with no clear philosophy and this is what you get: defeat.

The election of Obama was not a referendum against small government and tax cuts. It was a referendum on competence. Republicans had seemingly gone out of their way to show an utter lack of it. From controlling two branches of government yet failing to reduce the size of it, to Sen. John McCain's lackluster campaign, the GOP had lost credibility as an agent of change. That moniker would belong to someone else.

Conservatives at CPAC would be sure to wonder, then, how to restore in the Republican Party a standard of competence and a core philosophy. That is, if it was at all possible.

Not that I or my brethren had answers. While most of my peers are young participants in the larger center-right movement, none of us were grassroots activists. Few conservatives are. But even this disconnect was troubling: Why was it so hard to think of ourselves as activists when all we did was live and breathe this stuff?

Within the next week, we planned and participated in a new American tea party—a snowballing popular *counter*revolution that encouraged people to speak up, people who never before considered playing an activist role in politics. In doing so, it was clear that the paradigm had shifted (as paradigms seem to do) and that conservatives were beginning to rethink their disdain for community organizing.

The Planning

We had media and event planning experience. But it never occurred to us that planning a protest in front of the White House would be a viable use of time. Then again, we never thought we would have to explain to people why the government shouldn't help people buy more house than they could afford.

We had also seldom participated in, let alone successfully planned, a protest rally. For many conservatives, rallies are the tools of the left, a notable exception being the March for Life. The stereotype fit: Conservatives are busy working and don't have the time or inclination to paint signs and stand outside cheering and jeering. And Libertarians never show up for anything except dinner and drinks—if they like the company and what is on the menu.

We weren't grassroots activists or community organizers. Our jobs, while in "the movement" were not particularly well suited to planning a rally. I was working at a nonprofit as a fund-raiser. Freire was a magazine editor. In less than a week we needed to procure a venue, a permit, speakers, and equipment—all while simultaneously promoting the event so that people would show up.

Both of our workplaces were flexible but skeptical. While both of our organizations were philosophically on board, it is not the mission of a magazine nor a think tank to do this sort of thing—an important point that I'll address further when confronting claims about some sort of right-wing conspiracy. (A preview: If the tea parties are a well-funded movement, we're still figuring out who to bill.)

Freire did the vast majority of planning for the event. He procured the permit for Lafayette Park in front of the White House, set up a web site from scratch, and began to plug the event in media appearances. I started making phone calls to see who else would want to participate.

There was also the fact of visibility. Washington was a fantastic media environment, and it would be easy to lure cameras to the front of the White House. If we coordinated with others having similar ideas in other towns, we could make an even greater impact—if there was one tea party, it would look like a half-baked neighborhood watch. But if they happened across the country on the same day, that might be newsworthy.

The site, NewAmericanTeaParty.com, started attracting viewers. When Freire was interviewed about it on FOX News, the server was flooded and crashed. All the while, a number of other web sites were available—from the more anonymously-run ReTeaparty.com to Pajamas Media's site, to a site run by the founders of Top Conservatives on Twitter (a ranking system for conservatives on the trendy microblogging site). No site could claim an "official" distinction. The variety of sites simply meant a wider spread of information. Whatever potential for rivalry was immediately superseded by a realization: Interested people were logging on to the Web and trying to figure out where the closest event was to them.

For NewAmericanTeaParty.com, I sought sponsorship. Not financial sponsorship—a web site is cheap if you know how to design one—but sponsorship that imparts the "seal of approval" and sense of legitimacy from organizations with name recognition, ones that had a following and could help pull more people into the event.

This led to involvement from think tanks, grassroots organizations, and advocacy groups like Americans for Tax Reform, Americans for Prosperity, FreedomWorks, and the National Taxpayers Union. Many groups gave their support in name only but were eager to do more. But we had no idea what they *could* do. We'd never done this before, either.

As planning for the event progressed, Freire got on a conference call with members of Top Conservatives on Twitter to suggest a date—February 27th, that Friday, at 12 noon—in the hopes that the buzz about Santelli's rant wouldn't die down. Others on the call agreed. Individuals across the country could plan simultaneous protests from their hometowns.

NewAmericanTeaParty.com was flooded with requests to post events that were cropping up across the country. The site quickly went from the home for the D.C. event to a hub for citizens to post and search for events in their cities or towns. And, again, it wasn't the only one. Thousands of e-mails flooded in, announcing another event or requesting information about nearby events.

Here's a typical e-mail from a fellow unwilling to use Facebook. Joe wrote:

Thanks for taking this cause and running with it. I have been saying for quite some time now that a leader needs to step forward, get people organized, and show these sorry asses in Washington that the people back home, the ones they are supposed to represent, can be a force to be reckoned with.

I will gladly be one of the "troops" in this battle for our country's survival.

Good luck and thanks again!

Katherine in Minnesota wrote:

Please keep up the excellent work! This is exactly what we need. When is there going to be an event in Minneapolis/St. Paul?

I will e-mail your web site to all my friends and family. God bless.

Mike from Maryland penned:

I would like to find out more about this event, but every time I click an information link, it's an invitation to sign up for Facebook.

I don't want to sign up for Facebook, I just want to find out about the Washington, D.C., tea party. Could you do this some other way?

Thanks and best regards with best wishes for all success.

People were actively seeking out this web site on their own, without the direction of a Rush Limbaugh or a Matt Drudge. They weren't picked up off of an activist e-mail list. These were organic hits. People *wanted* this badly enough to pursue it on their own. They wanted to do something.

The irony was that while people referred to us as leaders in a number of these e-mails, we were flying by the seat of our pants. We certainly weren't the only people on the planning side, either. We barely had enough time to keep track of everything happening on our end.

The speaker lineup was no exception. Freire was prepared to do a good deal of speaking and had gotten a megaphone from a friend who, appropriately, only used it for an annual Fourth of July celebration. We grabbed a couple of friends representing think tanks, and at the last moment met Joe the Plumber at a breakfast and puckishly suggested he participate.

Again, nothing could have prepared us for planning a rally in front of the White House to address government mismanagement of the financial system alongside Joe the Plumber. It still seems a little surreal.

Politicians played no role in the event. Originally we wanted a few principled folks. We asked a few of the usual suspects—fiscal conservatives, those who voted against the bailout. A few responded that they were out of town; otherwise, calls were rejected or not returned. Interestingly, one month later they'd be scrambling to speak at any event with the words "tea party."

Details were so haphazardly managed that even the permit for the location wouldn't be solidified until two days before. Originally, we had planned on using space in front of the Washington Monument. But the location was far from a metro station, and we were hoping to make it easy for CPAC attendees and commuters to show up.

At one point we discussed using the tidal basin and perhaps a boat with some sort of symbolic action—like dumping tea *a la* the original Boston Tea Party. But dumping tea in a national park seemed like a bad idea when a friend had recently been arrested for dancing at the Jefferson Memorial. Known as the Jefferson 1, she was part of a larger group of freedom lovers who brought iPods to the Jefferson Memorial to dance in silence on the Founding Father's birthday. It was apparently unnerving for the police who had no idea what was happening (while my peers have little community organizing experience, apparently we do have a dash of Merry Pranksters about us).

The threat of rain on the 27th was also a concern, and we discussed bringing the event indoors. Former Speaker of the House Newt Gingrich was also scheduled to speak at the same time the tea party was scheduled.

Eventually, we decided to keep it outside for maximum impact. Ideas for a gimmick at the event were numerous, but we settled on doing nothing, just having folks show up with signs, have a few speakers talk, and let the rally go from there.

Leading up to the event, we received a number of e-mails about sending tea bags to the Hill or to the White House. Particularly for folks who couldn't make it to the D.C. tea party or a concurrent one in their town, this seemed like a great alternative. While we didn't endorse or run the effort, it certainly was admirable. We didn't have the heart to tell enthusiastic patriots that due to post-9/11 safety measures and anthrax terrorism, their tea bags would likely end up scanned and discarded at a scanning center in Maryland or Virginia.

Within 24 hours of the event, we determined that there would be significantly greater impact and it would be more appropriate to have the event in front of the White House or the Capitol. The White House has a park where up to a few hundred could easily gather. So the location was changed, and the word disseminated via new media and e-mail, and surprisingly, the word got out.

To spread the word and to track projected participants, we created a Facebook page for the New American Tea Party Coalition and for the February 27th D.C. event itself. By game day, we had over a thousand Facebook supporters and a few hundred people planning to attend the event. The coalition page allowed people to discuss starting a tea party in their city or town or to discuss the news of the day and how it fit into the theme for the rally.

From there, event pages sprung up across the country with people joining in support of or to attend an Atlanta tea party or a Chicago tea party.

I cannot stress enough the role that online networking tools like Twitter and Facebook played in these rallies' success. Freire and I hardly knew or know 400 free-market people we could call on to show up outside the White House with a week or less notice. A decade ago there would have been absolutely no way to make this possible. The multiplier effect of Facebook, for example, was amazing. To be able to forward an invite to 10 friends who could in turn forward it collectively to 100 and so on was invaluable. Folks that barely knew how to check their e-mail were signing up for Facebook just to stay in the loop on protests in their area. This phenomenon continued exponentially into the April 15th events.

Game Day

February 27th was predicted to be overcast and rainy. We decided to plow ahead without a rain location, hoping for the best and realizing that even if attendance was cut in half due to rain, even 100 people turning out would be significant.

We arrived with the recently procured bullhorn and our permit. The rally was scheduled for noon. It was 11:45 A.M. and there were hardly 30 people there. It was obvious that the location change and the weather had affected attendance.

Freire began to gather people around with the bullhorn while I liaised with Secret Service and the park police regarding the rules of the road.

By noon there were 100 people gathered and the speeches began. We had tapped our coalition members to provide speakers and had no more than five lined up.

Logistics-wise, the event went off almost without a hitch. We had to move the rally 100 yards or so due to the specifics of the permit. The only other incident involved balloons. Megan Barth, an Irvine, California, resident who flew in to participate and who was an invaluable volunteer for the rally, had purchased about $300 worth of pig balloons to symbolize pork. After distributing them, we were informed that balloons weren't allowed in front of the White House for security reasons. The police and Secret Service were understanding about the entire thing, and quietly asked me to collect them.

Two friends took the majority of them and stuffed them in a car around the block. I was asked to collect the remaining balloons, held by a few young children and conservative author Michelle Malkin. Malkin kindly obliged, and I coaxed the balloons from the children and walked across the street and appropriately popped the pork balloons with a mini American flag's point.

By 12:30 P.M. more than 300 people had gathered. When the speakers we had lined up were finished and the crowd was still pumped up and calling for more, Freire waded into the crowd with the bullhorn. We heard from a woman business owner concerned about the cost of doing business and hiring people. An electrician gave an impassioned speech about the fiscal situation we'd be handing to our children and grandchildren.

Off to the side of the protest, a family was dressed in Revolutionary War garb playing the era's music on fiddle, drum, and pipe.

The participants consisted of men, women, teens, and families. Democrats, Republicans, and Libertarians waved Gadsden flags and signs decrying bailouts and pork or calling for the Fed to be audited.

It was beautiful, it was real, and it was entirely unscripted. It couldn't have gone better.

We're All Community Organizers Now

While the event was scheduled for two full hours, we closed it after about an hour while the momentum was still going strong.

Following the event, the mood was not one of anger but of hope, but it was a different flavor of hope than promised during the recent election. The event, while only a few hundred strong, showed those present and those watching at home that they were not alone. Little did we know this last-minute, first-time rally of ours would spark a nationwide "million-man" taxpayer protest.

For an hour or so after the crowd dispersed, Friere, as head planner and MC of the event, was overwhelmed with media requests. I acted as a press agent, lining up everyone from Joe the Plumber to PBS to do interviews with Freire.

Cable and network news coverage was disappointing. One cable network in particular provided ample coverage of the event, but that was expected. But many major networks ignored the events. In a time where a half a dozen Code Pink protestors make national news, why would a few thousand taxpayers protesting major government expansion not make cable headlines?

That said, coverage was fairly wide in traditional media, from the *Washington Times,* to the *Washington Post,* the *New York Times,* and *Investor's Business Daily.*

The Tax Day Tea Parties

By mid-March, the tea party movement was a formidable force. Thousands had turned out in Orlando and Cincinnati following the February 27th events. What we heard from many groups and individuals during the planning for the February tea parties was that they wished they'd had more time to rally the troops, to get off from work, or to arrange for transportation to an event in whatever major city was closest to them. The one-week notice for the first event in D.C. was too short. While we were happy with the turnout in February, particularly given our timeline, it seemed like a no-brainer to shoot for a large-scale, national concurrent tea party on a highly symbolic day like tax day. On April 15th the average American is faced with the reality of how much of their hard earned money is going to the Leviathan instead of to their 401(k), a child's college fund, or a family vacation. In other words, on April 15th, every American is a fiscal conservative.

Hundreds of cities and towns began to plan tax day tea parties. Again, we saw the movement fully utilizing the Internet and new media like Twitter and Facebook. Many existing think tanks and grassroots organization set up networks far more sophisticated than our original coalition web site that allowed individuals to find a tea party organizer in their city or town, print off posters and talking points, or volunteer to take the lead on getting something going in their town. Many of these groups had weekly conference calls in each city and nationally to discuss logistical concerns, press opportunities, and so on for the tax day events. One impressive site that was organized was TaxDayTeaParty.com. It was a very sophisticated version of the hub we had tried to produce for the February events.

Institutional Organization

We were excited to see this movement take off, although we were skeptical of people co-opting it. This was genuinely a grassroots movement—something quite rare on the left or the right. It is one thing for an organization to pull together an event. It doesn't take away the validity of its points, but in a sound bite world, a more organic grassroots uprising is a lot more impressive and largely immunized from fallacious leftists attacks—or so we thought.

In the February effort, we were eager to have the event endorsed, for it to look legitimate in order to get boots on the ground for the protest. Skeptical but willing organizations signed on and sent out notes to their members. This was good for the event and good for them. Many of them have the explicit mission of aiding grassroots movements like this. We, on the other hand, needed the infrastructure to get the word out to protestors and the press.

After the success of the February events, people were coming out of the woodwork with "official" tea party organizations, web sites, and events. With the change of administrations paired with the struggling economy there was no shortage of out of work, entrepreneurial individuals in libertarian and conservative camps looking to make a name for themselves. We're market guys, this makes sense. Our concern was, however, that any group, or groups, claiming to be *the* tea party was antithetical to both the broad, grassroots nature of the movement and the core principles of the movement. On the one hand you have Democrats, Republicans, small and big "L" libertarians and independents who were frustrated with runaway spending and the state of the nation we'd be passing on to the next generation. To associate these principled concerns with one organization is problematic. Frankly, many center-right think tanks turn off Democrats and Independents, regardless of the fact that they may see eye to eye on virtually every fiscal principle and beyond. A dishonest SourceWatch entry is enough to make many people, rightly or wrongly, quite skeptical. Even if the average tea party protestor didn't care, there was always the concern of the media. Local or national media outlets, if they didn't like the flavor of any one organizing group, could write it off as "Astroturf"—a term for fake activism playing off "grassroots." This was, after all, a constant—and legitimate—criticism of many protests on the left, funded by George Soros and the like.

Secondly, there is the fact that any sort of command and control infrastructure was against everything these protests stood for. Thousands of people were turning out to protest an ever-expanding, heavy-handed federal government command and control. To take a similar approach to the protest of this Leviathan would be absurd. There were people claiming to be *the* tea party coordinators at the national, state, and local levels. There were "official" t-shirts, talking points, posters, and web sites. There were official spokesmen who had never officially spoken for anything in their entire lives, let alone the millions of Americans frustrated with the various implications of the federal government's fiscal imprudence. That said, there you have the free market at work.

Striking a Balance

Fortunately, in the vast majority of cases, the will of the people prevailed. It was an interesting case study that illuminated why central planning simply doesn't work. It is nearly impossible for one person or group to dictate to a highly motivated, distant, and disparate force of individuals, rather like trying to herd cats.

The impractical prospect of a far-off puppet master controlling several hundred thousand or even a million or more protestors of various individual temperaments with varying political gripes, paired with the philosophical incompatibility of a command and control approach to organizing a grassroots effort made for a nice free-market solution to many of the organizational issues.

For example, back in Chicago at this time, I found myself at the reigns of the Chicago effort almost overnight. Having burnt a solid week of personal and work time on the February efforts, I was ready to retire as a tea party organizer. However, it became apparent that there was nobody taking the lead on a tax day tea party in Chicago. Eric Odom's TaxDayTeaParty.com that spearheaded a lot of national coordination was based in Chicago. Its volunteer PR person, a young PR professional, was tasked with also planning the Chicago effort. She was, however, overwhelmed with the task of coordinating national media. She wasn't able to focus on actually getting the event off the ground in her home city—the city where Santelli famously blasted the bailout and called for a Chicago tea party.

Only a few weeks out, there was no location, no time, no speakers, and no permit. This is arguably the easiest part. Getting people to the rally is the hardest, and there were already thousands signed up to attend on Facebook.

I volunteered to help coordinate in my free time with my friend and colleague Brian Costin. We found that what really worked was institutions offering aid—financial, logistical, PR help, but not branding or controlling events. When that happens, ancient organizational rivalries, prima donna personalities, and general PR issues cloud the message of the movement.

Internal Complications

The Chicago protest would eventually go off without a hitch, but there were plenty of bumps along the road. I was handed an interesting brew. For one, the only speaker that was confirmed was the previous organizer's boss, a conservative commentator who ran a professional public relations firm. And he posed a problem. It was well known in Illinois Republican circles that he was feeling out a race for governor. The last thing this effort needed was to be branded as Republican, particularly as a springboard for a campaign. This was a genuine concern and it spoke to the movement's commitment to keep the protest focused on the issues and not about parties. He understood, and stepped down as a speaker.

Then I was told that a local radio station was promised exclusive cosponsoring rights. I was flabbergasted. This was going to be an event with people in the thousands. Any and every local radio and TV outlet would be covering it. That day I had gone on FOX News Channel and its local affiliate to promote the event. What did this radio channel bring to the table? Would they *not* cover it if they weren't cosponsors? It turned out that our previously scheduled conservative commentator speaker was a paid commentator for the station. I eventually decided to move on, as the spot as promoter had already been promised before I took the reins.

I proceeded to line up speakers from Illinois state think tanks, a female business owner, and a young man who worked on Hillary Clinton's campaign who was disenchanted with his party.

No, Really, We're Nonpartisan

As momentum built, Eric Odom received a call from the Republican National Committee. It was RNC Chairman Michael Steel's scheduler.

The caller mentioned that Steele would be in the area on April 15th and wondered if he could speak at the rally. Odom stuck to his guns and said "thanks, but no thanks." He told them Mr. Steele was welcome to attend, but that no political figures would be sharing the stage in Chicago.

This was a gutsy move. In many other cities, politicians were speaking at rallies. However, organizers for the most part limited themselves to fiscally responsible, antibailout officials. In the case of Steele, he stood for a party that millions of people felt had let them down. Steele rightly saw this as an opportunity for him to pick up the mantle and reclaim fiscal responsibility for Republicans. But this was not the point of the rally. This was a chance for the people to speak to the politicians for a change. Odom made the right call respectfully declining. He then sent out a press release hailing the decision, which was gutsy insofar as it was touting a dissing of sorts of the one party that, at least on paper, had some sympathy for the protesters' beefs. This move alone should have provided ample proof that the rally was not partisan and was not about the GOP. We had, after all, rejected the *head* of the GOP. Our naiveté was showing; this factoid would, of course, be overlooked by many in the media later.

Bureaucrats and Permits

The permitting issue was a huge concern. For one, the original site for Chicago was the Daley Plaza. This site required a $1 million insurance policy. Thankfully, the folks at FreedomWorks, one of the top grassroots facilitators in the country, helped out.

As the expectations grew from 1,000, to 2,000 attendees or more, we realized the Daley Plaza wouldn't hold the crowd. To further complicate matters, the city of Chicago required 30 days notice and more insurance for staging, among other requirements. But thousands of attendees were planning on showing up at that location. I knew from the weekly conference calls we were running that folks in the suburbs were chartering buses to come in. We needed to nail down a location and permits as quickly as possible.

I went with Brian Costin to the Kluczynski Federal Building, the plaza of which could hold up to 5,000 people safely. As one might imagine, getting a permit approved was a tiresome bureaucratic process (giving us some sympathy with our community organizer/protest brethren on the left). Two other groups had permits for the location. One was an antitax group that needed limited space. That group's organizer said, "sure, they can join the party." The other was an antiwar group that expected up to 100 people and wanted half the plaza. Efforts to contact the organizer went unanswered. With days until the event, if the location was going to change it had to change quickly. I sent our press releases and Facebook messages to thousands of attendees and press. On the day of, we would have volunteers redirecting people from the original location. Now all we needed was the permit.

The day before the event there was still no word from the Federal building. Costin and I went to the Federal building and waited for the supervisor. At 1:45 P.M., she was still at lunch. When she finally arrived, we made a good case for our permit being approved. More than 4,000 people were showing up the next day at that plaza, permit or no permit. Additionally, the existing protestors had similar beefs. The folks with fiscal concerns could be easily integrated. We then argued that since the antiwar protestors had a complaint with the spending on the war, that, too, was quite compatible. Besides, they expected 100 at the most and likely were to have about 6 people show up. Finally, she slapped on the seal of approval and we were in business.

April 15, 2009: The Million-Taxpayer March

Around the country on April 15th, the much anticipated tax day tea parties took off in all forms. Every capital and every major city had one. Some were also held in small towns. The final count for attendees was conservatively estimated at over 500,000. And for every man, woman, and child in the street, there were at least a dozen Americans at home or at work cheering them on.

As the *Christian Science Monitor* reported:

> By some estimates, over half a million Americans took to the streets
> last Wednesday to protest taxes and Washington spending—the largest
> single-day turnout of protesters in the U.S. since 750,000 people

marched in Los Angeles in support of rights and protections for immigrants on March 25, 2006.[4]

Prior to the event there was significantly more press coverage than
with the first event in D.C. I received two calls from a producer—one
was to ask "is this a Fox event?" I responded that it was not, that it was
newsworthy and many outlets were covering the lead-up to the event
and planning on attending the events themselves. I asked if he wanted
to talk to any organizer or participants; he said "no."

I received a second call a couple hours later and was asked why
the permitting was not in order for Daley Plaza. Well, as the press
release explicitly stated, the event was not taking place there but at
the Kluczynski Federal Building plaza. "Why has Chicago not heard
of any permit?" I patiently gave the CNN person a brief civics lesson,
explaining that the great city of Chicago doesn't oversee federal property.
The confrontational tone and lack of knowledge foreshadowed the CNN
interaction that would take place and make news itself just one day later.

The Chicago speakers and participants represented a broad spectrum.
Speakers at other events included concerned taxpayers, grassroots organizers, and fiscally conservative local and state Republicans and Blue
Dog Democrats. Some events procured folks like Ted Nugent, and a
couple were covered live by the likes of Sean Hannity and Glenn Beck.

The Chicago event went off without a hitch. The speakers were passionate, the crowd was excited. There was no violence, no disruptions
from ACORN as that group had promised.[5] A few strange folks showed
up in masks, but outnumbered about 1,000 to 1, they did nothing.
Afterward, the crowd cleaned up the plaza, impressing the law enforcement so much that it made news the next day on Rush Limbaugh's
radio show.

All told, the nationwide estimates were 250,000 to 500,000. Americans for Tax Reform compiled a master list of the turnout in all cities,
specifically asking for conservative estimates for each. All told, it counted
over half a million participants.[6] Cities the group reported as having
5,000 or more participants are listed on page 20. I'm confident the numbers are rounded down as police estimates in Chicago put the number at
5,000 to 7,000 and on this list, Chicago doesn't make the conservative
estimate cut.

Location	Attendees
Atlanta, GA	15,000
San Antonio, TX	13,000
Overland Park, KS	10,000
Sacramento, CA	10,000
St. Louis, MO	10,000
Madison, WI	8,200
Dayton, OH	7,500
Fresno, CA	7,500
Columbus, OH	7,000
Nashville, TN	7,000
St. Paul, MN	7,000
Woodland, TX	7,000
Austin, TX	5,000
Baton Rouge, LA	5,000
Birmingham, AL	5,000
Bossier City, LA	5,000
Cleveland, OH	5,000
Dallas, TX	5,000
Denver, CO	5,000
Ft. Meyers, FL	5,000
Ft. Worth, TX	5,000
Lansing, MI	5,000
New York, NY	5,000
Oklahoma City, OK	5,000
Olympia, WA	5,000
Phoenix, AZ	5,000
Portland, OR	5,000

SOURCE: Americans for Tax Reform. "People Attended Yesterday's Tax Day Tea Parties." www.atr.org/people-attended-yesterdays-tax-tea-parties-a3138.

What's more, the tea parties were viewed favorably by a majority of the nation with a Rasmussen Reports poll indicating 51 percent approval and 32 percent of respondents reporting *very* favorable views of the events.[7]

Unfortunately, as we would discover, the political class, the media, and the Hollywood elite didn't share America's view.

CHAPTER 2

HOW WE GOT HERE

ABANDONING PRINCIPLES AND THE PEOPLE

There are many men of principle in both parties in America, but there is no party of principle.

—Alexis de Tocqueville

Ours is a nation unmoored from history.

Conservatism, the political philosophy most responsible for maintaining that link, has fallen politically inert. That is not to say that it has failed, that it is irrelevant, or that it is outdated. Instead, it has been drowned out, watered down, or thrust to the side. That unmooring has allowed the debate about good government to lose important context: The founding principles of this country and their steady abandonment.

Bring it up, and some will think you're trying to bring the tri-corner hat back. The hat is cool and all, but the principles are more so. While the Founding Fathers made an effort to give limited government command of the ship, every passing day brings with it another attempt at mutiny.

The entire point of the American Revolution was the preservation of individual liberty against an overbearing state. Today, this view is treated as an anachronism.

The trouble is that conservatives have been unwilling to act as counterrevolutionaries, to vigorously defend against these revolts. It takes a lot of energy to withstand each wave. Believing that government should not intrude on one's life includes having a life worth defending against intrusion. In short, we're too busy to make a fuss. Life's too short.

Yet a fuss is exactly what is needed. Nothing else will communicate to party leaders that the conservative base isn't merely a block of votes ripe for the taking. It is a principled opposition to the use of politics as a way of life, as a solution without a problem. Those among the tea party protestors realize this and are finally learning how to fight. The political landscape will only change if conservative activists demand it.

It is for this reason that Ronald Reagan's ascent to power is so important. It is not so much the realization of a conservative dream, but rather it is only the beginning. What followed was the adolescence of newfound political power, and the realization of just how difficult this fight would be.

I don't intend to embark on a rehashing of "How the Conservative Movement Sold Out," nor a deification of the right-wing pantheon. Political and intellectual forefathers were goodly, but they were men, who must be taken for all in all.

Instead, here I separate the conservative success from the myth and extract the lesson from it. That lesson is simple: Baby steps toward changing the debate in Washington are as good as national mandates get.

Touting versus Learning from Reagan

Conservatives have delegated the defense of their principles to politicians and pundits with varying degrees of success. But the last 20 years especially have illustrated the consequences of success and failure. Having skin in the game has moved conservatives from complacency to consistency. Not that complacency has been a failure. When it's Ronald Reagan in 1980, it's a stunning victory. When it's George W. Bush, it's a mixed bag. And when it's the chattering class of television and newspaper pundits, it's a popularity contest.

When it's the primary for the Republican nomination in 2008, it's almost like a vaudeville show, one that could be titled, "Will the Real Ronald Reagan Please Stand Up?" Sen. John McCain described himself as a foot soldier in the Reagan Revolution. Mayor Rudy Giuliani brandished his Reagan Justice Department credentials. Gov. Mitt Romney leaned on the rhetorical three-legged stool that was central to Reagan's legacy. Everyone wanted the shine, but no one wanted the substance. That politicians have caught on to conservatism as a great brand identity is certainly a sign of progress. That conservatives are so willing to go along with it is not.

The rewards for going along with it are nowhere more apparent than the results of the 2008 election. Sen. McCain, the Republican nominee whose prohibitive stances against freedom of speech and other conservative orthodoxies, was so unfamiliar with free-market philosophy that he couldn't confidently assert himself once the financial crisis came to a head. Sen. Barack Obama, on the other hand, came off as cool and collected. Not once did he have to explain his own economic approach in detail.

Voting for Obama, then, was an exercise in risk aversion. The policies born from that exercise, however, were anything but. Suffice it to say, the lesser of two evils was the freshman senator from Illinois. One whose stated policies on taxes and the size of government sounded reasonable.

Even Obama loaned himself to the Reagan chorus saying:

> I think Ronald Reagan changed the trajectory of America in a way that Richard Nixon did not and in a way that Bill Clinton did not. He put us on a fundamentally different path because the country was ready for it. They felt like with all the excesses of the '60s and the '70s and government had grown and grown but there wasn't much sense of accountability in terms of how it was operating. I think he tapped into what people were already feeling. Which is we want clarity, we want optimism, we want a return to that sense of dynamism and entrepreneurship that had been missing.[1]

Obama was right. People did want clarity, people *did* want optimism. But they also wanted substance. And here Obama was just like others who used Reagan as a rhetorical flourish: He had no intention of following through with Reaganesque policy.

But do many Republicans?

You can't go to a right of center dinner or luncheon without hearing at least one Ronald Reagan reference. The Conservative Political Action Conference (CPAC), the Mecca for conservatives run by the American Conservative Union (ACU) has its main dinner dedicated to the Gipper. Many other organizations do the same at annual gatherings. There, one can expect to hear from a conservative congressman who was inspired to run for office because of Reagan, or one who wants to simply ruminate on the principles Reagan espoused—small government, individual liberty, and fiscal responsibility—principles, our Founding Fathers intended our government to protect and shelter, not chip away and smother. Prominent political pundits and writers often go right to a Reagan quip and apply it to the political status quo.

The problem is that many in the center-right movement, and many looking in from the outside, get the message that the good old days have come and gone for conservatism and its ideals. Additionally, the hero-worshiping of one individual is eerily similar to the creepy idolatry that abounded amongst the masses that swept Barack Obama into office. Either we draw lessons from the Reagan era, or we ignore it entirely. At the moment, Reagan appears to be a good source for speaking material.

As Stephen Slivinski aptly describes in his book *Buck Wild: How Republicans Broke the Bank and Became the Party of Big Government* (Thomas Nelson, 2006), Reagan does matter, and more importantly, what he did matters. The case must be made clearly, however, that it is not the past that we are looking to recreate. Conservatism is not a philosophy that yearns for what is past. It is a philosophy that devoutly wishes to never repeat the mistakes of the past. Progressivism is quite the opposite, suggesting that no matter the past follies of government intervention, this time we'll get it right.

This is a hurdle our movement faces and we oftentimes unintentionally reinforce it with tributes to this great man. Speaking with political activists and journalists on the right, many often confuse remembering a great man and his principles with living in the past. The left frames, often quite successfully in the media and minds of Americans, that Democrats and the left are "progressive" while Republicans, the right, and conservatives are "static" or even "regressive."

Heck. Reagan has a good enough response for this, to which I'll ironically refer. Conservatives don't want to go back to the past, but rather, we "want to go back to the past way of facing the future." Despite what Rachel Maddow may have you believe, conservatives aren't interested in reverting to the cookie cutter towns of yore and Jim Crow. What appeals to conservatives about times past is the rugged individualism and personal responsibility that went along with them—characteristics that both predicated and encapsulated the formation of our country.

Reagan's legacy does no good if we don't use it as a guide for political success when the dinner or luncheon is over. Reagan was a very popular president who charmed the nation. But you can be charming and not get a thing done. This is the best way one can explain Sen. John Kerry's popular support in the 2004 election. Reagan fought for principles that resonated with a nation.

Recent history of the Republican Party is about one question: Do we want to stay in the game, or do we want to change the game? Since Reagan's victory, the party has moved to the latter question, but it has frequently faltered, as it was bound to do. To examine this is to learn how far the conservative movement has come, and how much further we need to go. The movement's ascendancy is only in its adolescence, and learning how to deal with power has been a hard lesson.

Reagan was a fiscally conservative shining light in a recent history of big-spending, big-government Republicans and Democrats. His GOP predecessors Richard Nixon and then Gerald Ford were wary of conservatism, thinking its ideological discipline was both a straightjacket and an unrealistic assessment of how politics worked as "the art of the possible." Government, after all, expanded out of pure inertia. To negotiate from a position of "no" meant to forget one's surroundings. The whole point of Congress was to haggle, not cut.

Reagan's election represented a moment where the country signaled a desire to get the government back to the basics of governing with the smallest cost and least interference possible. Slivinski makes two crucial points about Reagan. One, his success was based on solid principles for which there was a great deal of support. Polling data and election returns made it clear that his message of reducing the size of government resonated with the American people. His commonsense conservatism spoke to millions of Americans, but he wasn't able to immediately and consistently implement his ideas by chopping off arms of the Leviathan whose reins were handed to him. This leads to the second point: He was not perfect.

There were tangible lessons to be learned about his presidency as well. Reagan's failures (and there were a few) must be recognized in addition to his successes, but they are not lessons on giving up. It is a lesson that change is incremental, it can be done, and most importantly, *Americans want it.*

Reagan slowed the growth of government dramatically down to 2.6 percent from 4.0 percent, cut taxes from 70 percent to 30 percent, and kept 8 cabinet agencies' spending under inflation, all while building up the Department of Defense and winning the Cold War.

Where Reagan fell short was really where he left the fight for another day. Reagan's goal was to slow things down. By the time he took office, government was taking on too fast a pace. Large, budget-busting programs were enjoying huge increases in funding, and few in Congress stood against them. In fact, before Reagan arrived on the scene, cutting the size of government was hardly a topic for debate. Republicans and Democrats alike focused on the Cold War and on inflation and jobs, but the view that "government was the problem" was unusual. Congressional fights were less severe because saying "no" was mostly a matter of haggling, not principle.

If anything, the fights Reagan took on and lost, or ones he simply didn't address, provided a checklist for expectations over the next decade. Eliminating the Departments of Energy, Commerce, and Education, rolling back the welfare state, and cutting gargantuan pork projects were battles waged and lost by Reagan's director of the Office of Management and Budget. But fighting these fights was more symbolic than successful. As Alfred S. Regnery notes in his book *Upstream*:

> Critics who like to point out that Reagan did not actually accomplish much, that his programs did not achieve what he had promised, fail to understand that Reagan ran for president in order to change the American people's concept of the role of government.[2]

Here was a popular president proposing a radical departure from business-as-usual. And he didn't seem radical in his pursuit. Instead, he seemed more real than his predecessors—because he believed in something. After his 1981 budget resolution passed, the battleground had shifted severely. No longer did you have to justify cuts alone. You also had to justify spending.

All of this is to say that Reagan's work was a blueprint for substantive change. The tale shows that even with the White House on their side, conservatives cannot wait on the change they ordered. They need to deliver it, too.

If conservatives do not hold the reins tightly, moderates roam free. George H. W. Bush, elected in the warm glow of Reagan's legacy, was in many ways representative of the party prior to Reagan. When soliciting ideas from a friend about cutting issues for the 1988 campaign, the friend suggested he go take some time alone to figure out where he wanted to take the country. Bush replied, exasperated, "Oh. The vision thing."[3]

Robert Novak reported, "As it became clear late in the 1988 campaign that George Bush would be elected comfortably but saddled with big Democratic majorities in Congress, he reverted to his liberal Republican roots." The only thing Bush would be clear on during campaign rallies (to Novak, the only "beef" in "a bland campaign-ending stew") was his dedication to not raising taxes.

Without a core philosophy, Bush had no reason to embark on an ambitious program with the same fastidiousness as his predecessor. But he did have the imprimatur of being Reagan's vice president, giving him the gravitas of a Reagan Revolutionary. Following any other Republican president, Bush would have looked sterling—experience in foreign policy, legislative experience, well-spoken.

But Bush followed Reagan—thus his campaign pledge, "Read my lips: No new taxes." The country expected from him a continuation of the Reagan Revolution. But Bush had run against Reagan, describing the Gipper's fastidious love of free markets as "voodoo economics." Instead, Bush asked for the resignation of every Reagan appointee. He spoke of a "kinder, gentler" nation on foreign policy, even as the Communist Manifesto still had the gravitas of nuclear warheads. He eventually would sign the Omnibus Budget Reconciliation Act of 1990, diluting the Republican brand and retarding Republicans' small-government credibility among voters.

In short, Bush's administration would be the first major swing back to the old party approach of compromising for clout. It would also last as long as the last moderate Republican: one term.

It would also be an important lesson, one that would not be learned for a long time—don't waste an opportunity.

1994: The Revolution That Wasn't

Conservatives cannot campaign on the ideas of fiscal responsibility and small government only to switch paths once inside the Beltway. The temptation, as Slivinski aptly points out, is to take the reins of the federal beast and somehow control it for conservative ideals.

Rather than killing the beast, many politicians—and many with good intentions—decide it more expedient and more prudent to make the beast work for them. This is a temptation that must be avoided. It is big government itself, it is the intrusions of government into people's everyday lives and the financial consequences for future generations that get to most Americans.

When Congress was overtaken by a new Republican majority, it was due in large part to the architect, Newt Gingrich. He scouted out candidates, helped develop the "Contract with America," and capitalized on the dissatisfaction with President Clinton's leftward drift in government. It was also due to ideas that he maintained and along with several others, adopted from Reagan's 1985 state of the union address, in the form of a Contract with America.

Slight tremors presaged the Republican takeover in 1994. The off-year gubernatorial elections in New Jersey and Virginia, and mayoral elections of New York City and Los Angeles were undergirded by conservative principles. Christie Todd Whitman won over a Democrat in New Jersey on the promise of lower taxes. George Allen scored big among the Christians in Virginia, which was hardly a surprise. But Rudy Giuliani's victory in New York City indicated that some had had it with liberal governance.

News reports played down the possibility of a House takeover. Democrats thought that health care was unquestionably their winning issue, and that Republican obstruction would only mean defeat. They were, of course, dead wrong. Even House Speaker Tom Foley was kicked out of office. Democratic heads were spinning.

First Lady Hillary Clinton unwittingly took every possible action to make sure Democratic victory would not be the case. Even though moderate Republicans in the Senate were willing to make a deal, she had made it clear that it would be either her way or the highway.

Republican House member Dick Armey would write an Op-Ed in the *Wall Street Journal* assailing her health care plan, alleged to be a "streamlined and simpler system" as it promised to create "59 new federal programs or bureaucracies, expand 20 others, impose 79 new federal mandates and make changes in the tax code." William Kristol, who led the Project for the Republican Future, started issuing strategy memos to Republican congressmen and activists. The strategy was all about replacing the welfare state with free-market initiatives. The Heritage Foundation and other groups got on board.

Soon, there was an entire movement dedicated to defeating a single policy: health care. The pump was primed for something more. Theda Skocpol, a liberal Cornell professor, writes in *Boomerang*, her chronicle of the health care reform effort:

> . . . Right-wing government haters could argue that this set of reforms would hurt businesses, individuals, and health providers, interfering with their "liberties." Proclaimed threats of possibly rising taxes and governmental inefficiency could be spiced with pronouncements that big, intrusive government would destroy our freedom and the quality of the best health care system in the world. Designed to get around and trough the antigovernment and fiscal legacies of the Reagan era, the Clinton Health Security proposal—in its ultimate irony—gave new life to the outcries of "governmental tyranny" that Barry Goldwater had once presented so ineffectively.[4]

Those outcries became Gingrich's revolution.

This revolution as it is referred to today is a mirage. Like any other, this was an election of opportunity, not simply ideas. The president's party always loses seats in off-year elections. Many members retired or switched parties.[5] Out of the 52 House seats picked up by Republicans, only 34 of these were victories over Democratic incumbents. It's substantial, clearly, and not possible to ignore, but it only speaks to the opportunity.

Of course, that opportunity was amplified by the president himself, who had throttled the trend. David Brady of the Hoover Institute notes that incumbency advantage had greatly declined, given the smaller-than-usual second-election boost experienced by 1992's freshman class.

The more the Democratic incumbent voted in support of Clinton's positions, the worse he or she did. This is particularly true in conservative districts. In those districts (defined as those where Clinton had won less than 40 percent of the 1992 vote), 63 percent of the incumbents who most strongly supported the president's positions lost their reelection bids. In contrast, none of their counterparts who supported Clinton's positions less than 60 percent of the time lost. The same pattern holds, although it is less dramatic, as expected, for Democratic incumbents representing more moderate districts (those in which Clinton got 40 to 50 percent of the 1992 vote).

This doesn't bode well for President Obama in general (something to be addressed later), but it's also important that we recognize that at this time, voters did not feel that they were truly represented in their districts. 1994 was a time when districts had grown conservative and didn't find their representative capable of abiding by it.

The Republican gains in 1994 came from conservative and moderate districts with liberal Democratic incumbents. The pattern of Republicans replacing Democrats too liberal for their districts had been going on since at least 1978, and 1994 was the culminating election. In short, the Republican victory was the result of a long-term trend, especially prominent in the Southern and border states and in the Midwest, wherein conservative constituencies and Republican representatives were matched and sorted.[6]

In other words, while the party won, it won owing a great deal to the opportunity set out before it rather than on pure ideas. This isn't a denigration of the achievement. In fact, it is a demonstration of realistic strategy. It rebuffs those who classically suggest that if conservatives ran on ideas, they would win. Even with ideas that resonated with the

American public, a victory would not have been possible without the political winds blowing favorably.

The program itself was certainly ambitious. According to Slivinski, then-Rep. Christopher Cox of California read David Stockman's memoirs four times and arrived at the conclusion that it wasn't the radicalism of the ideas, but the timing that was important. "Revolutions have a very short half-life. If you don't ask for [what you want] early, you won't get it."

Momentum would, in fact, be the very thing to get in the way of the agenda. The Republicans appeared to be aware of this, including in their Contract with America a promise to make a number of reforms on the very first day of Congress. Term limits on committee chairmanships, opening committee hearings to the public, and more were promised.

Watching all of this transpire on television with our parents when we were young, my generation couldn't have possibly understood the political significance of these changes. But our parents and "social studies" teachers were visibly affected. It was a shock to the system—Congress finally seemed to be restored to the people.

But the revolution was stymied. In fact, it has become more difficult to distinguish between the walkers and the talkers in conservatism. Because of the expansiveness of the term and the growth of the movement, the spectrum of conservatives, including the more opportunistic among the crowd, has grown. Conservatism has become less of a church and more of a confederacy. And in so doing, it has fallen prey to politicians with alarming philosophical flexibility.

Indeed, it became clear that one of the chief opponents was, shockingly, the house speaker himself. Gingrich was enjoying his position at the helm of the conservative voyage into power. As soon as he arrived in his new position, he received a $4.5 million book advance from HarperCollins he was reluctant to let go. He even appointed Rep. Bob Livingston (R-LA) to be House Appropriations committee chairman, who would argue to keep Democratic staffers on the committee.

The House Appropriations Committee is where the worst part of political deal making happens. To make an enemy on the committee is to commit political suicide—any funds necessary to complete a project would be in jeopardy.

When Robert Novak went to meet with Livingston for the first time, he was shocked to learn that Livingston was hardly a strict conservative. It would appear that Gingrich had picked him to put a fresh face on the committee, rather than undermine its abilities.[7]

It's no surprise, then, that the House Appropriations Committee became resistant to budget changes. Rep. John Kasich (R-OH), the fiscally pure House Budget Committee chair, feuded with Livingston. Whereas Kasich was set on the goal of eliminating the federal deficit by 2002, Livingston was a touch dismissive. "He'll run his business, and I'll run mine."[8]

Other victories did occur. Welfare reform returned power to the states in distributing cash assistance to the poor. Nondefense discretionary spending was cut by 4 percent. And a phaseout of farm subsidies was (if only temporarily) initiated. The Contract with America, out of which Congress passed just 9 of 10 items in the first 100 days, would remain a figment in a very active conservative imagination, as the last time a group of conservatives came together and got something done. Unfortunately even that memory is wrong—the majority of these items failed to pass the Senate and many were eventually rolled back by future Republican majorities.

The slipups of the revolution are still hard to ignore. Looking at the priority list for Republican reform, one gets the feeling that the whole thing was a show in order to access power. The combined budgets of 95 of the major programs that the Contract with America promised to eliminate increased by 13 percent in 2000. A moratorium on all new federal regulations died in committee. A constitutional amendment to require the government to run a balanced budget failed in the Senate. Over the years, congressmen would forgo term limits. Congressman George Nethercutt (R-WA),[9] who had proudly branded himself a term-limited congressman, explained: "I didn't realize I'd be in the majority."

When Francis Fukuyama referred to the "End of History," he could have just as well had his eye on Republican rule. It was a promising, ideologically strict revolt around which so much feverish nostalgia still hovers. It turned into a transaction-based economy. Republicans would continue this trend for years.

Though Congress has continued down the path of reckless spending, the terms of debate have changed even more in the direction Reagan had hoped for. In other words: We are watching the ebb and flow of a political movement, one that barely stood on the radar 50 years ago. Movements go through periods of growth and decline, but every time conservatism has been described as in decline, it has grown back stronger.

Treating this as an inevitability, however, is a mistake. That the movement has expanded in the number of organizations, scholars, media outlets, and even politicians, has really only made it clear that conservatives are an easy demographic to target. That the debate has changed doesn't mean that the actions have.

The Quasi-Conservative Presidency of George W. Bush

There were two options in 2000. One was Al Gore, and one was George W. Bush. It didn't take a subscription to *National Review* to figure out which candidate would espouse policies closer to conservative ideals.

Not only did Bush run as a conservative, however, but he ran as an everyman in the mold of Reagan. Whereas Al Gore's technical know-how and wonkish experience allowed him to be easily cast as the out-of-touch candidate, then-Governor Bush's Texas swagger had the markings of "one of us." He had the accent, the glibness, and the pedigree.

Sen. McCain, his arch nemesis during the Republican primary, was actually at a disadvantage because he was so familiar to so many. Whereas Bush could reasonably pose as the harbinger of the conservative agenda, McCain maintained appeal amongst Democrats and Independents. But Bush's gambit was based on "compassionate conservatism," an almost satirical reconfiguration of his father's "kinder, gentler nation."

The need to tone things down was apparently so palpable, conservatism needed the modifier. Bush's evangelical Christianity appeared to be sincere, and this appellation appeared to be a way of subtly bringing it up, but it also made non-social conservatives curious as to whether he would cater to all branches of conservatism.

Over time, compassionate conservatism appeared to be simple Republican establishmentarianism. Thankfully, it had far more conservative overtures than in years past, but it still wasn't the ideal for a nation 20 years after Reagan. But it's meaningful that President George W.

Bush would be the first Republican moderate to swing conservative because the political winds were blowing in that direction.

It may sound funny, but it's no joke that this actually marked an achievement. That conservatives would need to be pandered to in such a way meant that their segment of the voting populace was expanding. And because politicians were framing the debate in terms of who would spend more, hike taxes more, invade your life more, conservatism had gone from nerdy wonkery to a lexicon for the national discussion.

The tragic events of September 11, 2001, interrupted Bush's weird moderation, however, and animated the national security wing of the movement. Those who had previously been mobilized against the Soviet Union had a new threat to guard against. The nation was united behind its government in seeking retribution for terrorist attacks against those working in the Twin Towers and the Pentagon.

But this brought up yet another contentious issue for an ever-expanding movement. Do we subjugate rights in time of war? Do we set limitations on the executive? The discussion between libertarians and neocons was a fascinating exercise in internecine warfare. Conservatives were steadily becoming emboldened and hawkish when traditionally they had sought a humble foreign policy.

This new environment, rather than unite conservatives and libertarians, provided a brave new world of debate. Conservatives accused libertarians of being stuck in an ivory tower. Libertarians accused conservatives of becoming unmoored from their principles. Both were right. Both were wrong. But that the conflict was happening signaled a fracture in the "fusionist" coalition that brought the two together.

Bush's handling of Katrina also became an issue. While in principle, the local and state governments should have leapt into action, the federal government was woefully unprepared to address the disaster. Whether Bush had screwed up or not wasn't the issue. It undermined every effort then-Republican National Committee Chairman Ken Mehlman had made toward pulling the minority demographic into the party. Pictures of destitute people losing their homes indicated not only a lack of seriousness, but a callousness toward the plight of the impoverished. A longtime stereotype of Republicans was only reinforced.

How to Pretend You Are Something You Aren't

The 2006 elections brought heavy losses for Republicans. Not that they were undeserved. By this time, Republicans held two branches of government and couldn't shrink government at all. This was an opportunity that never existed under Reagan or Gingrich. Yet the Department of Education was thriving rather than being abolished. The budget was continually expanding rather than shrinking. The only obstacles that stood in the way of Republicans making change were Republicans standing against change. The revolutionary zeal from 10 years earlier had been lost.

As Tommy Thompson aptly stated, "We went to Washington to change Washington. Washington changed us."[10] True. But people change according to their environments. That Republicans hadn't established a steady flow of candidates to ensure that policy would remain limited and closer to the people was sign enough of the lack of Republican commitment to principle. Either you valued open, participatory government, or you didn't. Since Bush had arrived in office, the answer to that question was clearly "no."

Democratic victory, on the other hand, had been engineered by Rahm Emanuel, who had no problem pulling more conservative Blue Dog Democrats into the fold. While these Blue Dogs would provide the Democrats with a majority, they would also prove to be a constant thorn in their side. The Democrats had their talking point—that the American people had resoundingly repudiated the Bush message. But they also fibbed to get there—the Blue Dogs had campaigned on conservative issues like fiscal discipline.

That's right: When Democrats are running like conservatives in order to stay in power, it's a sure sign that things are looking up. But how to turn that into something real? How to use that to truly reduce the size of government?

Meltdown

It's all fun and games until the economy tanks and you're suddenly faced with the prospect of a run on the banks. That thought must have been the thought running through every market-minded conservative at the time of the first cracks in the U.S. economy.

But rather than exemplify selfishness, stirrings among conservatives about the financial crisis were rooted in deep-seated frustration that market forces had been led so far astray by government incentives. As the American Enterprise Institute's Peter Wallison writes:[11]

> What is required instead is an appreciation of the fact—as much as lawmakers would like to avoid it—that U.S. housing policies are the root cause of the current financial crisis. Other players—greedy investment bankers; incompetent rating agencies; irresponsible housing speculators; shortsighted homeowners; and predatory mortgage brokers, lenders, and borrowers—all played a part, but they were only following the economic incentives that government policy laid out for them. If we are really serious about preventing a recurrence of this crisis, rather than increasing the power of the government over the economy, our first order of business should be to correct the destructive housing policies of the U.S. government.

These destructive housing policies were arguably borne out of a genuine desire to help the impoverished. While Democrats had done little to look into the consequences of such disastrous fiscal (and social) policy, conservatives in Congress were equally culpable for failing to address what would become the flame that lit the economic powder keg.

2008 Election

History repeats itself, and conservatives are not immune to this immutable law. In many ways, as the excesses of his predecessor, Ford, laid the groundwork for Reagan's common sense, small-government conservatism, so did the straying of the Republican party following the elections of 1994 and 2000 tarnish the conservative movement and allow for the election of one of the most radical presidents our nation has ever seen.

Barack Obama won by playing to the middle by promising tax cuts while simultaneously saying he planned on "fundamentally transforming the United States of America."[12] Many—including those in the White House—saw the election of Barack Obama as a referendum on small government.

This was not the case, as campaign rhetoric showed. If he was talking to certain crowds, he was happy to emphasize the importance of small government and low taxes. While Obama promised to protect 95 percent of Americans from any tax hike, Sen. McCain pushed the case for taxing health care, the government buying up bad mortgages, and the first round of bailouts (corporate handouts) being necessary to save our economy. When the economic crisis hit with full force, McCain "suspended his campaign" (fat chance) and returned to Washington to help broker a deal to help the country. But it was naked political opportunism, and the Obama campaign's charge that McCain had acted erratically and irresponsibly started to stick.

McCain's stance thoroughly hurt and diluted the Republican almost-tradition of standing on principle. More practically speaking, it made distinguishing between the two candidates on many issues nearly impossible. As both men ran to the center, the only distinguishing characteristic involved their age and party affiliation. Why not pick the guy who didn't suddenly pull a political *Ferris Bueller's Day Off*? McCain had never sounded coherent on economic policy and his chickens were coming home to roost.

Democratic strategy was smart. By pandering to the middle, they locked in the greatest number of votes they could muster. Those who were on board with Obama and were sick of the Bush years were going to vote no matter what. And those who considered themselves more independent minded would wonder about what happened to the old John McCain while pulling a lever for a man they couldn't be sure wasn't espousing policies contrary to their own values.

As Peggy Noonan remarked in a *Wall Street Journal* Op-Ed, speaking of the Democrats and the Obama administration, "Their 2008 win left them thinking an election that had been shaped by anti-Bush, anti-Republican, and pro-change feeling was really a mandate without context."[13] As Noonan states, there *was* a context. There was the context of Republicans losing their way paired with an empty suit who promised "change" and "hope."

The House and Senate also took heavy losses as Republicans finally saw an end to their own revolution. One wonders whether, as the election returns came in, any congressmen wished they had voted for fewer government bills.

Hope and Change We *Can* Believe In

A major part of the 2008 campaign, one that I'd be remiss not to discuss, was the rise of libertarian sensation Ron Paul. Congressman Ron Paul ran for and lost the Republican nomination in 2008. Paul was an unlikely sensation to drum up grassroots support. His campaign focused on the most radically assertive hope that the Republican Party could once again take up the mantle of limited government and fiscal responsibility.

Congressman Paul, then 73 years of age, was the Republican change candidate. As part of the Liberty Caucus, a group of Republicans that advocate for limited government, he sought to infuse those ideas into the broader Republican party and take them to the national stage. Paul had a highly motivated network of grassroots supporters who held rallies and fundraising events across the country. By the summer of 2007, he would have more cash on hand than John McCain.[14]

It would be difficult, however. Paul had been accused in news reports of including racist content in his newsletter.[15] Blocked out of many of the primary debates, and with impressive gains but not enough delegates to clinch the GOP nomination, Paul withdrew from the race, refusing to endorse the Republican or Libertarian candidate.

His support only galvanized, culminating in a concurrent convention in Minneapolis during the GOP convention at which McCain was nominated. Paul's alternative convention drew plenty of press and crowds of over 10,000.[16]

It wasn't that Paul had originated new ideas. It's that he finally arrived at a time when they resonated with an increasingly restive public. If waking the GOP up and shaking the establishment is what he wanted, he certainly made an impact. By 2009, as the GOP would begin to reassess the political landscape after the losses of 2008, Ron Paul's message and grassroots tactics were touted by the GOP elite as preconditions for future success.[17]

A Center-Right Nation

A cursory examination of this brief history illuminates that the United States is a center-right country that typically favors individual liberty, smaller government, and personal responsibility. While elections exhibit the pendulum effect, an often healthy mix of the two parties controlling different branches, the fact remains that people generally prefer less government intervention than more.

The election of Barack Obama was an overcorrection toward a gilded path. That he could get elected promising fiscal responsibility is, by today's lights, hilarious. While the current path toward hegemony is uncertain and in disarray, it is one that Obama seems more than happy to expedite by increasing the size of the budget. What he doesn't realize is that for every notch he increases it, people react viscerally.

The tea parties represent the opening of Americans' eyes to this reality. They represent the collective wisdom of the people—not populism, not the rule of might makes right, but the collective desire to be true to founding principles—a union of individualism, if you will. This is a beautiful self-correcting force built into our democratic process and protected by law—the right to speech, the right to protest. It is these aspects that those in power fear, as indicated by their reactions to the protests on which we will later elaborate.

It is *because* of the fear and the adverse responses elicited from runaway spending, freedom-restricting big-government politicians, and their special-interest constituents who pull their strings and ride their coattails to pad their lecherous lifestyles, not in spite of these reactions, that the methodologies and principles embodied in the tea parties and the permutations thereof can and should lead to a genuine resurgence of small government conservatism and the preservation of the founding principles, which that philosophy of governance promotes and protects.

During the financial crisis, great stress has been placed on the need for fairness, for extreme measures, for abandoning a reckless free-market system that has left too many Americans economically traumatized. This hardly bucked a trend.

Big-government advocates could be easily relied on to use any event as an occasion for government to "do something"—whether or not there was a crisis in the air. Drastic times call for drastic measures, sure, but how drastically politicians have moved shows how poor their grasp of the idea.

Defending the idea is not a fight exclusively against admitted liberals and big-government advocates. It's really against all of those who use the rhetoric of capitalism, of limited government, of free markets, while abiding by the exact opposite. It's those who have promised to lead the march against the Leviathan, but have settled on a strategy that merely resists—rather than repeals.

In other words, it's about coming to terms with the myth of a Republican party that is led by conservatives and libertarians informed by free market, liberty-oriented principles. It is not. But it can be. Doing so is only one part of a larger strategy, however, one that emphasizes that the only way to maintain American liberty is to be willing to fight for it.

Republicans lost their principled ground and thus lost elections. Their voters typically identify as conservative or free-market oriented. Their allegiances lie with principles not personalities. Thus, when the principles fall by the wayside, so does the electoral support. Voters don't show up, or show up for the other guy, rolling the dice on "change." As the purveyors of the empty change would soon find out, empty or misguided principles can be as big a weakness as principles lost.

Enter the tea party counterrevolution: by the people, for the politicians.

CHAPTER 3

THE WHISTLING TEAPOT

THE FINANCIAL CRISIS AND THE BAILOUT NATION

True, governments can reduce the rate of interest in the short run. They can issue additional paper money. They can open the way to credit expansion by the banks. They can thus create an artificial boom and the appearance of prosperity. But such a boom is bound to collapse soon or late and to bring about a depression.

—Ludwig von Mises, *Omnipotent Government:
The Rise of the Total State and Total War*
(New Haven, CT: Yale University, 1944)

Ludwig von Mises' quote succinctly sums up what led the country into the financial crisis: The financial crisis that led to trillions of dollars in bailouts also created a robust counterbailout movement. But what made millions of Americans take to the streets and tune in at home for the tax day tea parties and the thousands of rallies and protests that followed?

A brief review of the financial crisis and the bailouts, handouts, and spending that followed puts the backlash the nation saw in perspective.

The Original Sin: The CRA

Despite the facts, members of the media and the Left eagerly sought to spin the collapse of the housing industry and the ensuing financial crisis as a failure of the free market. These ill-informed big-government advocates worked hard to lay the blame at the feet of the Republicans who were in charge and on a set of economic principles that had guided and developed the most dynamic and robust economy the world has ever seen. This wasn't new. For years, the Left had tried and failed to change the predominant economic theory in the country away from the principles of capitalism and free markets. The Left had been losing this fight miserably but with an economic crisis occurring under a Republican president the Left began to feel that this was their opening to finally produce a paradigm shift in the United States.

It doesn't take much digging for one to find the real culprits of the housing and financial collapse. The mandating of lending to noncreditworthy individuals through the Community Reinvestment Act (CRA), manipulations of the tax code in favor of home ownership, the Federal Reserve keeping interest rates artificially low, and two ill-conceived government-sponsored enterprises (GSE) all share some of the blame, along with some wacky regulations. These public policy blunders created and expanded by Democrats and Republicans alike artificially built up the housing industry to unnatural levels. It was only a matter of time before the housing bubble had to pop.

The CRA, originally signed by President Jimmy Carter and revised numerous times afterward, was created to force banks into lending in low-income minority neighborhoods. Later, the CRA played a key role in forcing banks to allocate housing loans to people who wouldn't otherwise be creditworthy enough to get a loan for a home.

Robert Litan, an economist for the liberal Brookings Institution, who advised the Clinton administration on financial industry deregulation told the *Washington Post* that "If they [banks] wanted a merger approval, they had to show they were making a conscious effort to make loans to subprime borrowers. If the CRA had not been so aggressively pushed, it is conceivable things would not be quite as bad. People have to be honest about that."[1]

The Tax Code

The abundance of tax breaks and tax subsidies provided through the tax code to homeowners and prospective homeowners certainly fueled the housing boom. According to a study completed by Gerald Prante, the senior economist at the Tax Foundation, if you combine everything "from the mortgage interest deduction to the deduction for real estate taxes paid to the capital gains exclusion for primary residences, the federal tax code funnels more than $100 billion dollars annually into the housing sector. That's nearly 10 percent of total federal income tax collections, enough so that if the subsidies were repealed, we could cut every personal income tax rate by 14 percent."[2]

This overabundance of housing tax breaks lobbied for by the housing industry in the tax code helped to influence its fair share of renters to become home buyers regardless of their financial standing. The incentives to buy a house as a substitute to renting were made so lucrative that it was hard to say no, especially since the return on investment was shooting through the roof.

Easy Money

In the wake of 9/11, the Federal Reserve began sharply reducing interest rates out of fear that the economy was in danger. The interest rates were cut down from 6.25 percent to a record low of 1 percent in 2003. Lawrence White, the F. A. Hayek Professor of Economic History at the University of Missouri–St. Louis, summed up the Federal Reserve's involvement best. "Our current financial turmoil began with unusual monetary policy moves by the Federal Reserve System and novel federal regulatory interventions. These poorly chosen public policies distorted interest rates and asset prices, diverted loanable funds into the wrong investments, and twisted normally robust financial institutions into un-sustainable positions."[3]

With money being loaned out to banks at interest rates lower than inflation, the Federal Reserve was handing out essentially free money, a disproportionate amount of which went toward pumping up the housing industry.

Take a Loan off Fannie

While there is plenty of blame to go around, another instigation of the financial crisis was imprudent public policy that created the mortgage giants Fannie Mae and Freddie Mac. These government-sponsored en-terprises (GSEs) have roots that date back to the Great Depression in an effort by the federal government to increase home ownership. Iron-ically, these organizations would play a significant role in *causing* the financial crisis we face today by the government indirectly subsidizing and implicitly guaranteeing mortgages and securities thereby increasing overinvestment in the housing industry.

As GSEs, Fannie and Freddie have enjoyed significant benefits not afforded traditional lenders. In addition to a direct credit line from the U.S. Treasury, they receive billions of dollars a year in indirect federal subsidies.[4] What's more, these organizations on their own ac-cord and through prodding from Congress took an already backward, anti-market mandate—to expand low-income home ownership—and lowered their standards. They lowered their standards for recipients of mortgages, they increased how many people they leant to, and they lowered their own internal standards for leveraging their actual capital.

There is a reason many low-income individuals can't afford a home or get approved for a good mortgage rate: They don't have enough income and don't have the credit to get approved for good mortgage rates. The first part should be simple, and it is something many politicians glaze over: Don't buy what you can't afford. You can't create affordable housing. You can find housing at a lower cost, but you can't *create* housing, for example, overlooking Central Park that is affordable for low-income families. It either costs what the market dictates—a lot—

or it is subsidized by other taxpayers, artificially lowering the cost for the purchaser.

The second component should also be easy to understand. Many people don't qualify for "good" mortgages (that is, lower priced interest rates) because they *shouldn't*. Mortgage lenders need to manage risk, otherwise they would go out of business—or in today's political climate, if they are big enough, get a bailout from, you, the taxpayer. The fact of the matter is many people don't qualify for better rate mortgages because they have a high rate of defaulting on said mortgages. Thus, mortgage lenders need to have a system to mitigate these inevitable loses. This comes in the form of higher lending rates. The market adjusts for this reality through various lending standards that take into account income, credit rating, et cetera. Fannie and Freddie are great examples of how government-induced market meddling does not solve problems, but creates problems. Turning a blind eye to statistics, these two lenders eventually had to face facts. Although, instead of the political enablers and the shortsighted leadership of the mortgage behemoths bearing the consequences—the taxpayer is on the hook.

In his testimony before Congress on February 24, 2004, Alan Greenspan even warned of the fast pace that Fannie and Freddie had been growing at and how their presence was distorting the housing market. In his prepared remarks, Greenspan said "in the event of a crisis involving Fannie and Freddie, policymakers would have little alternative than to have the taxpayers explicitly stand behind the GSE debt,"[5] and that is exactly what the federal government ended up doing.

It was both Republicans and Democrats with their minds focused on home ownership as a center stone for public policy in the United States that helped fan the flames that Fannie and Freddie originally sparked. Congress, under both a Democrat and a Republican president, took steps to lower the standards for loans and encourage them to buy up more risky mortgage-backed securities in order to get more people into homes. As Dan Mitchell, senior fellow at the Cato Institute explained, "In 2000, Bill Clinton's Department of Housing and Urban Development made a bad situation even worse by imposing so-called affordable-housing quotas on Fannie and Freddie. The government-sponsored enterprises responded by becoming huge purchasers of securities containing sub-prime mortgages. This further contributed to systemic instability and the housing bubble. The Bush administration added fuel to the fire in 2004 by increasing the affordable-housing quotas, and Fannie and Freddie responded by lowering the standards for mortgages they would purchase for securitization."[6]

With all these public policy incentives in place to subsidize and promote the housing industry, the price of real estate grew astronomically. The blind encouragement of the housing market through any means necessary led countless individuals to begin stretching their money out in real estate and running up huge mountains of debt they couldn't afford. In far too many cases, many people even began learning how to "flip" a house into a quick and risk-free investment by watching get-rich-quick real estate infomercials.

Crisis

The combination of public policy blunders, which created the rapid rise in housing prices, and our public officials and special interest groups promoting home ownership as if it were the be-all and end-all of the U.S. economy, all contributed to the housing industry's demise. With a perfect storm of government interventions it was only a matter of time until this house of cards came tumbling down. In its ruins was a devastated financial market, a tanking stock market, and millions of people left wondering what happened?

With the banking industry on the edge of bankruptcy we began to see solutions reminiscent of communist Russia percolate in Washington, D.C. Normally calls for more government intervention and socialist-based ideas were crucified and not given much thought outside liberal academia and extreme liberal policy wonks. This was different, and with many Americans scared and worried about their 401(k)s and their families' well-being, many of these ideas unfortunately began to take hold on Capitol Hill.

As Newton's Third Law of Motion says, "For every action, there is an equal and opposite reaction." The same is true with political movements—especially ones that take a country toward socialism. It was in response to Washington's adoption of an increasing number of heavy-handed government "solutions" that the tea parties unwittingly grew.

As evidenced by the eventual size and strength of the tea party backlash, it is obvious that many Americans weren't buying big government as the solution. Maybe, as in the Bernie Madoff scandal, it was government that helped cause—or at least enable—the problem in the first place.

Bailouts, Handouts, and Corporate Welfare

The first shoe dropped as the liquidity of subprime mortgage companies such as Countrywide Financial was beginning to be compromised by defaulting mortgages.

In June 2007, CNN.com reported that two Bear Stearns-run hedge funds with large holdings of subprime mortgages ran into large losses and were forced to dump assets. The trouble spread to major Wall Street firms such as Merrill Lynch, JPMorgan Chase, Citigroup, and Goldman Sachs, which had loaned the firms' money.[7] When the financial sector began posting billion dollar losses due to the collapse of these mortgage-backed securities and investments, the federal government started to respond.

At this point, the financial market was teetering on the edge and the federal government began supporting the takeover of weakly positioned banks by stronger banks. The ball started rolling in January of 2008 when Bank of America bought Countrywide Financial for $4 billion. From there JPMorgan took over Bear Stearns and Washington Mutual; Bank of America also bought up Merrill Lynch, and Wells Fargo took control of Wachovia.

The first legislative shoe dropped on July 30, when President Bush signed the Housing and Economic Recovery Act of 2008, which included $300 billion in new loan authority for the government to back cheaper mortgages for troubled homeowners. On September 7, Fannie and Freddie were officially placed under full-blown government conservatorship by the Treasury, which put up $200 billion in order to back their assets. Less than 10 days later, the Federal Reserve offered up an $85 billion bailout to the collapsing American International Group (AIG) and pushed $70 billion into the nation's financial system in an attempt to loosen up credit.

Congress, feeling the need to fix the financial crisis, on October 3 passed the Emergency Economic Stabilization Act of 2008, a $700 billion bailout of the entire U.S. financial system proposed by Treasury Secretary Hank Paulson.

Baby You Can Buy My Car

Bailouts are like Lays potato chips—you can't have just one! Once you open that bag and taste the sweet goodness of special interest reciprocity, you can't stop. So when the CEOs of the failing auto companies flew from Detroit in their private jets to make the case for an auto bailout it was a mere formality. The real question was not if they would receive taxpayer funds but how much of a bailout they would receive. With the combined auto bailout tab reaching $80 billion there is little assurance that taxpayers will see that money back or that the American car companies will be able to survive without even more government intervention. In September's Congressional Oversight Panel for the Troubled Asset Relief Program's (TARP) report the government watchdog group disclosed that it was unlikely that all that money would be paid back to the taxpayers.[8] It is about time government got out of the auto industry and leave these struggling companies to restructure their contracts, innovate according in response to market, and compete without the crutch of taxpayers.

Newspapers Bailouts

As if the auto bailouts weren't enough, liberal politicians decided to target another noncrucial sector of our economy that they owed alms to: newspapers. Liberal politicians rely heavily on liberal newspapers for free PR. As bailout fever progressed, newspapers, struggling to survive under the auspices of delivering unbiased news, began to eye a piece of the federal bailout pie. Leading the way was Sen. Ben Cardin (D-MD) who has actually put the bailout into legislation by introducing S. 673 or the Newspaper Revitalization Act. The bill would give newspapers the ability to restructure as a nonprofit 501(c)(3) corporation, which

President Obama has said he would be open to. With the rise of the new media and its knack for scooping newspapers, it is wrong for government to give preferential tax treatment to one type of media outlet. I love *Car Talk* as much as the next guy, but do we really need print versions of NPR?

Balance Sheet

Neil Barofsky, the special inspector general of TARP, testifying before the House Oversight and Government Reform Committee on July 21, 2009, said that, "Since the onset of the financial crisis in 2007, the federal government, through many agencies, has implemented dozens of programs that are broadly designed to support the economy and financial system. The total potential federal government support could reach up to $23.7 trillion."[9] While this amount is the worst-case scenario, as he puts it the sheer size of the total would make almost any taxpayer's heart skip a beat. Bloomberg's detailed analysis of the total costs said that, "The U.S. government and the Federal Reserve have spent, lent, or committed $12.8 trillion."[10] This number is higher than the national debt ($11.7 trillion not including unfunded liabilities). Some big-government types might argue that this amount is inflated, but actually it is the most accurate because it not only includes the bailouts but also the preferential tax treatment handed out to failing companies and both stimulus plans. What this means for you and me is that the federal government has committed $42,666 for each of the roughly 300 million men, women, and children in the United States.

Account Overdrawn

These handouts to banks and other failing companies struck a chord with Main Street Americans who were seeing their government spend and spend while leaving them by the wayside. The spending racked up by both the Bush and Obama administrations in the aftermath of the housing and financial crises was more than was spent, even when adjusted for inflation, on the New Deal and World War II combined!

With bailouts building and billions of dollars flying out of the Federal Reserve and Treasury daily people started to ask, "How are we going to afford this?" These same people were sitting around dinner tables with their families discussing how best to budget during this fragile economic period. Parents had to tell their children that Santa Claus wasn't going to be able to bring as many presents this year. Trips and luxuries that they had been enjoying before the collapse were now being cut because they knew they had to be responsible and not run up debt.

While families were making sacrifices at home they witnessed their own government printing and spending money as if it grew on trees, they saw two presidents handing over billions of dollars to failed companies, and they saw people who bought houses they obviously couldn't afford in the first place get a free pass.

In the end, government had created a huge moral hazard and it wasn't merely theoretical. It was real, and real expensive. Government was now telling us that if you make bad decisions running your family business sorry that's business, but if you were "too big to fail" and make even worse decisions that government would be there to bail you out.

This "too big to fail, too small to succeed" philosophy was a pill many Americans were unwilling to swallow.

CHAPTER 4

THE POLITICAL CLASS REACTS

The price good men pay for indifference to public affairs is to be ruled by evil men.

—Plato

Not surprisingly, reactions from politicians to the tea parties ranged from praise to apathy to downright hostility. What was surprising, however, is the intensity with which the Left reacted—and not just obscure, freshmen congressmen. Democratic leaders including House Speaker Nancy Pelosi, Senate Majority Leader Harry Reid, and the commander-in-chief himself lashed out at protestors.

When White House Press Secretary Robert Gibbs was initially queried about the president's response to the tea parties, he said the president wasn't aware of the hundreds of thousands of people expected to turn out on tax day. Recall Bush Sr. not knowing about scanners at the grocery stores? The media latched on to this to show how out of touch he was with ordinary Americans.[1] Later, George W. Bush[2] and

Sarah Palin[3] were assailed for not reading newspapers or not reading the correct newspapers. Where was Obama getting *his* news?

Gibbs wasn't the only one in the Political Class[4] who remained ignorant—intentionally or otherwise—of the widespread tea parties. According to a Rasmussen Reports poll, 25 percent of Americans personally knew someone who attended a tea party.[5] This is in sharp contrast to the Political Class, 1 percent of whom reported knowing someone who attended a tea party. It seems clear that our politicians are staggeringly out of touch with their constituents.

Through interviews and press conferences to supporter-stacked town halls, partisan opponents of the tea parties attempted to undermine the protestors, questioning everything from their motives to their right to speak out.

It was shocking. As Rick Santelli had said less than half a year before, "This is America!"

Memo from the White House: You Just Don't Get It

One day after Santelli's on-air rant, White House Press Secretary Robert Gibbs was asked about the brewing frustration of Americans over the president's foreclosure plan, which promised that only people who acted responsibly would be helped. Gibbs' reply initially pointed the finger back at Santelli, "I've watched Mr. Santelli on cable the past 24 hours or so. I'm not entirely sure where Mr. Santelli lives or in what house he lives."[6] As if Santelli's financial situation and house had anything to do with the merits of his argument?

Gibbs eventually got around to answering the question, stating:

> Here's what this plan will do. For the very first time, this plan helps those who have acted responsibly, played by the rules and made their mortgage payments. This will help people who aren't in trouble yet, keep from getting in trouble.
>
> You can't stay in this program unless you continue to make mortgage payments. That's important for Mr. Santelli and millions of Americans to understand.
>
> Here's what this plan won't do: It won't help somebody trying to flip a house. It won't bail out an investor looking to make a quick

buck. It won't help speculators that were betting on a risky market. And it is not going to help a lender who knowingly made a bad loan and it is not going to help—as the president said in Phoenix—it is not going to help somebody who has long ago known they were in a house they couldn't afford. That's why the president was very clear in saying this was not going to stop every person's home from being foreclosed.

Of course, Gibbs can't prove that. And doesn't anyone in trouble *by definition* seem to have been taking out mortgages for houses they couldn't afford?[7] A second reporter pushed this point:

> The criticism that's common on the housing plan is similar to the criticism that came on the bank bailout, both before you came into office and in phase 2, which is, there are people who were irresponsible who will be helped. Period. . . . People are going to use that to say this is not fair.

Gibbs replied:

> There is—there will be people that made bad decisions that in some ways will get help. This plan, though, I think it's important for the American people to understand, was designed to help those that have been responsible.

So this program is not supposed to reward bad decisions, but don't worry, it is *designed* to help people on the brink of facing the consequences of their bad decisions that they thought were responsible.

The nuances and PR spin of this (and other) bailouts differ. Sometimes the pitch is that we have to bail out reckless individuals and corporations because it is for the "greater good." Other times, as with Gibbs in this case, it is that we are only going to shield the helpless and innocent victims of said reckless behavior. No matter how you cut it, though, somebody has to pay for these solutions. That "somebody" is inevitably someone who made more prudent decisions. These people are likely living more income-appropriate lifestyles than the very people they are bailing out. That is where the outrage is, and that is something that neither the Obama administration—nor the Bush administration, for that matter—have an answer for.

Gibbs also repeated the president's analogy about putting out a fire at your neighbor's house. "You don't debate it, you get a hose and try to put the fire out. That's what's most important." Except in this case, it's like putting out a fire with water that *you* have to pay for. To run with Gibbs' analogy, let's compare underwater homeowners to victims of a brush fire started by neighborhood kids. The rage is about forking over taxpayer money to those who made stupid decisions, like having open bonfires in the family room and recklessly flicking lit cigarettes onto booze-soaked carpets. This is not a sympathetic picture.

This analogy illustrates a strategy the Obama administration has used repeatedly: Stress the urgency of the issue to avoid deliberation and criticism. The American people just don't buy this trick; we live in a representative democracy with checks and balances for a reason. It doesn't always make for swift, nimble government, but it helps prevent radical deviation from our founding principles.

Gibbs ended the press conference with the following:

> But I also think it's tremendously important that people who rant on cable television be responsible and understand what it is they're talking about. I feel assured that Mr. Santelli doesn't know what he's talking about.

For the millions of Americans at home frustrated about being punished for their good behavior, the White House had a simple message: You don't know what you are talking about.

From the Department of Homeland Security: A Preemptive Strike

On April 7, just one week before the tax day tea parties, the Department of Homeland Security released an internal report titled "Rightwing Extremism: Current Economic and Political Climate Fueling Resurgence in Radicalization and Recruitment."[8] The report was put out by the Extremism and Radicalization Branch of the Homeland Environment Threat Analysis Division in coordination with the FBI and released April 12 by the Liberty Papers blog.[9] The report was unclassified, which is a bureaucratic distinction that allows the document to be specified as sensitive and for certain eyes only, without limiting the distribution too narrowly to say, those with "Top Secret" clearance. This allows agencies within the federal government to internally specify things they believe should be exempt from Freedom of Information Act (FOIA) requests for press or taxpayers.[10] In this case, the report was specifically intended "for official use only." The document reads that the information is "Law Enforcement Sensitive," and portions of the release of the document may be exempt from Freedom of Information Act requests from citizens.

The report, initiated under the Bush administration, was filled with references to current events potentially instigating a rise in domestic right-wing extremism. It ran the gamut from racism, xenophobia, militias, and domestic terrorism to conspiracy theorizing. I do not seek to defend the indefensible racism and conspiracy theorizing; rather, it is the timing, scope, and release of this report in reaction to the tea parties by politicians and media that are my concern here.

The report starts off with a chilling section on the scope of the report, the last sentence of which reads: "Federal efforts to influence domestic public opinion must be conducted in an overt and transparent manner, clearly identifying United States Government sponsorship." Just why the feds are in the business of influencing taxpayer opinions is not clear. They shouldn't be—they're in the business of working for the taxpayers, not working the taxpayers like an infomercial pitchman. That said, Uncle Sam keeping an eye on social movements is nothing new. In the days of COINTELPRO (an acronym for Counter Intelligence Program), the FBI ran covert operations to gather intelligence on and to actively subvert communist, socialist, women's rights groups, and civil rights groups. The group's explicit mission was "protecting national security, preventing violence, and maintaining the existing social and political order."[11] This would not be the last instance in which the Obama administration may have stretched civil liberties to make its political ends meet. Following the tea parties, questions would arise as to whether the government broke the Privacy Act of 1974,[12] passed following Nixon's extensive use of federal agencies for personal political purposes.[13]

Interestingly, the first paragraph of the report calls into question the need for the creation of the report itself:

> The DHS/Office of Intelligence and Analysis (I&A) has no specific information that domestic right-wing terrorists are currently planning acts of violence, but right-wing extremists may be gaining new recruits

by playing on their fears about several emergent issues. The economic downturn and the election of the first African American president present unique drivers for right-wing radicalization and recruitment.

"Right-wing," as defined by the report, includes "those groups, movements, and adherents that are primarily hate-oriented (based on hatred of particular religious, racial, or ethnic groups), and those that are mainly antigovernment, rejecting federal authority in favor of state or local authority, or rejecting government authority entirely." The idea that those who "favor state or local authority"—often appropriately and legally so—would be characterized as not only right-wing but in the same group as militant white power groups is nothing short of bizarre. It's called federalism, and it is a basic tenant of our system of government.

What's more, the report does not name a single current incidence, group, or individual as evidence. Instead, the report associates the current increase in civil discontent with previous militia activities and domestic terrorism:

> The current economic and political climate has some similarities to the 1990s when right-wing extremism experienced a resurgence fueled largely by an economic recession, criticism about the outsourcing of jobs, and the perceived threat to U.S. power and sovereignty by other foreign powers.
>
> During the 1990s, these issues contributed to the growth in the number of domestic right-wing terrorist and extremist groups and an increase in violent acts targeting government facilities, law enforcement officers, banks, and infrastructure sectors.
>
> Growth of these groups subsided in reaction to increased government scrutiny as a result of the 1995 Oklahoma City bombing and disrupted plots, improvements in the economy, and the continued U.S. standing as the preeminent world power.

As an example, the report cites an April 4, 2009, incident in which a man shot three police officers in Pittsburgh, Pennsylvania. His reaction, according to the Department of Homeland Security, "reportedly was influenced by his racist ideology and belief in antigovernment conspiracy theories related to gun confiscations, citizen detention camps, and a Jewish-controlled 'one world government.'"

What is odd about the inclusion of this incident is that, with the exception of two incidents involving plots against the president that are later broadly referenced, it is the only specific case the report cites as evidence of a trend or uptick in right-wing activity. What's more, this particular incident took place only three days before the release of the report. So what exactly inspired someone to write it in the first place?

The report then cites the election of Barack Obama as an instigating force behind said resurgence in right-wing extremism. Following the election of Obama, there was a spike in gun and ammunition purchases. Newly-installed Secretary of DHS Janet Napolitano was no friend of second amendment rights,[14] and law-abiding citizens were concerned—given her and Obama's track record on the subject—that their constitutionally guaranteed right to keep and bear arms might be restricted. The DHS report implied that this *could* signal a resurgence in militant activity:

> Many right-wing extremist groups perceive recent gun control legislation as a threat to their right to bear arms and in response have increased weapons and ammunition stockpiling, as well as renewed participation in paramilitary training exercises. Such activity, combined with a heightened level of extremist paranoia, has the potential to facilitate criminal activity and violence.

Again, the report cites no current indicators, but refers to the past:

> Prominent among these themes were the militia movement's opposition to gun control efforts, criticism of free trade agreements (particularly those with Mexico), and highlighting perceived government infringement on civil liberties. . . .
>
> During the 1990s, right-wing extremist hostility toward government was fueled by the implementation of restrictive gun laws. . . .

The state of the economy is cited as a motivator for right-wing extremists as well:

> Historically, domestic right-wing extremists have feared, predicted, and anticipated a cataclysmic economic collapse in the United States. Prominent antigovernment conspiracy theorists have incorporated aspects of an impending economic collapse to intensify fear and paranoia

among like-minded individuals and to attract recruits during times of economic uncertainty.

This report muddies the water between legitimate critics of fiscal policy and black helicopter conspiracy theorists. The state of the economy *was* bad at the time of this report, and the outlook on the future state of the economy, according to countless experts, is quite dire in light of the heavy-handed government intervention into the marketplace we saw with bailouts, handouts, and regulations. In a *New York Times* Op-Ed published just one day after the tea parties, economist Paul Krugman stated that "the most you can say is that there are scattered signs that things are getting worse more slowly—that the economy isn't plunging quite as fast as it was." He went on to caution: "Don't count your recoveries before they're hatched."[15]

And many of those concerned about the constitutionality of the government takeover of banks and federal stimulus dollars are reasonable people. But the report goes on to cite concerns of illegal immigration, a highly volatile topic whose debate has its fair share of xenophobes but also plenty of reasonable people who see our broken immigration system, see its consequences, and want to see reform that works.

One of the more striking parts of this report is buried at the end under a section entitled "Disgruntled Military Veterans."

> DHS/I&A assesses that right-wing extremists will attempt to recruit and radicalize returning veterans in order to exploit their skills and knowledge derived from military training and combat. These skills and knowledge have the potential to boost the capabilities of extremists—including lone wolves or small terrorist cells—to carry out violence. The willingness of a small percentage of military personnel to join extremist groups during the 1990s because they were disgruntled, disillusioned, or suffering from the psychological effects of war is being replicated today.

Like much of the report, the supporting evidence is shaky if not lacking, citing the 1990s, an anonymous musing from a civil rights group, and a report from the previous year:

> After Operation Desert Shield/Storm in 1990–1991, some returning military veterans—including Timothy McVeigh—joined or associated with right-wing extremist groups.

A prominent civil rights organization reported in 2006 that "large numbers of potentially violent neo-Nazis, skinheads, and other white supremacists are now learning the art of warfare in the [U.S.] armed forces."

The FBI noted in a 2008 report on the white supremacist movement that some returning military veterans from the wars in Iraq and Afghanistan have joined extremist groups.

Not one specific case or statistic was mentioned. As could be anticipated, many veterans were offended at being singled out, particularly in light of no trend of veterans committing such crimes. David K. Rehbein, national commander for The American Legion, a nonprofit, community service veterans organization, wrote DHS Secretary Napolitano a letter that included the following:[16]

> On behalf of the 2.6-million-member American Legion, I am stating my concern about your April 7 report, "Rightwing Extremism: Current Economic and Political Climate Fueling Resurgence and Recruitment."
>
> ... The best that I can say about your recent report is that it is incomplete. The report states, without any statistical evidence, "The possible passage of new restrictions on firearms and the return of military veterans facing significant challenges reintegrating into their communities could lead to the potential emergence of terrorist groups or lone wolf extremists capable of carrying out violent attacks. ...
>
> Your report states that "Right-wing extremists were concerned during the 1990s with the perception that illegal immigrants were taking away American jobs through their willingness to work at significantly lower wages." Secretary Napolitano, this is more than a perception to those who have lost their job. Would you categorize union members as "right-wing extremists"?
>
> ... I would be happy to meet with you at a time of mutual convenience to discuss issues such as border security and the war on terrorism. I think it is important for all of us to remember that Americans are not the enemy. The terrorists are.

Rehbein eventually accepted Napolitano's apology, although other veterans and veteran organizations remained skeptical.[17]

The report's closing section referenced "echoes" of the 1990s, concern of strict firearm regulation in the pipeline, and the uncertain economy "may be" stoking the fires of right-wing extremism.

That's a lot of work for a closing assessment of "may be." The threat assessment of the theoretical crimes of the Right seems odd when compared to the actual crimes of the Left. While this report was formulated and released, the Left's "activists" were actually hitting the streets with their radical tactics. Code Pink rushed stages,[18] ACORN "foreclosure fighters" were breaking into houses,[19] activists were storming Bear Stearns,[20] and violent, anticapitalist G20 hoodlums clashed with police in London.[21]

The report, regardless of its original intent, fueled the unfounded claims that the tea parties were somehow racist protests. In their loose affiliations, vague references, and in what the report said and did not say, it was easy for the Left to run with it as an implicit report on the tea parties and dossier on tea party participants. Secretary Napolitano eventually apologized for the report, stating that that infamous footnote defining "right wing" would be the main thing that she would have changed.[22]

The fact is that the timing was odd, the scope was too large, and the tenor of the report was much different than comparable reports. In January of 2009, a DHS report[23] detailed tangible examples of wing nut activity like environmental groups that bombed car dealerships and animal rights groups that attacked laboratories. This report citied specific groups and specific crimes that occurred, thus giving tangible, actionable intelligence to law enforcement officials. This is in sharp contrast to the right-wing report that consisted largely of vague, incendiary insinuations from a politically opposed administration that gave plenty of ammunition for allied Left-wing media and operatives to attack their critics.

Such extreme behavior on the Left is often ignored or even rewarded. Paul Watson of the Sea Shepherd Conservation Society and his merry band of seasick hippies board the ships of and harass Japanese whalers with guerilla tactics like glass stink bomb and acid attacks.[24] They've even rammed ships[25] and interfered in sailor rescue attempts.[26] Watson believes the human species is a "virus"—the "AIDS of the earth"—in need of drastic reduction.[27] These ecoterrorists have their own show glorifying their exploits on *Animal Planet*.[28]

While the DHS report was certainly suspicious, a report that made its way to the media on tax day at least seemed to be aimed directly at the movement. On April 15th, it was revealed that the Maryland National Guard specifically named tea party attendees as potential threats. The report, dated April 9, 2009, was entitled "Planned TEA Party Protests (FPCON Advisory 09-004)."[29]

> This Maryland Army National Guard (MDARNG) Force Protection advisory is in response to nationwide planned protest activities scheduled for April 15, 2009. Although there is no known direct threat to MDARNG facilities and MDARNG members, they may become a target of opportunity during planned protest activities throughout Maryland. . . .
>
> Numerous entities have formed recently to express displeasure/anger over recent federal/state government actions: more taxes, increased spending, higher deficits, a surge of borrowing to pay for it all, bailout of the financial institutions, etc. This movement can be identified by different variations of "TEA Party" or "Tea Party." Past "TEA Party" events have been peaceful. There was a "tea party" event at Solomons, Maryland, on March 22, 2009. "TEA" stands for "Taxed Enough Already."

Just why are peaceful protests and their philosophical nature important to the National Guard? Did any state's National Guard posts take a similar pre-emptive action toward antiwar protestors? There is no evidence that they did, and the media outcry would have been (justifiably) boisterous.

The Maryland document continued by listing "known locations" in the metro-D.C. area. The announcement then gave advice on what to do should protestors harass personnel or trespass. Guardsmen were encouraged to "Keep family members informed. Talk to other service personnel to share information. Practice OPSEC [Operational Security]. Don't provide personal information to anyone you don't know. Avoid high risk areas." The strangest part of the entire document was that at the end, the point of contact for the warning was the "antiterrorism program coordinator."[30]

Thus, it doesn't seem a stretch to think that just months later as taxpayers protested congressional town halls and spoke their minds, the media would bring up the largely baseless claim—again—that the rallies were "hate fueled."[31]

Congress Claims We're All Astroturf

Speaking of tea parties and attendees on *KTVU* on tax day, Nancy Pelosi said:

> What they want is a continuation of the failed economic policies of President George Bush which got us in the situation we are in now. What we want is a new direction. . . . This initiative is funded by the high end, we call it Astroturf, it's not really a grassroots movement, it's Astroturf by some of the wealthiest people of America to keep the focus on tax cuts for the rich instead of for the great middle class.[32]

This unfounded claim was repeated by pundits and politicians for weeks and resurfaced during the town hall protests during the August 2009 congressional recess. Like many criticisms of the movement, this was false.

Hundreds of thousands of Americans expressed their discontent over excessive spending and government expansion on April 15, 2009. They didn't do it for money; they did it *because they cared*. Many organizations played a role in facilitating, not funding protests. You can't get people off their couches and out of their houses to protest because an organization says so. You can get the word out through networks on Facebook and Twitter and through web sites and e-mail. Hundreds of thousands of highly motivated citizens make up and utilize these networks created by people at groups like Americans for Prosperity and FreedomWorks. Their explicit mission is to facilitate genuine grassroots movements. They do not need to, desire to, nor have a history of paying people to protest. In fact many citizens and governors rejected what they saw as unsustainable, inequitable wealth distribution in the form of the stimulus and rebate checks.[33,34]

It is not surprising that Pelosi and others assumed that protests were Astroturf. Manufactured protests funded by billionaires are the *modus operandi* of many on the Left. Most liberal groups (like MoveOn.org and the Center for American Progress) and the protests they support are funded by liberal billionaires George Soros[35] and Herb and Marion Sandler.[36] Soros, to the disillusionment of many on the Left should they find out, made and continues to make much of his wealth as a speculator.[37] The Sandlers made much of their fortune dumping toxic mortgages on soon-to-collapse Wachovia, although they don't appreciate the insinuation they had anything do with it.[38] President Obama made his own political bones working within the Leftist Astroturf model as a community organizer.[39]

Backroom deals and arm-twisting aren't the only Chicago exports to make their way to the Beltway. David Axelrod, Obama campaign strategist turned senior adviser, previously made a living as a high-end Astroturfer. He's deployed the strategy in his home community of Chicago through two extremely secretive organizations: AKPD Message and Media consultancy and ASK Public Strategies. The latter organization's goals are anything but in the public interest. According to 42nd Ward Alderman Brendan Reilly, Axelrod's ASK Public Strategies is "the gold standard in Astroturf organizing. . . . ASK has made a name for itself in shaping public opinion and manufacturing public support."[40]

Support for the highest bidder, typically corporations looking to drum up public support through shell consumer groups. Think of him as a public opinion mercenary. While Axelrod sold his share in the companies upon taking his job at the White House, his son remained. By August of 2009, ASK would be one of the firms signed to push Obama's health care agenda in an alliance with Leftist financiers, lobbyists, unions, and the pharmaceutical industry.[41]

David Axelrod went beyond his boss' casual air of divisiveness to an outright attack on the protestors. Here is Axelrod in a *Face the Nation* interview on April 19th with Harry Smith:

Smith: What do you make of this spreading and very public disaffection with not only the government but especially the Obama administration, the tea parties this week? You even have the governor of Texas using the word secession. Should Texas be allowed to secede?

Axelrod: Well, I don't think that really warrants a serious response. I don't think most Texans were all that enthused by the governor's—

Smith: But what about the first part of the question, this growing disaffection?

Axelrod: I think any time that you have severe economic conditions, there is always an element of disaffection that can mutate into something that's unhealthy.

Smith: Is this unhealthy?

Axelrod: Well, this is a country where we value our liberties and our ability to express ourselves. And so far, these are expressions. Now, one thing I would say is the thing that bewilders me is this president just cut taxes for 95 percent of the American people, so I think the teabags should be directed elsewhere because he certainly understands the burden that people face.

Did Axelrod really mean that tea consumption could be unhealthy—perhaps because of the caffeine? Just another example of liberal nanny-statism? Or did he mean that when productive members of society go to rallies, they can't make money during that time and thus can't be overtaxed to subsidize the democratic base, thus suggesting that the protests were unhealthy *for the economy?*

Or did Axelrod mean that speaking out against the president is unhealthy? If so, then it's fair to say that he doesn't believe in the First Amendment right to free speech if it means criticizing his worldview or policy ambitions. This may be the case, and it wouldn't be that unusual in that it's human nature to be for something in principle but against it in actuality, but it would be an unlikely thing for such a sly operative to admit on national television. Further, an all-out assault on protesting in general would be hypocritical and easily revealed as such coming from someone whose boss, after all, was a community organizer. Besides, protests have been a sacred ritual of the Left for decades.

Better to cast *these* protests as unhealthy. The implication seemed to be that they were unconstructive, violent, maybe even racist as insinuated in the Department of Homeland Security report. Whether Axelrod meant to disparage protests he didn't agree with or First Amendment rights in general, Americans heard a candid statement from the president's right-hand man and a glimpse at a mind-set that is, one might say, unhealthy for democracy.

Straight from the Economist-in-Chief Himself

Just eight weeks after the successful tax day tea parties, President Obama gave an address at a town hall meeting where the audience provided preassigned, preapproved questions.[42]

I know you've been hearing all these arguments about, oh, Obama is just spending crazy, look at these huge trillion-dollar deficits, blah, blah, blah. Well, let me make a point. Number one, we inherited a $1.3 trillion deficit—that wasn't from my—that wasn't me. [Applause.] That wasn't me.[43]

The Obama administration inherited a $1.3 trillion dollar debt from an 8-year administration that had prosecuted two wars. Even Paul Krugman admits that the vast majority of the deficit is due to failure to get Medicare and Medicaid under control and the wars in Iraq and Afghanistan.[44] A good chunk, of course, would in the 11th hour of the Bush administration be spent on the Troubled Asset Relief Program (TARP) and the federal takeover of Fannie Mae and Freddie Mac.[45] Obama writes off the fact that his administration doubled this inherited debt within months of being in office as irrelevant, as if two wrongs make a right.

... There is almost uniform consensus among economists that in the middle of the biggest crisis—financial crisis—since the Great Depression, we had to take extraordinary steps. So you've got a lot of Republican economists who agree that we had to do a stimulus package and we had to do something about the banks.

Democrats love using a false consensus to make a point. It has been deployed especially nicely by Al Gore and company in order to make the case for the existence of catastrophic, human-induced, climate change and the need for immediate action. Obama does the exact same thing, citing agreement among experts as a reason to go against all reason.

"Almost uniform consensus" is an odd turn of phrase. Consensus is by nature uniform, and it either exists or it doesn't, making "almost" unnecessary, unless of course one is trying to make a strong point with a little breathing room so as not to be called a liar.

Those are one-time charges, and they're big, and they'll make our deficits go up over the next two years. But those aren't the problem that we face long term.[46]

"One-time charges," sounds like a gym membership—"don't worry, this is a one-time initiation fee." Which begs the question, what is Obama selling? He's selling the idea that these short-term, large deficits don't matter. On closer analysis, Obama's pledge[47] to halve the national deficit after his first term is laughable.[48]

But deficits "aren't the problem we face long term." What is, then?

> What we face long term, the biggest problem we have is that Medicare and Medicaid—health care costs are sky-rocketing, and at the same time as the population is getting older, which means we're using more health care. You combine those two things, and if we aren't careful, health care will consume so much of our budget that ultimately we won't be able to do anything else. We won't be able to provide financial assistance to students; we won't be able to help build green energy; we won't be able to help industries that get into trouble; we won't have a national park system; we won't be able to do what we're supposed to do on our veterans. Everything else will be pushed aside because of Medicare and Medicaid. That's the problem that we really confront.[49]

In other words, if we don't spend a ton of money right now that we don't have, Yosemite National Park will shut down, nobody will go to college, we can't subsidize T. Boone Pickens' windmill boondoggle, and we can't "do what we're supposed to do on our veterans," whatever that means. Of course I kid; Obama is correct that Medicare and Medicaid are financially unstable. So is Social Security, and we need to sustain and improve care for our veterans. If only we hadn't let those greedy speculating private sector Enron-types run those programs into the ground. Wait a second, those are all government-run programs. Yet Obama and his allies are looking at further government intervention and more government bureaucracies to *solve* the problem. On top of that, not one of the health care plans put forward at this time actually effectively dealt with the underlying issues like the unfunded liabilities of Medicare and Medicaid.[50]

Even if they could, just how does increasing the national debt not matter? The Congressional Budget Office estimated that congressional health care plans would be revenue neutral *at best*. In other words, they will either bring us about to the same state of financial instability or worse.

> So, you know, when you see—those of you who are watching certain news channels on which I'm not very popular [laughter] and you see folks waving tea bags around [laughter] let me just remind them that

I am happy to have a serious conversation about how we are going to cut our health care costs down over the long term, how we're going to stabilize Social Security. Claire [McCaskill] and I are working diligently to do basically a thorough audit of federal spending. But let's not play games and pretend that the reason is because of the Recovery Act, because that's just a fraction of the overall problem that we've got.[51]

Obama's first job was that of a community organizer. That he would have such disdain for the millions of Americans protesting the "almost uniform consensus" that our debt is too high is rich. You'd think a man who started his short career as a community organizer would at minimum respect the right of Americans to protest. Instead, he mocked the millions of people exercising their constitutionally guaranteed right to organize and express their opinion. A classier approach would have been to recognize the millions of frustrated Americans, and somehow spin it that he was trying to speak to them and trying to help them, and ask them to give his policies a chance. There was no such effort—he simply dismissed them outright and in similar vein as the silly pundits like Janeane Garofalo, Rachel Maddow, and Keith Olbermann.

Obama closed with what sounded like a nod to fiscal responsibility but morphed quickly into an unfounded and irrelevant Bush bash:

We are going to have to tighten our belts, but we're going to have to do it in an intelligent way, and we've got to make sure that the people who are helped are working American families. And we're not suddenly saying that the way to do this is to eliminate programs that help ordinary people and give more tax cuts to the wealthy. We tried that formula for eight years. It did not work, and I don't intend to go back to it. [Applause.]

For one, as was established when Obama started his speech in defense of his own spending, government did, in fact, grow under Bush. This included augmented programs to help the needy—programs Obama endorsed, then tweaked and expanded.[52] Furthermore, it was Bush and Hank Paulson who twisted congressional and bank leadership arms to start the spending spree—a spree that Obama was continuing. It would be funny if it weren't so serious.

The Obama administration's lack of tolerance for dissent—and respect for freedom of speech—was in sharp contrast to his predecessor's administration, often assailed as "fascist." Google and Lexis Nexus searches for the variously combined terms "Rove," "Bush," "antiwar protestors," "un-American," "unhealthy," and "mock" yield no such evidence. In fact, one of the biggest criticisms of Bush's handling of antiwar protestors was that he wouldn't meet with Cindy Sheehan, a leading activist in the antiwar movement whose son died in combat. Tea party protestors weren't asking for meetings with the President of the United States, just not to be attacked and ridiculed by him and his administration.

Interestingly, Obama's lack of respect for popular protests for democracy weren't limited to those within the borders of the nation he governs. A few months later, we would see a belated, timid endorsement of the millions of Iranians protesting a heavy-handed government and what appeared to very likely be a rigged election.[53]

The Response from the Right

The GOP did not and likely could not have garnered the momentum necessary for the tea party movement to take off. The question of why is largely answered in Chapter 2. The recent phenomenon of Ron Paul rallies was the closest popular movement to core principles that could compare. The reactions of Republican politicians to the tea party movement were mixed and interesting.

Lou Dobbs reported on April 20 that many so-called conservatives got lukewarm to hostile receptions in their districts. Republican Gresham Barrett, who supported the Bush-initiated bailouts, was met in Greenville, South Carolina, by constituents who turned their back on him—literally. Representative Barrett assured attendees that "It's about people being heard. It's about your voice. And I shall promise you one thing, guys, you may boo, you may turn your back, but I have devoted my life to the conservative cause." At which point, one man shouted, "Go home!"

Then there was Michael Steele. A major disappointment to the GOP, Steele had failed to give the shot of adrenaline to the party that was expected. A number of gaffes stood out as the sole distinguishing characteristics of the early days of his term as chairman of the Republican National Committee.[54],[55]

Leading up to the tax day tea parties, Steele's scheduler reached out to Eric Odom, a disaffected libertarian whose Twitter handle's profile picture was a "no politicians" sign modeled after a no parking or no smoking sign. Confused when he didn't accept the invite, one can only imagine how foolish he felt when it was publicized that he was turned down. While Odom may have pushed the dramatic element, he certainly had a point.[56]

Where was Michael Steele and the RNC in February? In March? Did they simply make the calculation once the movement was going strong that they should be involved? What took so long? To make matters worse, Steele's shop denied the conversation ever took place.[57]

Why not just say "we respect that this is a time for the people, not politicians to talk. Chairman Steele will be there in the audience fully participating"? Steele then canceled plans to speak at a Young Republican event taking place that evening, lest it look like he went to a less cool party.

A month after the tax day rallies, the Republican Governors Association (RGA) hosted "Tea Party 2.0" with South Carolina Gov. Mark Sanford, of foreign affair fame, and Texas Gov. Rick Perry. It was billed as a tele-town hall for the fiscal conservatives to get in touch with grassroots activists and take their ideas into the public policy realm—a novel concept, and one that should be commended.

Calling it a Tea Party 2.0, though, was strange and arguably detrimental. Usurping the tea party mantra does two things: It annoys the protestors who turned out, and it fuels the false claim that the tea parties were GOP run, sponsored, endorsed, funded, and so on.[58]

Sanford and Perry's idea was fantastic. These rallies aren't ends in and of themselves; the goal is to *accomplish* something. What that means is making a difference where the rubber meets the road, with politicians who make policy. The fact that two prominent governors were listening and acting was good, but they needed to show something for it, not just throw a party.

Sanford eventually did just that. He was one of a few governors (including Rick Perry of Texas, Bobby Jindal of Louisiana, and Haley

Barbour of Mississippi) to reject stimulus funds. Eventually, he lost the debate to the South Carolina legislature, took a break to go "hiking," and it was eventually revealed that he was having a long-distance affair with an Argentinean woman. So that was that.

Others Show a Healthy Respect

Other politicians realized the value of a hands-off recognition of the protests. Representative Mike Pence of Indiana, head of the Republican Study Committee, is a self-proclaimed conservative with a record to match. On tax day in an appearance on MSNBC's *Hardball* with me, Pence deftly addressed how the protests were not partisan, but principled. When guest host Mike Barnicle questioned why the tea parties were only springing up now, after years of increases in government spending, Pence replied:

> Well, you know, I think it's a fair question, Mike. But candidly, now I know how the old settlers back in the West felt when the cavalry came riding over the hill. Those of us that have been fighting deficit spending, the growth of government over much of the last decade under Republican administrations, and continuing to fight it under a Democrat administration, are heartened to see people like John stepping forward, millions of people across this country today that know we can't borrow and spend and bail our way back to a growing America. . . .[59]

Pence makes a valid point without attempting to brand the tea parties as GOP backed. Some in the GOP, himself included, *have* been principled. Pence is quick to admit that this has been the exception, and that bipartisan outrage from taxpayers is well-founded. Barnicle pushed the point, asking why now under Obama and not under Bush. Pence responded:

> You know, when I came out against the Wall Street bailout last fall, I thought I'd be in a distinct minority in the Congress. And then in one week, Mike, after I came out against it and a majority of House Republicans opposed our own president on the Wall Street bailout, I got 10,000 e-mails in 5 days. And that's just what got through.

You'd have to ask John, who's one of the leaders of this grassroots movement in the country, what motivated him. But I really think something happened last fall when the American people saw the prior administration and the Democrat Congress willing to get out our grandchildren's credit cards and bail out bad decisions on Wall Street. And the stimulus bill and the budget that was just passed are all adding steam to that anxiety.

Pence's recognition of the principles behind the tea parties while keeping the GOP at arm's length was constructive. He showed that the GOP can not and should not take credit for this grassroots surge. This was in sharp contrast to the RGA and Steele's attempts to insert themselves into the movement. Ironically, his healthy respect is more likely to turn out votes for candidates like him within the GOP that stick to their guns on important fiscal issues important to the millions of Americans that make up this movement.

Out of the Loop

With a few notable exceptions, the vast majority of politicians on both sides of the aisle found themselves outside the tea party movement. From outside the movement, many that fancied themselves reborn fiscal conservatives tried to jump on the bandwagon, only to fall off and land face first in the mud. Those without a hope—mostly on the Left—cried loudly to not pay attention to the thousands of citizens behind the curtain, they're only hate-mongering racists, after all.

The nonpolitician movement spoke to not merely the nonpartisan nature of the movement, but to just how severely out of touch those that occupy the marble offices of the Beltway and state capitols really were with the principled concerns of the electorate.

The vast majority of the news media, rather than speaking truth to power, opted to serve as enablers of the defunct status quo, choosing to protect the political elite in lieu of leveraging and magnifying a powerful movement of citizens attempting to keep them in check.

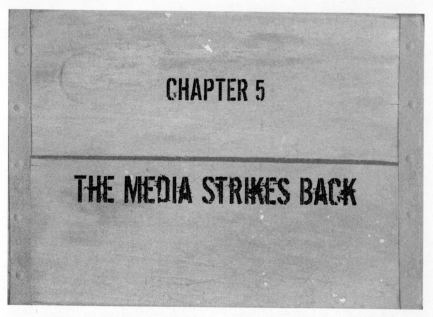

CHAPTER 5

THE MEDIA STRIKES BACK

I read . . . chiefly the advertisements, for they contain the only truths to be relied on in a newspaper.

—Thomas Jefferson, Letter to Nathaniel Macon,
Monticello, January 12, 1819

It didn't take long.

The press had been so caught up in the excitement about President Obama's election that the only opposition coverage it provided was of a demoralized Republican Party. Where in one photo, the new occupants of the White House were smiling and attending balls, another photo would depict neutered GOP leaders.

Worse, the same GOP leadership that was around during the last disastrous 10 years was receiving coverage as it discussed rebuilding. It was as though the election had happened in a vacuum and Republican incompetence had nothing to do with it. Concerned columnists would advise the Republicans what was really needed to make a comeback. It was the end of an era and the start of a new golden age.

In conservative and libertarian circles, it is widely claimed that most journalists and outlets in the news media are biased toward the left in varying degrees. Nine times out of ten, the average news article or broadcast is implicitly, if not explicitly, sprinkled with commentary that taints the news. Facts are frequently twisted or intentionally omitted so the story fits a more liberal mold. While the nature of this bias can range from ferociously critical to blatantly ignorant, no one believes the press can always get it right. What matters, however, is whether they try.

If any reader takes issue with this premise, the tea parties make for an excellent case study. Much of what was seen from the media went beyond the typical bias of nuanced word choices. Many times, the coverage was outright hostile toward the organizers and participants of the rallies. Worse, the media didn't even seem to want to try to get it right or be fair.

When all was said and done, the negative coverage would prove to be a double-edged sword for the Left. The coverage may have rallied its base, but it further alienated the protestors who already had a grievance with the press. Not giving them their due was only going to make them more enthusiastic. It also led Independents and those in the middle to be more sympathetic to the tea party protests.

Media Blackout

Some 300 protestors of all political stripes stood in Lafayette Square Park facing the White House in February. Across the country, thousands more protested. As a multicity event with a fair number of participants organized at a grassroots level in less than a week, you would think this would have been a newsworthy event. The headlines would have been easy: Working Americans speak out! Fed up! Mad as hell!

This was, after all, an organic protest of the largest explosion of federal spending in the history of printed money let alone the United States. News organizations covered the stimulus largely from the perspective of *something* needing to be done—our protest was the perfect opportunity to balance that reporting.

Besides, this was happening mere weeks after the inauguration of a popular president, during which time it was said that the opposition of big-government forces was in disarray. The allegedly dispirited fighters for smaller government were picking up bullhorns and taking to the streets. This new president who would usher in a new era of bipartisanship had already genuinely raised the hackles of your neighbors. Whether you saw it as a big deal or not, it was clearly something of a deal. This was more than anonymous rants by who knows how many or how few individuals on blogs.

Instead, most of the coverage of the February event was limited to one cable news network and a few print media outlets. The coverage was more than we expected for our humble efforts, but vastly undercovered given what took place. The press missed a story of note: Americans were mobilizing in an unprecedented way, one that would change the terms of the debate. And while the press initially took the events to be a non-story, they would soon realize their error—and punish us for their early omission. It was almost like the reaction against Bush over the war in Iraq when the press seemed to repeat the party line about weapons of mass destruction instead of investigating and reporting. When there were no weapons found, the press punished the White House for their omission.

Mr. Obama, Are You Watching?

Due to the size and scope of the tea parties on April 15th, it was nearly impossible for the local and national media to ignore them. Rather than cover the events accurately, however, many outlets, commentators, and hosts attempted to undermine the events. Some downplayed the significance of the tea parties. Some branded them with the scarlet letters "GOP," as the last dying breaths of a defunct political party out of ideas and out of energy. Others simply giggled and made fun of them, invoking a double entendre that describes a sexual act.

Opinion pages reflected mixed reviews and television commentary was hardly definitive. Either it was some kind of opportunistic populist outcry, or it was a tax revolt. Or maybe it was a Republican thing? Or maybe it was angry white people. The media's ambiguity on the message was a testament to how centrally unorganized and real the event was.

Half a million Americans took the day off or took a long lunch break on short notice to protest runaway government spending and expansion. Millions more tuned in at home to watch the coverage. That's a significant movement, no matter how you cut it. Those in the media who wrote it off as "fringe" or cracked jokes were missing a piece of the puzzle: Fringe or not, understood or not, what was happening was worth covering. Speaking to these people would have made that much clear. But because they didn't, they lost an important detail: This was a very real, very serious backlash from a large segment of American taxpayers.

One of the most outrageous reactions from the media came out of Chicago, from the very office that had called me prior to the event with two strange questions and no desire to talk to participants or organizers in advance. CNN's Susan Roesgen, in covering the events, picked out a man holding a sign stating that Obama was a fascist, complete with a picture depicting him as Hitler. Regardless of the merits of President Obama and his radical policies, it was a strange and offensive sign. Oddities make news but, and this is important, that one sign was not representative of the signs, sentiments, or spirit of the rallies. Yet, out of over 5,000 people in attendance, Roesgen chose the one nut in the crowd. As Dennis Miller remarked to me afterward, one could walk into a deli and likely find a wacko out of a line of 10 people.

Roesgen was clearly singling out the oddest guy in the crowd to fit her agenda and to shape, not report, the news. She wanted to frame the crowd as hateful, extreme, Obama haters. "This is a party for Obama bashers," she reported, "this was organized by three different conservative groups." Of course, neither comment is accurate. The event was about principles, not personalities. It was about the unprecedented expansion in the power and scope of the federal government, and the consequences, both philosophical and practical for future generations. Furthermore, the slide in principled governance was not started, and will not end, under Obama. What was being discussed here—the financial crisis and ensuing bailouts, was started under the administration of Republican President George W. Bush. Signs and speakers—not to mention historical fact—contradict Roesgen's assertion.

The latter half of her comment is equally unfounded. She knew full well that the event was not organized by conservative groups. A few people organized the event in their own time with the help of dozens of volunteers. Many groups sent out notices, but the power of this event was in the thousands of people who called for it and then called their neighbors and friends to attend, be seen, and be heard. E-mails were sent by ordinary citizens to other ordinary citizens, none of whom were affiliated with a party or an institution. I worked nights and weekends and lunch breaks to make the event a success. There was no overarching organizational support. The same was done at events throughout the country. Interestingly, I clearly articulated as much to the CNN producer who called me before the event. Furthermore, the fact that no organization sponsored or owned the event was stated explicitly in the event's press release and demonstrated in both the breadth of speakers who spoke and individuals who attended the rally.

It is interesting to put that individual's inappropriate sign into historical context. Particularly given that we can easily compare it to another instance in which Roesgen encountered such extreme rhetoric. Bush Hating Derangement Syndrome (BHDS), while not technically recognized by the American Psychiatric Association's Diagnostic and Statistical Manual of Mental Disorders, is widespread and well known. The hypocrisy of coverage in this instance is quite stunning. On January 13th, 2006, Roesgen herself covered a rally in which a protestor dressed up as President Bush, with a Hitler mustache and devil horns. Did she call the protestor out for his radical behavior? No. In fact, she implicitly endorsed the outfit stating "while a look-alike showed up with a wad of cash, Mr. Bush did not."

What happened at the tea party after the encounter with the oddball sign holder was the most telling interaction of all. Roesgen's attempt at news made news around the country. After speaking with the sign holder, she went up to a man named Norm, standing in the crowd with a young child holding a sign that read, "I'm two years old and already in debt," and asked, "Okay, let's see, you're here with your two-year-old and you're already in debt, why are you here today, sir?"

Norm responded, "Because I hear a president say that he believed in what Lincoln stood for . . . Lincoln's primary thing was he believed that people had the right to liberty. . . ."

Roesgen interrupted, "Sir, what does this have to do with taxes, what does this have to do with your taxes? Do you realize that you're eligible for a $400 credi-"

Norm interjected, "Let me finish my point. Lincoln believed that people had the right to share in the fruits of their own labor and that government should not take it, and we have clearly gotten to that point."

But Roesgen had the last word: "Wait, wait, did you know that the state of Lincoln gets $50 billion out of this stimulus, that's $50 billion for this state, sir ... [looking back toward camera] I think you get the general tenor of this. It's anti-government, anti-CNN, since this is highly promoted by the right-wing, conservative network FOX."

Roesgen's behavior was strikingly different at a liberal protest she previously covered. Earlier, leading up to the inauguration, she reported on a protest of Veterans for Peace and Democracy Now in President Obama's neighborhood. "Small in number, big in spirit," Roesgen swooned, speaking of the six to eight individuals from "activist groups" standing near candidate Obama's Chicago home. Roesgen's piercing reporting that we saw on tax day 2009 hadn't quite yet been honed, hence insightful comments like "it's cold out here!" She also didn't quite yet have a handle on separating herself from the story, ending the segment with "Mr. Obama, are you watching?"

The difference in tone is amazing. The idea that a handful of protestors would be worthy of not only coverage, but also a prerecorded spot with voiceover, is laughable. Why did it happen? This particular protest fit the mold of appropriate, CNN-endorsed protests. They had reinforced a liberal political agenda, specifically keeping Obama accountable to left-wing campaign promises.

For a half a dozen liberals ensuring that the president kept his word on liberal promises, Roesgen's coverage was softball fluff—like a panda birth. For thousands of Chicagoans protesting said massive government spending (liberal tendencies), Roesgen acted like a rabid bulldog. She went after a father and child with the ferocity of Geraldo Rivera confronting a pedophile or a murderer. It was ... strange.

The exchange between the CNN reporter and Norm shows much more than mere media bias. It highlighted two important aspects of the tea parties. For one, the feds' hush money was of no interest to Norm and tea party goers. Here, where Roesgen thought she had a "gotcha" moment, she was actually making Norm's point for him. His concern was that in tough economic times, Americans tighten their belts and cut back on spending. Why wouldn't government do the same? Secondly, Norm had the wisdom that many of the politicians and pundits lack: Someone will have to pay for this (my child?). The idea that government would raise taxes, print money, and redistribute wealth indiscriminately was unconscionable to him. The idea is equally reprehensible to thousands of Americans, even if they are the short-term beneficiaries of said redistribution; they realize that there are long-term fiscal and philosophical repercussions of this type of reckless behavior.

The CNN run-in became a cause célèbre and eventually a tangible victory for the tea party protestors. Shortly after the event, Roesgen went on leave. Protests took place outside CNN offices across the country. By the summer of 2009, CNN opted to not renew her contract.[1] One can only surmise that her reporting talents will be better applied to local, human interest stories . . . like panda births.

Propaganda and Disinformation

More dishonest than Roesgen's reporting were the propagandizing Op-Ed pieces masquerading as factual reporting. One came from Paul Krugman, Nobel Prize winning economist. (Don't be too impressed by this; Al Gore has a Nobel Peace Prize for his work on global warming/climate change/global cooling. Like everything from toasters to bicycles to cars, they don't make Nobel Prize winners like they used to.) In an April 2009 Op-Ed in the *New York Times*, Krugman tore into the Republican Party:

> Today's GOP is, after all, very much a minority party. . . . Republicans have become embarrassing to watch. And it doesn't feel right to make fun of crazy people.
>
> One way to get a good sense of the current state of the GOP, and also to see how little has really changed, is to look at the "tea parties" that have been held in a number of places already, and will be held across the country on Wednesday. These parties—antitaxation demonstrations that are supposed to evoke the memory of the Boston Tea Party and the American Revolution—have been the subject of considerable mockery, and rightly so.[2]

A *minority* party! That's great news, conservatives have been trying to widen their appeal for a while . . . oh wait. Note that Krugman begins the article about nonpartisan protests by cavalierly eliminating the very real distinction between the protestors and the GOP. This is intellectually dishonest.

Exactly why Krugman thinks the tea parties deserve mockery is not clear. Of course he describes the tea parties as "antitaxation"—not the more apropos "fiscal responsibility" demonstrations. The tea parties were not antitax. This is an exaggeration the Left used *ad nauseum* to oversimplify the tea party movement. Few people are antitax, many people are for lower taxes and for preventing impending higher taxes—like the higher taxes a cap-and-trade regime would inevitably bring down on the American public. While fighting excessive taxation is certainly a noble crusade, this was not the only tenant of the tea parties. Rather, they sought to protest the expansion of government as a whole and reinforce the larger idea that government works for the people, not for itself, not for specific interest groups, not for select organizations. For the people, by the people.

Krugman goes on to undermine the protests as fake:

> . . . it turns out that the tea parties don't represent a spontaneous outpouring of public sentiment. They're Astroturf (fake grass roots) events, manufactured by the usual suspects. In particular, a key role is being played by FreedomWorks, an organization run by Richard Armey, the former House majority leader, and supported by the usual group of right-wing billionaires. And the parties are, of course, being promoted heavily by FOX News.

Krugman's assertion that the tea party movement is a sad, GOP, Astroturf effort is disingenuous and provably false. FreedomWorks, like a handful of grassroots organizations, aided protestors on the ground with similar philosophical leanings. That is what they do. It hardly undermines the hard work of thousands of unpaid activists who made these rallies a reality. Much like thousands of volunteers across the country, I worked late nights and weekends, unpaid, to make the tea parties I was involved in a success. Attendees and organizers ran the policy gambit from liberals, to independents, to conservatives, to libertarians. If the movement was Astroturf as Krugman asserts, wouldn't Dick Armey, chairman and founder of FreedomWorks, jump to take credit for it? It would make sense. Nonprofits survive based on what they *can* take credit for. Yet he did not. Armey had this to say on *Meet the Press:*

> One of the fascinating things... about the tea party movement is it is an enormously impressive grassroots uprising across the country of loosely affiliated people, and there's probably 100, 200 different web sites by different people. Somebody in Oregon's got one, somebody in Illinois—we had a situation with somebody in Connecticut that we did not know and who did not know us put out something that was mischaracterized and then attributed to us by somebody who obviously didn't have enough diligence in their ability to do their research to get their facts straight. These things happen. People get blamed for what other people do. The fact is that just causes further aggravation, especially when you start talking about elected officials, people that have the privilege of having new shows under the license branded by the federal government. They should at least have the adult discipline to get their facts correct.[3]

With the Left, Astroturf is the status quo, so it is no surprise that they assume any protest is fake or funded by some man behind the curtain. It has long been known that this is the *modus operandi* of Saul Alinsky's brainchild and Obama's first employer, Association of Community Organizations for Reform Now (ACORN). The organization has a history of accidentally employing criminals who engage in voter fraud and financial funny business.

Months after the tea parties, as the health care debate heated up during the 2009 Congressional August recess, left-leaning ObamaCare groups would begin to place ads on Craigslist for people to help organize for hourly, daily, or weekly payments. The tea party protesters were not being paid. So who is Astroturf?

With regard to the rallies being GOP-run, Krugman ignores that Michael Steele was rejected as a speaker in Chicago. The fact is, this movement, like the frustration millions of Americans are feeling, transcends partisan politics. Hundreds of thousands of people turning out to protest unprecedented government spending is neither fringe nor sad, Mr. Krugman. What's sad is that the Left resorts to petty name calling and belittling when Americans are facing such serious problems.

Sexual Slurs

In an attempt to avoid any real discussion of real issues, some commentators decided to change the subject . . . to sex! On the left, talk of taxes and government expansion was dropped—arguments liberals seemed to be losing (perhaps because they didn't know much about the topics)—and turned instead to something they seem to know something about: ridiculing hardworking Americans and talking about obscure and obscene sex acts, like tea bagging.

For those of us not familiar with homoerotic fraternity hazing, (MSNBC and CNN associate producers, please bear with us for a minute), tea bagging is sexual slang for an act involving a part of a male's genitalia and another person's mouth or face. (For more detail, see the Wikipedia entry.) As of this writing, one third of the entry is dedicated to this subject in terms of the tea parties.

The movement expected substantive criticism. What we got was the mainstream media equivalent of a boozed up fraternity brother drawing male genitalia on our foreheads. It was weird.

A number of commentators turned out to be experts on both the act and its incorporation into news. In a reach around to their college-humor days, they worked hard to insert the joke wherever possible, no matter how contrived it was. Commentators didn't shy away. It was like watching a bunch of kids discover that you could type dirty words onto a computer screen.

Snarky liberal commentator Rachel Maddow had this to say on April 9, 2009, on her show on MSNBC:

> The Republican Party controls no real levers of power in Washington. They have yet to settle on any national leadership at all. They did come up with a Republican budget proposal in the House of Representatives, and 38 House Republicans even voted against that.
>
> The GOP, in other words, is clearly in exile. But the conservative movement has found a reason to live. They have found something about which they feel very positive, something which they are ready to rally around. I speak of course of tea bagging.

Cut to a clip of serious news people covering the newsworthy events of thousands of people organizing protests, followed by these comments:

Tea bagging. After spending weeks mailing teabags to members of Congress, conservative activists next week say they plan to hold tea parties to proverbially tea bag the White House. And they don't want to tea bag alone, if that's even possible. They want you to start tea bagging, too. . . .

Maddow brought Ana Marie Cox of Air America into the discussion. Maddow, doubting the Boston Tea Party parallel, described the protests as an outcry against reverting to the Clinton-era tax rates for the wealthy.

Well, it's the parallel they're trying to draw, Rachel, But you know, it is true that tea baggers are grossly unrepresented in Congress. I'm trying to work on that personally. But one can only do so much. I think David Vitter really is the right spokesperson for the movement, though.

Maddow responded:

Well, that's a point well taken and which I was afraid to allude to. And that's why you're here because you're braver than I am. So many Republicans are addressing the Tax Day teabag parties. Michael Steele has been rejected. Is he not considered a true tea bagger by the movement?

Skipping over the fact that Michael Steele having been rejected spoke to the nonpartisan nature of the event, Cox proceeded to joke about homosexuals:

Well, you know, he said in that GQ interview that he thought tea bagging wasn't a choice, that you couldn't change whether or not you would be a tea bagger. I think the tea baggers now really believe that it's something they've chosen to do, that they could change if they wanted to. But they won't.

Maddow continues to then associate the tea party movement with white power groups and groups that support armed revolution. What starts as a reasonable assertion that you can't be held responsible for who agrees with you, turns into a less-than-subtle association with white supremacists and militant extremists:

Well, in terms of what's going to happen on tax day and what's been happening with the tea bagging of Congress, which has been happening through the mail, which I didn't even know was possible, I sort of never believed you can be held responsible for the people who say they agree with you.

So we had this enthusiasm expressed for the tea bagging events by white power groups like Stormfront and by the secessionists and by the armed militias. And I don't think you can really hold the tea baggers responsible for that. But is there a radical message here? I mean, the whole idea here is about revolution, sort of, right?

Fortunately, Cox takes the question about as seriously as most Americans take Maddow's political insight:

Well, yes. I mean, I think that the people—the tea baggers would like it to be more radical than it is. But the fact is people have been tea bagging for a long time and they probably will continue to do so.

Maddow's comment about extremist groups was actually part of a significant campaign to slander the taxpayer protests. At least she named names and gave the benefit of the doubt that tea party planners couldn't be held responsible for fringe endorsements. Unfortunately, as I will later outline, the Obama political appointees at the Department of Homeland Security explicitly attempted to link the tea parties to a resurgence in racist, militant extremism in an official government report.

Anyone who attended or watched the tea parties knows that the events were not about race and that any assertions to the contrary are sad attempts at hurting a strong movement many on the left fear. Maddow could have taken the opportunity to note the unhinged participants of the forum at Stormfront.org as being a source of trouble for tea parties.

(Don't take my word that race played no role here, just ask them. Posts at Stormfront.org, the site of the group mentioned by Maddow, spoke of usurping the tea parties for their sick cause. Wrote "waxwing": "If you live in Chicago, please help me by *infiltrating* [emphasis added] the event and holding an interesting sign." Further posts spoke of hijacking the tea parties to send anti-Israeli, anti-immigration messages.) These racists wackos didn't *align* with tea parties, they saw them as mass, high-profile gatherings where they could possibly hold up a sign and get attention. But that nuance doesn't fit into the narrative about disenfranchised racists descending upon government buildings en masse.

Maddow continued the interview, switching the subject to what the tea parties were *really* about: Obama bashing!

Fair enough. Most of the energy of these events seems anti-Obama. You saw all, you know, the Facebook and Twitter things, "Tea bag Obama. Tea bag Obama." But then, there's the rejection of Michael Steele and I wonder if there's also a chance that this sort of gets channeled into being tea bag Arlen Specter, tea bag John McCain, against Republicans who voted for any of the bailouts.

Of course the tea parties were about the growth of government and fiscal irresponsibility. But to address that would be to highlight the subjects as legitimate grievances taxpayers may have, and Maddow wouldn't want to devote valuable airtime to something like that. That would be irresponsible journalism. Cox plunged ahead running with the sex joke about John McCain:

> Well, who wouldn't want to tea bag John McCain—that's all I have to say. But I really think actually it's probably going to be more directed at Obama. And this is actually very much a part of, I think, the midterm strategy. You know, it's going to be tea bagging like 24/7 when it comes to midterms.

The interview ended with a few more schoolgirl jokes and this closing line from Cox: "I think the social tea baggers and sort of the fiscal tea baggers are really starting to move apart from each other."

In full disclosure, I'm not mad at Maddow, just disappointed. The guest's name was begging to be utilized for a joke.

Bad Comedy, Worse Commentary

Just what did this interview accomplish? It was a silly tone, okay. It wasn't particularly funny, aside from the shock value of appearing on an NBC channel in prime time. No new insights, no firmly grounded liberal principles. A movement can and should expect criticism, but this isn't criticism. It's just cynical immature guffawing.

David Shuster, while filling in for Keith Olbermann, struck similar notes. Here's a transcript from April 13, 2009. I numbered the double entendres to make sure you don't miss them:

> For most Americans, Wednesday, April 15th will be tax day. But in our fourth story tonight: It's going to be tea bagging day [1] for

the right wing and they're going nuts [2] for it. Thousands of them whipped out [3] the festivities early this past weekend, and while the parties are officially toothless, the tea baggers are full-throated [4] about their goals.

They want to give President Obama a strong tongue-lashing [5] and lick government spending [6]—spending they did not oppose when they were under presidents Bush and Reagan. They oppose Mr. Obama's tax rates—which will be lower for most of them—and they oppose the tax increases Mr. Obama is imposing on the rich, whose taxes will skyrocket to a rate about 10 percent less than it was under Reagan. That's tea bagging [7] in a nutshell [8?].

He went on to cite the aforementioned Krugman Op-Ed, closing with "if you are planning simultaneous tea bagging all around the country, you're going to need a Dick Armey."

Shuster, of course, drops the ball on his commentary by making a huge pair of false claims. For one, the idea that most tea party protestors will see a reduction in taxes is neither true nor the point of the protests. The protests were, as we know, about calls for broader fiscal responsibility and to decry the expansion of government power and size. Most people present at the events work for or own a small business, drive a car or buy things delivered on a truck, and heat or cool their homes. Under President Obama's agenda, they will all see tax hikes. In fact, at the time of these events, President Obama had already reneged on his promise to freeze or cut all taxes on 95 percent of working Americans. His promise to cut taxes on 95 percent is impossible according to experts, considered financial sleight of hand at best. As the *Wall Street Journal* editorial page noted, millions of Americans don't pay taxes, and thus an alleged tax cut is really a transfer of wealth funded by tax increases:

> The Tax Foundation estimates that under the Obama plan 63 million Americans, or 44 percent of all tax filers, would have no income tax liability and most of those would get a check from the IRS each year. The Heritage Foundation's Center for Data Analysis estimates that by 2011, under the Obama plan, an additional 10 million filers would pay zero taxes while cashing checks from the IRS.[4]

Obama's promise not to raise taxes on 95 percent of Americans was broken quickly when, within 16 days of being in office, Obama expanded the State Children's Health Insurance Program (SCHIP).[5]

This program, intended to serve poor children, often serves adults who aren't poor.[6] Furthermore, the bill raised taxes on a number of items Americans of all tax brackets consume.[7] By August of 2009, Treasury Secretary Timothy Geithner wouldn't rule out direct tax hikes on the middle class.[8]

Even if they saw no tax increase at all, many of the protestors who were present were rightfully concerned that their children will be saddled with the debt resulting from reckless bailouts and governance. The rant that gave voice to the concerns, Santelli's, was about people who took on more debt than they could service and then getting all of us to pay for it. In other words, the protests were about too much debt that we all end up paying for, and that led to financial crisis.

Shuster was able to work in both the cute jokes as well as to bring up solid (but wrong) points. But why not simply bring up the criticism and talk to a protestor? Why simply malign an entire movement or puckishly poke fun? When did MSNBC turn into Comedy Central?

Except this isn't comedy genius—this is childish blather.

While it is easy to simply focus on MSNBC, which is hardly circumspect about its alignment with the Left, CNN was surprisingly comfortable jumping onto the bandwagon. When Anderson Cooper asked David Gergen about how Republicans were positioning themselves, he quickly noted the one strategy that might get them far:[9]

Cooper:	And, David, where are Republicans kind of positioning themselves on all this at this point?
Gergen:	Well, Republicans are pretty much in disarray.
	They—they—the one thing they agree on is that they—they're warning about the deficits, that there's too much spending. And I think they will—I think they will be dragged kicking and screaming to any more intervention of the kind of Ali's talking about.
	But they have not yet come up with a compelling alternative, one that has gained popular recognition. So . . .
Cooper:	Tea bagging. They have got tea bagging.
Gergen:	Well, they have got the tea bagging.
	(Laughter.)
Cooper:	But there was an interesting Politico survey that was out today that said that, you know, the president—the trust level

in the president on economic issues is extremely high. And, you know, and everybody else in the administration is well below him. But the Republicans are a little below that. So, Republicans have got a way—they still haven't found their voice, Anderson. They're still—this happens to a minority party after it's lost a couple of bad elections, but they're searching for their voice.

Cooper: It's hard to talk when you're tea bagging.

Cooper proceeded to giggle as though tea bagging were a silly secret only he and his fellow commentators had discovered after a night of drinking at last year's Daily Kos Winter Solstice party.

Cooper later apologized, at least for the confusion and misinterpretation of his remark:

> I think it's an incorrect statement to say I was, in any way, trying to disparage legitimate protests. I don't think it's my job to disparage, or encourage, which oddly other networks seemed to be doing. Protest is the great right of all Americans, and it's not my job in any way to make fun of people or disparage what they're doing.
>
> If people took offense to that and felt that I was disparaging their legitimate right to protest, and what they were doing, then that is something I truly regret, because I don't believe in doing that. Having this discussion just takes away from the real story.

That's fair. It makes good sense to disparage something you respect with crude jokes. Those crazy tea baggers were just blowing things out of proportion.

Even accepting that Cooper was just seizing on the phrase out of context as a joke, he was still doing it on the air. If he felt the right to protest was so sacrosanct, why mock it with crude jokes? Does it really get so boring on the set that to have a little fun every once and a while you have to beat a dead horse like the tea bagging joke to get your jollies?

The Racism Straw Man

Not to be outdone by fill-in David Shuster, Rachel Maddow, or Anderson Cooper, Keith Olbermann covered the tea parties with reporting and commentary as illuminating as Nancy Pelosi's smile after a

Botox appointment. One day after the tea parties, on April 16, 2009, he ran a segment titled "Capitalist Tools" that featured actress-turned-commentator (and neuropsychologist) Janeane Garofalo. As a second-rate comic turned third-rate actress, who could be more qualified than Garofalo to discuss the news of the day and complex fiscal policy? Garofalo launched into a hate screed against the tea party protestors, conservatives, Republicans, and women in any of those groups. She managed to stun viewers with her theories of pop-psychology/eugenics and her fine-tuned barometer on racial relations by explicitly calling the tea party protestors "racist rednecks," an oft-insinuated sentiment of both Hollywood liberals and the Obama administration's Department of Homeland Security.[10] (I can't help but note that the nuance of the phrase suggests that Garofalo believes there are rednecks who are not racist, which I think is fairly open-minded of her.)

Olbermann kicked off the segment by playing a clip of a liberal blogger at a tax day tea party. Then a man took the stage and attempted to convince the crowd that Obama was going to cut their taxes. This is of course, not true. Within 16 days of taking office, Obama raised taxes through SCHIP that would affect all Americans.[11] Obama also favored cap-and-trade legislation, which would, by his and his administration's admission, result in higher energy prices.[12] The result, would be a de facto, if not outright tax on a number of goods.[13] This would only affect Americans who buy things produced in factories, heat or cool their homes, drive cars, or buy anything that is ever transported on an airplane or truck. In other words: everybody.

Regardless, Garofalo deduced that the crowd's rejection of false promises and the lack of a large crowd to believe one can spend their way out of economic turmoil was unadulterated racism.

Garofalo: You know, there's nothing more interesting than seeing a bunch of racists become confused and angry—

Olbermann: Yes.

Garofalo: at a speech they're not quite certain what he's saying. It sounds right and then it doesn't make sense. Which, let's be very honest about what this is about.

Olbermann: Uh hm.

Garofalo: It's not about bashing Democrats.

Olbermann: Yeah.

Garofalo: It's not about taxes, they have no idea what the Boston Tea Party was about.

Olbermann: That's right.

Garofalo: They don't know their history at all. This is about hating a black man in the White House. This is racism straight up. That is nothing but a bunch of tea bagging rednecks. And there is no way around that. And you know, you can tell these types of right wingers anything and they'll believe it.

Olbermann: Uh hm.

Garofalo didn't provide one instance of racism at these events, let alone evidence of racism being an instigating factor at these events. Sadly but not surprisingly, Olbermann did not question her outlandish claims. In fact, he actively *encouraged* her line of logic, yes ma'aming the most outlandish phrases she uttered.

Just when one would think the segment couldn't get any crazier, Garofalo launched into her theory on conservative brains. They are, after all, identical to white power brains, which is convenient because the subjects in this instance are one and the same:

> . . . except the truth. You tell them the truth and they become—it's like showing Frankenstein's monster fire. They become confused, and angry and highly volatile. That guy, causing them feelings they don't know, because they're limbic brain.

One can only assume this was a subject Garofalo concentrated on while earning her Ph.D. in neuroscience.

As any reasonable reader would surmise, one cannot *be* limbic brain anymore than one can "be kidney" or "be endocrine system." You couldn't say "liberals are spine," rather "liberals are spineless." Garofalo's insanity doesn't stop with this grammatical contortion:

> We've discussed this before, the limbic brain inside a right winger or Republican or conservative or your average white power activist, the limbic brain is much larger in their head space than in a reasonable person, and it's pushing against the frontal lobe. So their synapses are misfiring. Is Bernie Goldberg listening?

Usually a good dose of facts will wash away a liberal's house of cards. This is no exception. A brief science lesson reveals the absurdity of

Garofalo's claims. There is no limbic brain, rather, there is a limbic system or a limbic part of the brain consisting of the thalamus, hypothalamus, amygdala, and hippocampus.[14] The limbic system is located in the center of the brain, and Garofolo claims in "right wingers," it is pushing against the frontal lobe. The frontal lobe of the brain is associated with emotions but also higher reasoning and problem solving. Thus to claim that an individual's frontal lobe is being stimulated could be construed as a compliment, although a scientific misunderstanding.

The elements of the limbic system do contribute to emotional responses, but also long-term memory and sense of smell.[15] Perhaps Garofalo was confusing conservatives with elephants, the GOP symbol, said to "never forget"? This may or may not be true.[16] A finely-tuned olfactory system, however, would help alert one to her BS. While it is believed that emotion plays a role in partisan political decisions, some research doesn't point to one party or philosophy being more emotion-driven over another.[17]

Ironically enough, an MSNBC.com article (of all places) dispels Garofolo's assertion that this holds true only or significantly more for Republicans, conservatives, or "right wingers": "Democrats and Republicans alike are adept at making decisions without letting the facts get in the way."[18]

Other studies indicate that if any population trends toward making political decisions based on emotion, it is Democrats. In a research study using brain scans on Democrats and Republicans, Democrats elicited more emotional responses to both politicians they liked and disliked:

> ... One Democrat's brain lit up at an image of Kerry "with a profound sense of connection, like a beautiful sunset..." Brain activity in a Republican shown an image of Bush was "more interpersonal..."
> ... shown a Bush ad that included images of the Sept. 11 attacks, the amygdala region of the brain—which lights up for most of us when we see snakes—illuminated more for Democrats than Republicans...[19]

Olbermann prodded Garofalo to continue:

I don't think you do, for most of them. This is a—it's almost pathological or elevated to a philosophy or lifestyle. And again, this is about racism. It could be any issue, any port in the storm. These guys hate that a black guy is in the White House. But they immigrant bash, they pretend taxes and tea bags, and like I said, most of them probably couldn't tell you thing one about taxation without representation, the Boston Tea Party, the British imperialism, whatever the history lesson has to be. But these people, all white for the most part, unless there's some people with Stockholm Syndrome there.

Again Garofalo throws out the baseless racist claim, ascribing motive to people she doesn't even know that in any other context could be defined as slander, adding further that protestors are ignorant and don't understand history or taxation without representation. Garofalo reveals her own ignorance of history as she stumbles over the words masquerading as ideas in her knee-jerk rant. The protestors do understand the principle of taxation without representation and the idea that elected officials should work for the people and should be accountable to them.

Once more Garofolo inoculates herself from having to back up her racist claims by writing off any minority protestor as suffering from Stockholm Syndrome. I wonder if Kenneth Gladney suffers from Stockholm Syndrome? At a town hall protest during the August recess, Gladney passed out Gadsden "don't tread on me" flags. As Andrew Breitbart wrote in the *Washington Times*, Gladney "was viciously attacked by Service Employees International Union (SEIU) members. One called him a 'nigger.'" Who are the racists, exactly?[20]

Garofolo then accused right-wing media of influencing these events:

True, and Fox News loves to foment this anti-intellectualism because that's their bread and butter. If you have a cerebral electorate, Fox News goes down the toilet, very, very fast. But it is sick and sad to see Neil Cavuto doing that. They've been doing it for years, that's why Roger Ailes and Rupert Murdoch started this venture, is to disinform [sic] and to coarsen and dumb down a certain segment of the electorate. But what is really, I didn't know there were so many racists left. I didn't know that. I—you know, because as I've said, the Republican hype and the conservative movement has now crystallized into the white power movement.

Well isn't that calling the kettle black, as Garofolo and Olbermann foster anti-intellectualism and pseudoscience? Of course "disinform" is not a real word. Ironic that Garofalo would make such a blunder while ranting about conservatives' lack of intellectual prowess. We'll give her a bye, though. Her expertise is, of course, in sociology and neuroscience, not the English language. Olbermann accepted her premise, asked a follow-up question, then turned the conversation to political strategy.

Olbermann: Is that not a bad, long-term political strategy because even though your point is terrifying that there are that many racists left, the flip side of it is there aren't that many racists left.

Garofalo: They're the minority, but literally tens of people showed up to this thing across the country.

Tens of people? Of course there were over 5,000 in Chicago alone, 10,000 to 15,000 in Atlanta and other cities, for a net turnout of a quarter to half a million people.

Even if one were to accept their false premise that the tea party goers were such a small number of people, then why give so much attention to them, why all the vitriol from Olbermann and Garofalo? First, no one covered the protest and the movement, then they covered it and worked mightily to disparage it, then it was back to "but it's no movement."

Olbermann sensed the conversation was running out of unfounded dramatic TV fodder:

Olbermann: What happens if somebody who's at one of these things hurts somebody?

Garofalo: That is an unfortunate byproduct since the dawn of time of a volatile group like this of the limbic brain. Violence unfortunately may or may not ensue. It always, it's like a, the Republican Party now depends upon immigrant bashing and hating the black guy in the White House.

Olbermann brought up the prospect of violence at the tea parties, why? Was he praying for a tea party Altamont? Of course, one did not come. In fact, the protestors were extremely respectful and nonviolent. Countless law enforcement officers commented on how the crowds were both some of the largest and most controlled they had ever seen. In Chicago, people stayed after to pick up trash—so much for the anti-environment right-winger label. While it may seem like a minor issue, the controlled, respectful nature of the protestors speaks to a fundamental principle of the tea parties: a respect for the rule of law. The tea parties are not a revolution, rather a counterrevolution to uphold the law, most notably the constitutionally protected tenants of individual liberty and the pursuit of happiness.

By the Numbers

The line that these events shouldn't have received so much coverage flies in the face of journalistic standards. If an event is unusual, large, and timely, basic criteria are met for coverage.

As the *Christian Science Monitor* reported, the simultaneous events garnered more attendees than any protest since the March 2006 LA immigration march.[21] Americans for Tax Reform compiled a conservatively estimated list that logged over 500,000.[22] Nonpartisan blogger Nate Silver estimated at least 300,000 attendees.[23] Silver makes an important point that those leading the rallies had every incentive to exaggerate the attendance, which may be true. Estimating crowd sizes can be particularly difficult. But that there were crowds large enough to make it difficult was significant enough. In a Rasmussen poll released five days after the protests, 51 percent of Americans were reported to have a favorable view of the protests. Those who disapproved were only 33 percent.[24]

Clearly this was an event that had a lot of interest, not only from those participating but also from those simply asked their opinion of it. By what metric the punditocracy came to the conclusion that the event ought to be ignored is still unclear.

The Media Market Reacts

FOX News, chided by some as promoting the events, saw a dramatic jump in viewership during the tea parties. For the date of April 15, FOX News Channel logged 3,390,000 primetime viewers. This is compared with 2,879,000 viewers one week before and 2,663,000 one week afterward. Other networks' ratings, already limping behind FOX News, stayed relatively static or dipped. CNN gained a moderate bump on tax day, going up almost 30,000 viewers over one week earlier. They

Table 5.1 Cable News Network Ratings Comparison

	Wed. March 18	Wed. April 8	Wed. April 15	Wed. April 21
FNC	2,553,000	2,879,000	3,390,000	2,633,000
CNN	1,300,000	1,043,000	1,070,000	968,000
MSNBC	1,032,000	1,059,000	1,210,000	861,000
CNBC	209,000	150,000	167,000	143,000
CNN HLN	964,000	791,000	909,000	637,000

Sources: TVByTheNumbers.com, Cable News Ratings.
March 18: http://tvbythenumbers.com/2009/03/19/cable-news-ratings-for-wednesday-march-18/14897.
April 8: http://tvbythenumbers.com/2009/04/09/cable-news-ratings-for-wednesday-april-8/16415.
April 15: http://tvbythenumbers.com/2009/04/16/cable-news-ratings-for-wednesday-april-15/16892.
April 21: http://tvbythenumbers.com/2009/04/22/cable-news-ratings-for-tuesday-april-21/17238.

actually *lost* viewers from one month before, going from 1,300,000 to 1,070,000. See Table 5.1.

This is an interesting example of the market reacting to a desirable product. People simply didn't care that FOX was right wing, a characterization any American with a TV is aware of. Rather, people tuned in more than they normally did because they were interested in viewing, and in a way being a part of, the tea party rallies hundreds of thousands Americans participated in. Whether they were critical or approving, their eyes were voting "yes" on the question of whether the event was worth covering.

Nearly as many *additional* viewers tuned in to FOX News *Primetime* on April 15th (3,390,000) compared with March 18th (2,553,000) than tuned in to closest competitors CNN (1,070,000) or MSNBC (1,210,000). It is fair to say that the bump in ratings was likely due to the tea parties, given that no other major news—like the death of a pedophilic celebrity—was being covered. Additionally, it even appears as though the trash-talking on CNN and MSNBC actually *cost* them viewers following tax day. Just one week later, as FOX News settled in to March viewership levels, CNN shed nearly 100,000 viewers from pre-tax day levels while MSNBC lost nearly 200,000.

Specific shows saw ups and downs with the tea party coverage as well. Table 5.2 compares the month before the tea parties with one week after them (to account for wrap-up coverage).

Table 5.2 Cable News Show Ratings Comparison

6 P.M. to 7 P.M.

Network	Show	March 18	April 15	April 21
FNC	Special Report	2,289,000	2,401,000	2,005,000
CNN	Situation Room	858,000	942,000	735,000
MSNBC	1600 (Mar 18) / Ed Show	587,000	563,000	556,000
CNBC	Mad Money	342,000	228,000	234,000
CNN HLN	Prime News	344,000	341,000	281,000

7 P.M. to 8 P.M.

Network	Show	March 18	April 15	April 21
FNC	Fox Report	2,055,000	2,185,000	1,944,000
CNN	Town Hall (March 18) / Dobbs	1,302,000	870,000	816,000
MSNBC	Hardball	879,000	737,000	707,000
CNBC	Kudlow Report	256,000	238,000	236,000
CNN HLN	Issues	561,000	644,000	623,000

8 P.M. to 9 P.M.

Network	Show	March 18	April 15	April 21
FNC	Bill O'Reilly	3,298,000	3,980,000	3,409,000
CNN	Campbell Brown	1,242,000	892,000	742,000
MSNBC	Keith Olbermann	1,179,000	1,499,000	1,021,000
CNBC	CNBC Reports	241,000	203,000	129,000
CNN HLN	Nancy Grace	1,300,000	1,336,000	1,007,000

9 P.M. to 10 P.M.

Network	Show	March 18	April 15	April 21
FNC	Sean Hannity	2,246,000	3,239,000	2,443,000
CNN	Larry King	1,353,000	1,292,000	1,122,000
MSNBC	Rachel Maddow	1,161,000	1,149,000	985,000
CNBC	Specials	200,000	198,000	178,000
CNN HLN	Issues / Lou Dobbs (April 21)	735,000	590,000	259,000

Table 5.2 *(Continued)*

10 P.M. to 11 P.M.

Network	Show	March 18	April 15	April 21
FNC	Greta Van Susteren	2,107,000	2,947,000	2,046,000
CNN	Anderson Cooper	1,302,000	1,026,000	1,041,000
MSNBC	Keith Olbermann (replay)	758,000	981,000	577,000
CNBC	Special (March 18)/ On the Money	185,000	99,000	122,000
CNN HLN	Nancy Grace (replay)	874,000	848,000	686,000

SOURCES: TvByTheNumbers.com, Cable News Ratings.
March 18: http://tvbythenumbers.com/2009/03/19/cable-news-ratings-for-wednesday-march-18/14897.
April 15: http://tvbythenumbers.com/2009/04/16/cable-news-ratings-for-wednesday-april-15/16892.
April 21: http://tvbythenumbers.com/2009/04/22/cable-news-ratings-for-tuesday-april-21/17238.

As is shown in Table 5.2, many individual shows saw spikes in ratings on the 15th. Most notable were Bill O'Reilly, Greta Van Susteren, and Sean Hannity on FOX News Channel. O'Reilly saw a 700,000 bump on tax day while Van Susteren's ratings jumped 800,000. Hannity, who covered the Atlanta tea party live, enjoyed a *million viewer increase*. One week following the tea parties, their ratings dipped back to within 100,000 to 200,000 of pre-tax day levels.

CNN's Campbell Brown lost a staggering 400,000 viewers from one month before tax day, and another 100,000 a week after tax day, barely beating out the 10 P.M. Nancy Grace replay slot. As with the general network statistics, other individual shows saw static to moderately increased ratings. Only MSNBC's Olbermann enjoyed a significant bump of about 300,000 viewers. The tea party slander on tax day may have actually cost some individual shows viewers. Olbermann dropped half a million within one week of his coverage for a net 200,000 decrease from one month before tax day. Maddow and Cooper slowly lost viewership from one month before the tea parties through one week afterward.

So You Think You Can Politic?

Sadly, there really are no winners as far as informing the vast majority of the public is concerned. On any given night, over 20 million Americans tune in to see a snarky Brit critique a menagerie of singers on *American Idol*.[25] Of course this is more than any news channel receives, matched only by combined channel coverage of high-profile political events like presidential debates and press conferences, often in the high 20- to low 30-million viewer range. What's more, *Idol* draws more viewers than all major news channels combined receive in any two prime-time hours.

CHAPTER 6

RADICAL IDEAS

Lest we forget at least an over-the-shoulder acknowledgement to the very first radical . . . the first radical known to man who rebelled against the establishment and did it so effectively that he at least won his own kingdom—Lucifer.

—Saul Alinsky

I n order to best understand what the tea parties were and are about, it is necessary for both outside observers and those within the movement to understand what they are not about, or rather, what they were a reaction *to*.

One of the most important things the tea parties did was bring to the forefront of the political discussion the stark contrast between two competing worldviews typically, though not necessarily, represented by the two major political parties, or more broadly, the political Left versus the political Right.

Much of the frustration seen in the tea party movement was due to the Republican Party not effectively carrying the torch of fiscal responsibility and individual liberty, or not honestly representing the political center-right as it purported to do. The 2008 election cycle reflected this in the rise of Ron Paul and the failure of mediocre, conservative-light candidate John McCain who seemed not to care (or know) so much about free-market principles. The fading of principles since the 1994 Republican revolution to the runaway spending under the Bush administration exacerbated this sentiment among rank-and-file conservative and libertarian voters. The frustration began—and went from a simmer to a boil—as Bush pushed the first bailout package; TARP, which only spilled over as President Obama pushed the limits of the law; the Constitution; and eventually the American people to a boiling point.

The tea party movement was couched by the media and political elites as "radical." That label, however, more aptly describes the economic policies and practices adopted by the two most recent administrations. The tea party movement was and is a rejection of the radicalism visible in the statements and policies advanced in our recent political history. Bailouts composed of corporate welfare and union paybacks sparked the ignition of a counterrevolution. The spending of bailout money in the radical statements, proposals, and policies that specified how bailout money would be spent painted a draconian picture that continued to fuel the fire well after the tax day tea parties had ended.

Just days before being elected president of the United States, Barack Obama had this to say to his supporters: "We are five days away from fundamentally transforming the United States of America."[1] This is a frighteningly radical quote from a man whose background is in constitutional law. Given statements like this, though, the radical policies that followed his election should come as no surprise.

In what was seemingly an unintentional admission of opportunistic, ideologically driven governance, Chief of Staff Rahm Emanuel uttered an odd turn of phrase: "You never want a serious crisis to go to waste."[2] But the intention for foment was all there, and Secretary of State Hillary Clinton echoed this sentiment when advocating recommendations for climate change.[3]

FOX News' Major Garrett asked White House Spokesman Robert Gibbs what Emanuel meant. Gibbs responded:[4]

Well, I did not see Secretary Clinton's comments, and I've not spoken specifically to the chief of staff about this. But what I think what—the mind-set that the administration has brought to our governing choices is what I enumerated earlier, and that is that for far too long many of the problems that we understand undermine our potential long-term economic growth—whether it's dealing with our health care crisis, whether it's our increasing dependence on foreign oil, despite president after president after president discussing the dangers—and as I said, he'll outline tomorrow some ideas for reform on education, because unless or until we meet those challenges and take those steps, we're sort of muddling around the edges; that we have to take some concrete, bold action to deal with the many challenges that we face; that our economy is not likely to grow in the long term unless or until we deal with them.

In other words, he meant that the administration plans to utilize the fact that the economy is in shambles to ram their dramatic policies down the throats of American citizens. These political tyrants see the financial crisis not as a problem to be addressed but as an opportunity for a campaign of political shock and awe. What began as a massive spending spree was transformed into a justification for government intrusion into virtually every aspect of Americans' lives.

Part I: You Earn It, We Spend It

That is the American way . . . the way that it's generally done is, you find some group that's small enough where they can't beat you up, and you tax them and you tell everybody else, "See? We didn't tax you."

—Todd Stroger, Cook County, Illinois Board President,
as reported by Eric Zorn in "Change of Subject,"
Chicago Tribune, April 2009

The spending spree begun in the Bush administration and carried on by the Obama administration was the first part of a radical and swift two-wave expansion of the size and scope of government. The philosophy that informed said spending and the policy moves that followed were the first sparks of the impending tea party counterrevolution. What started as an off-the-cuff campaign trail comment to a man who would come to be known as Joe the Plumber would be revealed to be a genuinely held, radical redistributive wealth philosophy of Barack Obama that would lead to an orgy of bailouts and handouts on Joe the Taxpayer's dime.

Obamanomics 101: Spreading the Wealth Around

On October 12, 2008, at a campaign stop in Toledo, Ohio, then-presidential candidate Barack Obama provided the nation with an uncharacteristically unscripted and candid response to a question from the crowd. The following was an exchange between Obama and Joe Wurzelbacher.

Joe: I'm getting ready to buy a company that makes about $250,000 . . . $270 to $280,000 a year.

Obama: All right.

Joe: Your new tax plan's gonna tax me more, isn't it?

Obama proceeded to walk Wurzelbacher down a path of twisted logic, supposing that if his plan had been enacted 15 years ago, Wurzelbacher would actually have more money now than he currently did. Obama told him that, in the big picture, he would be where he is currently faster—getting taxed more, or as Obama said in a long-winded "yes" to the original question, "you'd go from 36 to 39 percent, which is what it was under Bill Clinton."

Obama continued:

> The only thing that changes is, I'm going to cut taxes a little bit more for the folks who are most in need, and for the 5 percent of the folks who are doing very well, even though they've been working hard . . . and I understand that; I appreciate that . . . I just want to make sure that they're paying a little bit more in order to pay for those other tax cuts. Now, I respect your disagreement, but I just want you to be clear. It's not that I want to punish your success. I just want to make sure that everybody who is behind you, that they've got a chance at success, too.

Here Obama perpetuated the fallacy that the only way to cut taxes is to raise revenue elsewhere. As anyone who's taken even a peripheral look at the federal government knows, it is not usually a revenue problem that prevents tax cuts but a spending problem. The cost of government already presents an enormous burden on taxpayers. Every year Americans for Tax Reform marks the Cost of Government Day, defined as "the date of the calendar year on which the average American worker has earned enough gross income to pay off his or her share of the spending and regulatory burden imposed by government at the federal, state, and local levels." In 2009, this day fell on August 12. The report stated, "On average, working people must toil 224 days out of the year just to meet all costs imposed by government. In other words, the cost of government consumes 61.34 percent of national income."[5]

What was also striking about Obama's statement was that he had no problem saying he wanted to tax Joe the Plumber more to give the money to other people. Here it is from the horse's mouth:

> Because my attitude is that if the economy's good for folks from the bottom up, it's gonna be good for everybody. If you've got a plumbing business, you're gonna be better off if you've got a whole bunch of customers who can afford to hire you.

This is Obamanomics 101: We need to take your money, run it through the federal bureaucracy, let us wet our beak on your productivity, and then redistribute it to people so that they can pay for your services. It's a win-win-win! Then Obama uttered the words that should have sunk his candidacy: "I think when you spread the wealth around, it's good for everybody."

This was not a gaffe, but an honest statement of the true philosophy of Obama and more often than not, his liberal compatriots. Obama's running mate Joe Biden echoed his radical sentiment of wealth redistribution. Biden, speaking of the Obama tax plan, said, "We want to take money and put it back in the pocket of middle-class people." Here Biden ignores the reality of the situation. The middle class has not lost money at the hands of the wealthy, thus putting it back is a mischaracterization of what is plain and simple wealth redistribution. Biden continued, "It's time to be patriotic . . . time to jump in, time to be part of the deal, time to help get America out of the rut."[6] Again, the idea that wealthier Americans don't have skin in the game is an outright lie. Biden pretends that up until now, wealthier Americans are somehow not doing their fair share, as he defines it, not paying more than others. They are already—unfairly—paying a higher percentage of taxes.[7]

Obama spent a good deal of time promising every constituency that 95 percent of them would be taken care of—everyone from small business owners to Joe and Jane taxpayer to energy users to health care consumers, and that the few, the top 5 percent, would foot the bill for his audacious monster government plan. Class politics and fuzzy math aside, by summer 2009, not even Obama's Treasury Secretary, TurboTax Tim,[8] would rule out middle-class tax hikes.[9]

Bailouts: The New Earmark

Bailouts offered politicians a way to give money directly to constituents. This happened in two ways. First, bailout funds were literally apportioned for "shovel-ready projects," a bogus, artificial job creator that very well may add to infrastructure woes. Erik Sofge of *Popular Mechanics* explained:

> ...the term "shovel-ready" may have been introduced in the 1990s by New York-based electric utility Niagara-Mohawk Power, which later became National Grid (it is the current owner of the URL shovelready.com). There are no specific parameters or requirements that define shovel readiness....[10]

In the article, Professor Robert Bea of the University of California, Berkeley, stated that this might be a good program "if you want to patch some potholes in the road . . . But if you're hoping for anything long-term with this approach, throw away all hope. It can't happen." The 90-day restriction in the bill resulted in a hodgepodge of projects that were limited, outmoded, and often irrelevant.[11] Shovel ready quickly became a(nother) meaningless term cooked up by politicians to combat justified criticism that the bloated stimulus bill wouldn't even kick in until 2011.[12]

Secondly, direct handouts were given to friendly corporations and unions, like the GM auto bailout[13] or the original TARP that built in tax breaks for essential portions of our economy like rum producers.[14]

Why waste time earmarking an irrelevant appropriation when you can send the money directly!

Congressmen lined up behind the bailouts because they saw an opportunity to turn America's loss into their gain. Thinking quite selfishly and in the short term, they could take money from a Robin Hood treasury secretary and pass it out to constituents for shovel-ready projects—no wait—*green* shovel-ready projects. With a few exceptions,[15] governors gladly accepted the federal handouts, which were a combination of taxes collected from more productive states and newly printed money, the consequences of which future generations would bear. More often than not, the requisites of actual economic stimulation were stretched, and federal stimulus dollars were tapped as just another taxpayer-funded slush fund. The American taxpayers quickly became unwitting investors in millions of dollars worth of frivolous infrastructure improvements, cultural boondoggles, odd scientific studies, and more. Over $1.1 billion was disseminated for 50 airport projects that didn't meet stimulus criteria.[16] In Wisconsin, $15.8 million was apportioned for 37 rural bridges while in Elizabethtown, Pennsylvania, $9.4 million was doled out for a train station renovation.[17] These were just a handful of $5.5 billion in alleged stimulus funds detailed in a report by Sen. Jon Coburn of Maryland entitled "100 Stimulus Projects: A Second Opinion."[18]

In Chicago, new "green" buses were bought and programmed to proudly proclaim over an internal loudspeaker "this clean energy bus was purchased with federal stimulus funds!" The stimulus funds were supposed to create jobs for a factory in Minnesota. Unfortunately, a delay in the funds from Uncle Sam resulted in the factory announcing the layoff of over 300 workers by the close of the year.[19] Not to worry, $50 million did make its way to the factory, so Chicago is still going to get half the buses it wants to purchase with other peoples' money.[20]

Taxpayer money, it was revealed, was spent on even more absurd projects like studies about condom use and general human sexual behavior.[21] Stimulating indeed.

Stimulus.gov, the web site for taxpayers to track spending, is a self-contained example of nonstimulus, antitransparency absurdity. Launched and then relaunched, it served as its own large stimulus, bringing in over $18 million for the small firm that would run it. The contract was posted, per federal law, on the Government Services Administration (GSA) web site at 9 P.M. on a Friday night.[22] Releasing information late on a Friday is a great time to try to slip it under the radar. Why spend so much for a web site when many others have done more with less? David Fredosso at the *Washington Examiner* compared the site to other sites that track government contracts: USASpending.gov and Recovery.org.[23]

USASpending.gov is a searchable database of government contracts, with individual transaction-level details for contracts dating back to 2000. The Office of Management and Budget (OMB), which developed the software for its own web site, bought the software for that site from the group OMB Watch for $600,000. Recovery.org is a privately-funded site launched in March by the Onvia corporation. It also tracks all government contracts, with an initial cost of only $10,000.[24] While Recovery.gov spent millions of dollars on cool features, it is difficult to determine just how much transparency the web site allows for, as much specific information has been redacted. As reported by ABC, "sections titled 'Design Concept,' 'Site Navigation,' and 'Technical Approach' are largely blacked out. Come to the 'Conclusion' and you will find that it is gone entirely."[25]

Smartronix, the firm awarded the contract for Recovery.gov, also had a good friend in Washington.[26] Fredosso reported, "The company appears to have just one important political connection: according to Federal Election Commission records, Smartronix President Mohammed Javaid, Vice President Alan Parris, and Partner John Parris have together given $19,000 to House Majority Leader Steny Hoyer (D-MD) since 1999. There is no record of a Smartronix employee contributing to any other federal politician."[27]

There is no limit to the entitlements many liberals believe you should have. One played a large role in the very financial crisis that precipitated the bailouts around which these tea parties were formed: the *right* to own a home! It doesn't matter if you can pay for it or not, society will pick up the tab! Get an extra bedroom, get a pool even, who cares, you deserve it. With the money saved on putting no money down, you could buy a late model BMW. Ah, the American dream. Actually, in some places you don't even need to spend your own money on that luxury. Massachusetts literally gives out cars to welfare recipients, complete with insurance and

AAA.[28] In Denver, subsidized or free cell phones for the poor are on the table.[29]

Our Money "at Work"

Recovery.gov was designed to show taxpayers our "money at work." Most people would rather be letting their money work for them for food, clothing, vacations, college funds, or in the stock market than working its way into someone else's wallet.

The web site is designed to make government transparent:

> The American Recovery and Reinvestment Act of 2009 targets investments toward key areas that will save and create good jobs immediately, while also laying the groundwork for long-term economic growth. The charts and numbers below give you an idea of where the money is going.
>
> Over the upcoming months, we will provide more information on the distribution of funding by federal agencies. In order to give small businesses and Americans across the country a chance to apply for Recovery Act dollars to create and save jobs, some funding may not be distributed until this summer. New information on the allocation of funds will be posted on Recovery.gov as it becomes available.[30]

Here are some of the uses of stimulus money at work, as specifically highlighted by the administration. These aren't the worst things that could be dug up, but these reflect what the administration thinks is so fantastic it deserves to be front and center on the bailout web site:

> The Nevada Division of Forestry has begun a $1.3 million Recovery Act funded project in Lincoln County, creating 26 jobs and saving 3. The project will reduce hazardous forest fuels through the removal of pinyon and juniper trees encroaching on Highway 93 and State Route 319.
>
> By December 31, 2010, approximately 54 million one-time payments of $250 will have been made to persons who receive certain types of federal benefits. Have you received your check?

Nice. Have you received *your* handout?

Thousands of public housing units for lower-income residents, including the elderly and disabled, will be developed and modernized as a
result of approximately $1 billion in grants from the Department of
Housing and Urban Development. Most of the grant money will be
devoted to making the units more energy efficient, thus decreasing
utility costs to the residents.

What looks like a $1 billion housing grant is actually a "moderniza-
tion grant" to make public housing "green," likely creating (or saving)
"green jobs." Many people (if not most) have no issue with providing
less fortunate individuals with housing but this grant didn't do that. Instead of decent housing for those in need, it instead makes their housing
(good or bad) green.

When one attempts to drill down to specifics on Recovery.gov, a
map of where money is going appears. The site provides an "investment
bubble" for guidance, shown in Exhibit 6.1.

Intrigued by the $8 billion "other"? Every American should be
concerned. Unfortunately, they don't expand on that minor line item.
Additionally, note the footnote on "Tax Relief." In a transparent attempt
to make the spending spree look like tax cuts, billions of dollars that
would appropriately be put into other categories—like education and
training or energy—get counted as pure tax cuts.

Many nonprofit groups put together stimulus tracking web sites more
effectively and less expensively than their federal counterpart. Stimulus
Watch.org set up a comprehensive database for proposed projects that
would be eligible for stimulus dollars. The site allows you to search
by keyword, so that you can see, for instance, the millions of dollars
proposed by various states and localities for golf course renovations,
heritage centers, and other crucial shovel-ready projects.

Stimulus Fraud

Vice President Biden was tasked with overseeing the spending of the
federal stimulus money. In his typical frank fashion, he stated, "We
know some of this money is going to be wasted ... There are going
to be mistakes made ... Some people are being scammed already."[31]

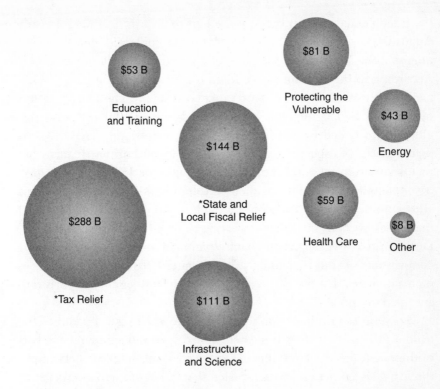

$53 B

Education
and Training

$81 B

Protecting the
Vulnerable

$43 B

Energy

$144 B

*State and
Local Fiscal Relief

$59 B

Health Care

$8 B

Other

$288 B

*Tax Relief

$111 B

Infrastructure
and Science

*Tax Relief includes $15 B for Infrastructure and Science, $61 B for Protecting the Vulnerable,
  $25 B for Education and Training and $22 B for Energy. This makes the total funds $126 B
  for Infrastructure and Science, $142 B for Protecting the Vulnerable, $78 B for Education
  and Training, and $65 B for Energy.

Exhibit 6.1   Where Is Your Money Going?
SOURCE: www.recovery.gov/?q=content/investments.

Neil Barofsky was appointed as a special inspector general overseeing
TARP distribution. He expressed grave concerns over the potential for
fraud and abuse, and testified that the Obama Treasury Department
refused to adopt his recommendations to combat said abuse and implement transparency reforms.[32] What's more, Barofsky's report put the
total taxpayer burden due to TARP at over $27 billion. Some analysts
predicted as much as $50 billion of the $700 billion TARP money could
end up in the hands of swindlers of one shape or another.[33] The FBI
and other federal authorities braced for what they, too, believed would
be an increase in white-collar crime related directly to the stimulus
cash cow.[34]

It didn't take long for Biden and others to be proven correct. In early August 2009, a Tennessee financial advisor was convicted of stealing $6.1 million from clients under the guise of a government bailout program.[35] According to the FBI, mortgage fraud is a burgeoning business.[36] Certainly government handouts won't increase this. . . . The Florida offices of Colonial BancGroup Inc. and Taylor, Bean & Whitaker Mortgage Corp. were raided by the FBI and TARP agents (yes, TARP has its own agents). No specific reason was given by authorities. It turns out they were up to no good and, surprise, in line for $500 million in tax-payer bailout money.[37] It was then revealed that they had a special deal with a mortgage firm that would provide a loan of $300 million to get the bank's assets in the range necessary to qualify for bailout money.[38] Less than two weeks later the bank would fail and be bought out by a competitor.[39] Fraud pertaining to the financial crisis and the bailout is such a concern that the FBI is shifting agents from counterterrorism to antifraud divisions.[40]

Sometimes criminals don't even need to try to get a piece of the bailout pie, they just find it in their inbox . . . or slipped under the bars of their cell. Nearly 4,000 inmates received $250 stimulus checks from the feds.[41] Even better, it was revealed that 2,000 of them would get to keep the checks because, as the Social Security Administration's Mark Lassiter clarified, "The law specified that any beneficiary eligible for a Social Security benefit during one of those months was eligible for the recovery payment."[42] The other checks were an error. Strictly speaking, they could be used to stimulate the internal prison economy. You must be able to get at least a few packs of cigarettes for $250.

Cash for Clunkers

Bailouts to financial institutions and car manufacturers paved the way for a host of ridiculous handouts disguised as stimulus programs. In the "voodoo economics" category, the Car Allowance Rebate System (CARS)—affectionately known as "cash for clunkers"—was announced in the summer of 2009 by the U.S. Department of Transportation.

The scrappage program was the brainchild of economist Alan Blinder, floated in a July 27, 2008, *New York Times* article. His enviro-economic malarkey convinced Transportation Secretary Ray LaHood, a former Republican congressman from Illinois, ostensibly eager to prove himself a different kind of Republican—the kind that doesn't understand basic economic principles. In the name of giving car buyers some relief and as an added incentive to go green, the federal government began offering up to a $4,500 tax credit for cars turned in for more efficient (better gas mileage) cars. The most egregious thing about this program was that it was a $3 billion[43] handout, run through the federal bureaucracy, to taxpayers and car dealers.

An entire book could be written on the absurdities of this program. Here are some of the highlights.

Not Green at All. The slew of unintended consequences came to light almost immediately. There were the practical concerns. For one, the cars need to be destroyed to get any alleged emissions reduction benefit. Critics rightly argued that there is no telling that cars traded in are actually not resold on the market here or beyond our borders, nullifying the environmental benefit. The government had to set up a system in which the cars are destroyed, but its ability to track this[44] and the environmental ramifications of destroying the cars were questionable.[45] Even if green jobs were created to oversee the immediate destruction of the turned in clunkers, wouldn't the environment be at a net loss? One car will have been taken off the road and into a landfill and another car created in its place. The real hook, of course, is global warming. Once one accepts the dogma that global warming is real, man-made, and will necessarily lead to impending disaster should we not take dramatic action, then no cost is too high to bear.

This is a $3 billion taxpayer subsidized plan to help other people get cars they don't need that will do nothing to alleviate a problem that doesn't exist. That is not a typo. As will be discussed, the case that global warming is real, man-made, and has catastrophic consequences that must or even can be addressed by humans is hardly definitive. In fact, quite the contrary is true. The largest consensus of scientists disagrees with this media-perpetrated political tripe, and most taxpayers see through it.[46] Taxpayers funded $3 billion in upgraded wheels for every Tom, Dick, and Harry who wanted a new ride. A wealthy family could hand in a $500 car, perhaps sitting in its driveway for use by a teenage driver, for a $4,500 credit, of which taxpayers would have to subsidize $4,000. This same family could then purchase a brand new car that gets only four more miles to the gallon.[47] Even environmentalists took issue with the program.

Professor Michael Gerrard of Columbia Law School's Center on Climate Law said: "It was sold as good for the auto industry, good for the environment and good for energy security," Gerrard said. "It was sold as a three-fer. It's more of a one-fer," referring to the boost in auto handouts . . . er, sales. Between the low minimum margin of emissions savings and the fact that the emissions made by *building* the new cars aren't factored in, Gerrard summed it up as "not a cost-effective way to reduce fuel use or greenhouse gas emissions."[48] That small margin of mileage savings wasn't helped by the fact that certain brands of Hummers, yes Hummers, counted as qualified new cars for traded in clunkers.[49] Senators Dianne Feinstein (D-CA) and Susan Collins (R-ME) opined on the pages of the *Wall Street Journal* that this wasn't what *they* had in mind:

> . . . The truth is, the House bill and its Senate counterpart are another big bailout. These bills are expertly designed to provide Detroit one last windfall in selling off gas guzzlers currently sitting on dealer lots because they're not a smart buy.[50]

Both Collins and Feinstein ended up voting for the bill that took effect July 27 and spent $1 billion of taxpayer dollars.[51] By the end of the program, the number would reach nearly $3 billion,[52] with Feinstein and Collins endorsing the extension.[53]

Special Interests. As the senators' stated, special interests did play a big role, but not only from automakers. The trade-in program heavily favored already bailed out businesses like Chrysler and GM. Flush with taxpayer investments, Chrysler dealers began offering *matching* cash back, for a net $9,000 taxpayer subsidy of new cars for trade-ins.[54]

This put functioning car makers making cars people want at prices they are willing to pay at a competitive disadvantage. Nobody saw this coming. Ford, not to mention the real American car producers Toyota, Honda, and BMW, were not in a position to match the subsidy.

Senator Chuck Schumer was a seemingly impartial proponent of the plan.[55] As the *Washington Examiner*'s Tim Carney reported, Schumer's intentions couldn't have been more selfish. The only greening he was concerned with was bringing dollars into his home state of New York:

> One lobbyist for this bill was Nucor Steel. In Cayuga County, N.Y., Nucor turns scrap steel into sheet metal and other steel products. The clunkers are now becoming a subsidized feedstock for Nucor, which helps explain why Sen. Chuck Schumer, D-N.Y., has led the push for $2 billion extra in clunker cash.[56]

A Spending Spree: Unintended Consequences. Cash for clunkers is a perfect example of economist Frédéric Bastiat's Parable of the Broken Window where destruction is beneficial because it forces the need for reconstruction, which in turn creates jobs and general economic stimulation. Programs like this that meddle with the market inevitably have unintended consequences. In this instance, the government encouraged people to take working cars and trash them, significantly altering the used car market for poorer people without cars to trade in. Say you are in the market for a used car. It is going to be a heck of a lot harder for you to find one below $9,000 if the owners of those cars in your area can instead take a $500, $1,000, or $8,000 car in for a new one. They'd be stupid to sell it to you at the market price if the government is inflating the value of the car in the name of environmental benefits and economic stimulation. This program benefited the middle class and wealthy and hurt the poor.[57]

What's more, any short-term benefit to car dealers resulted in losses for used car dealers. This program promoted taking their product out of the market and destroying it.[58] Salting the economic wound the program sparked a marked decrease in other consumer product sales, including consumer goods.[59]

The craziest part of the whole thing is that just as Americans were beginning to tighten their belts and rein in excessive spending at home, the government encouraged them to ditch what was a functional vehicle for a more expensive, enviro-holy-roller go-cart.

Just 30 days into the program, the government announced that it was putting it on hold due to funding concerns.[60] Breaking news: People like free money. The Senate rushed to approve an addition $2 billion.[61]

Problems persisted following the cash infusion. Dealers and buyers weren't sure they'd get their money. Meanwhile, the scrap yards that typically take old cars were reluctant to do so. See, the most valuable part of a scrapped car is its engine. Of course the engines are rendered useless in this program, making the profit margin for scrap haulers and scrap yards almost insignificant.[62]

In the waning days of the program, New York car dealers dropped out, citing major reimbursement delays.[63]

Detroit Can't Compete. Chrysler and GM enjoyed the added benefit of taxpayer bailouts that, paired with their taxpayer-funded bailouts, allowed them to match the CARS rebate.

Even this market meddling couldn't sway consumers to their products. Toyota overtook[64] Ford quickly to become the top beneficiary of the program.[65] Of the top five purchased car models, four were foreign.[66]

Why is this? Because a $4,500 subsidy on a Toyota goes farther than a $9,000 subsidy on a union made, overpriced, underperforming Chrysler.[67]

What's more, cars like Toyotas are as American as many of Detroit's brands. Three out of the top ten American-made cars are Toyotas.[68]

Policy Junk Yard. The CARS program was set to run until Labor Day, but was cut short, ending on August 24, 2009.[69] Thus, the most despicable strain of handout fever ended with numerous economic casualties only to be proclaimed a whopping success by its Democratic proponents as well as Republican Transportation Secretary Ray LaHood.[70]

The Department of Transportation had this to say:

> The CARS program has been a wild success. It has not only helped tens of thousands of consumers purchase new more fuel efficient vehicles, but has provided an economic boost to the car dealers, the auto manufacturers, the people who provide consumer loans and scrap yards.[71]

The *Wall Street Journal* editorial page stated the CARS program, inappropriately couched by the GOP as "ineffective," was bound to be successful:

> Now they get a taxpayer subsidy of up to $4,500, which on some models can be 25 percent of the purchase price. It's hardly surprising

that Peter is willing to use a donation from his neighbor Paul, midwifed by Uncle Sugar, to class up his driveway.[72]

The definition of successful is the sticking point. If it is wealth distribution, CARS was a smashing success. To pretend that it is a net gain for society, however, is as the *Journal* stated, "crackpot economics":[73]

> The subsidy won't add to net national wealth, since it merely transfers money to one taxpayer's pocket from someone else's, and merely pays that taxpayer to destroy a perfectly serviceable asset in return for something he might have bought anyway. By this logic, everyone should burn the sofa and dining room set and refurnish the homestead every couple of years.[74]

No sooner were those words written than an appliance subsidy program was floated out of the U.S. Energy Department.[75]

How about a political book subsidy?

But Wait, There's More! As with all free lunches there's often a catch. As citizens lined up to register their new green cars, they were told to their dismay that up to $4,500 in government handouts—er—rebates they took advantage of is *taxable* if their state chooses.[76] North Dakota, for example did just that. Someone should have informed the angry citizens who complained they were just being asked to do their patriotic duty to create green jobs associated with their green car purchase. Car dealers in North Dakota were equally frustrated when—surprise, surprise—they didn't get paid as quickly as the government promised.[77]

The Case of the Mythical Job Numbers

On the campaign trail, Barack Obama, like many a politician before him, promised to create American jobs. In January, as president-elect, his future administration and Congress assembled a multi-billion dollar stimulus package that put a number to that promise: three to four million jobs "saved or created" by 2011.[78] The administration justified the stimulus spending by saying such spending was a tourniquet on an economy hemorrhaging jobs at an alarming rate. In that month over half a million jobs had been lost, with the unemployment rate going from 7.2 percent to 7.6 percent.[79]

By September 2009, the administration declared "mission accomplished," estimating that the February 2009 stimulus package of $787 billion had saved or created one million jobs.[80] This alleged victory seems justifiably hollow to Americans amidst another quarter of a million jobs lost, a 9.8 percent unemployment rate. This is the highest unemployment rate in 26 years, and it doesn't include the more than 9 million workers who have been bumped down to part-time hours to save their employers money.[81] All told, 2.4 million jobs had been lost since Obama signed the stimulus bill in February.[82]

Besides the clear lack of results, the premise of the administration's argument is completely inaccurate. No politician will tell you this, but the government does not create jobs. More often than not, it takes our money and gives it to someone else to do something that either does not need to be done or could be done more efficiently by the private sector. There are a few exceptions: police, firefighters, the military, the postal system, infrastructure construction and maintenance, and the smallest amount of paper pushers possible are necessary functions of a civil society that most people are okay with government performing. That said, every one of these government functions has private alternatives: from plans for private police[83] and the leased Skyway in Chicago,[84] privatized fire districts,[85] to military contractors,[86] to government contractors and government privatization[87] to, of course, FedEx and UPS, which show that the private sector can and often does do a good job at supplementing or replacing certain functions of government.

All other government jobs fall into the sector of busywork. They are things private corporations are not willing to do because they aren't needed. They won't get a return on their investment. They aren't profitable because there is no demand for those services. In these instances, like so-called shovel-ready projects, the taxpayer shouldn't be interested in investing either. If there is no net productivity, why would anyone be interested in supporting it? Government creating jobs is the redistribution of wealth for busywork. They are work positions that result in the growth of government, period.[88]

A newer phrase, invented by the Obama administration, is the idea that government not only can create, but *save* jobs. In a clear attempt to give themselves cover for the inevitable failures of the bailouts, the administration repeats over and over again that it will create *or* save millions of jobs. As William McGurn deftly pointed out in the pages of the *Wall Street Journal*, the immeasurable nature of this metric is exactly what the Obama administration finds appealing:

> . . . no one—not the Labor Department, not the Treasury, not the Bureau of Labor Statistics—actually measures "jobs saved." As the *New York Times* delicately reports, Mr. Obama's jobs claims are "based on macroeconomic estimates, not an actual counting of jobs."
>
> . . . as a political formula "save or create" allows the president to invoke numbers that convey an illusion of precision.[89]

As Democrat Max Baucus stated, "You created a situation where you cannot be wrong. . . . If the economy loses two million jobs over the next few years, you can say yes, but it would've lost 5.5 million jobs. If we create a million jobs, you can say, well, it would have lost 2.5 million jobs. You've given yourself complete leverage where you cannot be wrong, because you can take any scenario and make yourself look correct."[90]

Is it too much to ask that the President of the United States actually confront the reality of rising job losses rather than playing a numbers game?

Part II: The Intrusion

> Government's view of the economy could be summed up in a few short phrases: If it moves, tax it. If it keeps moving, regulate it. And if it stops moving, subsidize it.
>
> —Ronald Reagan, remarks to the White House Conference on Small Business, August 15, 1986

The aforementioned hard money issues were only the first wave of the political shock and awe that stirred a nation into action. The fiscal sanity of the nation and the impact on its taxpayers is of crucial importance and significance to the tea parties. Spending taxpayer money irresponsibly rightly causes uproar. What cannot be forgotten or underestimated, however, is the moral bankruptcy that could result from the inappropriate insertion of government not merely into our wallets, but into our workplaces, our radios, and our homes.

The Return of the Fairness Doctrine

In 1927, the federal government created the Radio Commission, an agency that would become the modern-day Federal Communications Commission (FCC). The commission was tasked with giving out licenses for radio stations with the disclaimer that they "operate with public interest."

This pesky phrase would result in a series of First Amendment restricting measures for decades that would culminate in what is known as the "Fairness Doctrine." Introduced in 1949, the so-called Fairness Doctrine was a legal right, not obligation, granted to the FCC to ensure news outlets discussed controversial issues and all sides of the story were told. Unfortunately, this right, under the auspices of the government owning the airwaves or the right to broadcast on them, led inevitably to the invocation of the right by controlling government bureaucrats. Like young children asking for more ice cream or to stay up late, if you give the government an inch, it'll take a mile. The doctrine gave the federal government power to judge content for newsworthiness and insist on point-counterpoint discussion in the name of the common good and to best combat media scarcity.

Since 1929, the federal government has hemmed and hawed over the exact meaning of the doctrine and what constitutes the "public interest."[91] Eventually common sense prevailed and the Fairness Doctrine was abolished by Ronald Reagan's FCC Chairman Mark Fowler. This allowed for the public interest to be best represented by market forces instead of government bureaucrats. The media market reacted to tea party coverage, and the verdict was that coverage of tea parties brought higher ratings while disparaging them brought lower ratings. Talk radio is another example of the market at work. For years, conservative radio has dominated the airways. Why? Because those Americans who tune in to talk radio prefer a center-right approach, which may be a reflection of our politics. Most Americans are in the center to the right. According to a June 15, 2009, Gallup Poll, 40 percent of Americans identify as "conservative," 35 percent as "moderate," with a mere

21 percent identifying as "liberal."[92] Left-wing radio doesn't speak to as large an audience. Air America Radio, the Left's attempt at penetrating this market, is an abysmal failure.[93] Additionally, the Left already has outlets for their ideas through mainstream media outlets and Hollywood. And it just may be that liberals don't like talk radio.

The Left can't compete in the market so it turns to government for a fix. It's despicable. "They're disagreeing with us! They are numerous! We must use the law to shut them down! It isn't fair!'" they proclaim. An anonymous author on Daily Kos, ironically bearing the handle "America," stated the following:

> Have you been listening to talk radio? There you will learn that health reform—and the entire Obama agenda—is: socialist– communist–marxist–unconstitutional–tyranny. . . . We laugh at freepers but they are in control of the radio dial. . . . The shows consist of one angry caller after another, all agreeing with the host, and if any callers disagree [they] are given short shrift and/or put up against a break. That allows the hosts to say they take callers that disagree yet never engage them in conversation. But the airwaves belong to the public, not extremists, and our voices are not being heard. The answer is the Fairness Doctrine. . . . Why is this a controversial policy? The Fairness Doctrine can stop extremists, and probable extremist acts, at its source. Conservatives oppose it calling it an "attack" on free speech as if they have some right to use the airwaves for any purpose, and as an antiquated idea. They frame it as censorship of their ideas—as they censor our ideas.[94]

So it's about getting your ideas heard without getting cut off by a commercial; no one has a right to be heard on any privately operated radio or television station. A liberal caller has as little right to complain as this author does when cut off on MSNBC appearances. Tough luck. Speak up, get your thoughts out there when you can, but don't think for a second you have a right to airtime.

Equally laughable is the assertion that the doctrine is intended to combat extremism. These same people oppose waterboarding and wiretapping in the name of saving American lives, yet claim the government has a right to stifle political opposition in the name of safety? It is absurd.

Many politicians on the Left see the Fairness Doctrine as an excellent opportunity to gain an advantage. Liberal politicians don't like media outlets criticizing them, preferring instead those that cheerlead their every move so they seek to silence their opposition in the name of fairness. Such a transparently self-interested and eerily Orwellian ideology can be matched only by the arguments for taking away the secret ballot through union-backed "card check."[95]

Unfortunately the Fairness Doctrine is not a fringe issue propagated only by the Daily Kos. For Dan Fletcher of *Time* magazine, recent efforts to revive the free-speech stifling legislation that are "backed informally by congressional heavyweights including House Speaker Nancy Pelosi and Sen. John Kerry, raise old questions about the government's role in regulating the airwaves."[96] This is not a boogeyman invented by Rush Limbaugh and Sean Hannity; it is a constant threat that rears its ugly head in our nation's legislature. The attempt to revitalize the Fairness Doctrine is frightening. John Shu of the Federalist Society's Free Speech and Election Law Practice Group offers a helpful account of recent legislative skirmishes. In 2005, 24 congressmen signed on to a bill that would have required "that an FCC license holder cover important issues 'fairly'."[97] A second bill was also introduced that year and also defeated. As Shu reported, Sen. Norm Coleman and 43 colleagues proposed in 2007 to block any future resurrection of the Fairness Doctrine. On the House side, Congressmen Mike Pence made similar efforts with 208 colleagues cosponsoring. Neither measure made it to the floor of its respective house. The defeat of these protections for free speech is frightening in and of itself, paired with the fact that Fairness Doctrine proponents are hardly fringe elements of either house. Shu notes:

> . . . powerful Senate Democrats such as Dick Durbin, John Kerry, Debbie Stabenow, Tom Harkin, Jeff Bingaman, Speaker of the House Nancy Pelosi, and former President Bill Clinton have all repeatedly expressed their support of the Fairness Doctrine.[98]

Equally frightening is the reality of similar laws on the books already paving the way for such an unconstitutional aberration. In the name of campaign finance reform, the McCain-Feingold bill (Bipartisan Campaign Reform Act of 2002) is a shining example of do-goodery gone wild as a serious violation of the First Amendment.[99] Americans on the left, right and everywhere in between should find this and similar speech restricting measures alarming. Unfortunately, the Left, avowed champion of free speech, finds the opportunity to suppress the intellectual opposition under the guise of legislating fairness too tempting. Oddly enough, pornography seems to enjoy more protections than political speech.

As Fletcher reports, "the point might be moot without support from the Oval Office—which the doctrine does not currently enjoy.... Assuming the regulation doesn't get its renaissance this time, give it a few years. If history's any indication, the Fairness Doctrine will rear its head again."[100]

While Barack Obama explicitly denounced plans to reinstate the doctrine,[101] he doesn't hide his hatred of criticism from the media.[102]

Enemies of the First Amendment within his administration don't hide their disdain for the success of right-leaning radio either. The FCC's new diversity officer explicitly went after conservative radio before his appointment.[103] Brainstorming on the doctrine's reinstatement continues both inside and outside government ranks.[104]

Watch Your Pay

Capping compensation for executives from bailout-recipient firms was fairly controversial but easy for many to understand. The corporations accepted, for the most part willingly, taxpayer money and needed to be held accountable to their investors—the taxpayers. While this argument wasn't without its faults and may have been fueled more by PR than practical concerns, what it paved the way for was outrageous.

Congress and President Obama began speaking about capping pay in fully private industries—in companies that received no taxpayer money at all.[105] Obama called on finance CEOs to "show some restraint.... Show that you get that this is a crisis and everybody has to make sacrifices."[106] Eventually, the House passed a bill to *require* all corporations to allow shareholders to vote on executive compensation.[107] One wonders if Congress would have been amenable to an amendment to have the American people vote on congressional pay—or better yet—to hold proxy contests to vote out congressmen engaging in fraud or simply bad policies.

As the health care debate heated up in August 2009, congress began questioning the compensation packages of health care executives. As CBS' Stephanie Condon wrote, Congressman Henry Waxman, House

Energy and Commerce Committee chair, and committee member Congressman Bart Stupak wrote a letter to industry leaders calling for information on executive pay and general business practices.

> The letter asks each company to identify employees compensated more than $500,000 in any year from 2003 to 2008, as well as information on how those employees were compensated. It also asks for board member compensation, each companies' total revenues, net income, dividend payments, premium revenue, claims payments and other information.[108]

These politicians have no right to any of this information, but they believe they are entitled to it. This is certainly disturbing, but the reason they want it is even worse. They wish to use examples of private industry compensation to paint insurance companies as evil and excessive in talking points and advertisements to push their health care plans. House Speaker Nancy Pelosi summed up her side's view of insurance companies and health care issues thusly: "They are the villains in this."[109]

Cap and Trade

The Left has been steadily beating the drum of climate change for years, recently ramping up its efforts. Headed by Al Gore, many congressional Democrats and Republicans are on board, accepting his campaign against global warming as necessary and righteous. The basic premises are: anthropogenic (man-made) global warming is real, it is caused by carbon emissions (most notably, fossil fuels), it has catastrophic results that need to be immediately addressed, and it can be addressed by man. These claims are backed by a so-called consensus of scientists, politicians, and world citizens. The message has been hammered home through steady repetition in popular culture, by Hollywood, by politicians, and by corporations jumping on the green bandwagon encouraging us to lower our carbon footprint and go green. The solution offered by global warming alarmists is to massively reduce carbon output. This is done through regulations (mileage efficiency), upfront taxes (gas taxes), and complex Ponzi schemes like cap and trade, where companies would pay for permits that would give them the right to emit carbon.

The promulgation of this false consensus is a key tool proponents of a cap-and-trade regime use to pass legislation. Once the premise of catastrophic man-induced global warming is accepted, no price is too high to pay to fix the problem.

These premises are severely flawed. For one, global temperatures have been decreasing over the last decade.[110] Thus, the nomenclature of environmental alarmism has shifted from "global warming" to "climate change." Second, the notion that the fluctuation of earth's temperatures can be affected by human activity, let alone something specifically identifiable like carbon emissions, is highly contentious amongst scientists. Skeptics include Al Gore's mentor who taught the one science class he took on the subject. Roger Revelle reversed his position on carbon-induced warming.[111] Theories range from the sun, to water currents, to infinite combinations of the complex systems that constitute the Earth's environment.

Furthermore, alarmists have the hubris to suggest that we can easily come up with a fix for global warming. Ethanol was touted as the be-all-end-all of new fuel, only to be tossed out as foolhardy. *Time* magazine in the span of a year endorsed ethanol as the fuel of the future then reversed course to describe it as a boondoggle.[112] Ethanol for fuel was inefficient. The cost of energy that goes into processing the fuel exceeded the mileage and emissions benefits of the fuel itself.[113] What's more, the usage of corn for fuel was linked to food shortages around the globe.[114]

The bad, costly ideas just keep on coming. One suggestion is to force us to get smaller, more dangerous cars.[115] Another is the odd, glowing, light bulbs that are more expensive, more dangerous and potentially harmful for the environment long term.[116] Cap and trade would lead to higher energy prices (and who bears that burden the heaviest but the working class families Democrats keep telling us they and they alone are trying to protect). The Waxman-Markey bill passed by the House in the summer of 2009 would more than double prices across the board.[117] This isn't a straw man erected by political opponents. It is an explicit goal[118] expressed by President Obama himself:

> Under my plan of a cap-and-trade system, electricity rates would necessarily skyrocket. Even, you know, regardless of what I say about

whether coal is good or bad. Because I'm capping greenhouse gases, coal power plants, you know, natural gas, you name it, whatever the plants were, whatever the industry was, they would have to retrofit their operations. That will cost money; they will pass that money on to consumers.[119]

Gore and his allies get riled when their premises are criticized. In fact, Gore refuses to debate critics.[120] Instead, the alarmist camp cites a nonexistent consensus and the "shut and closed" case for climate change. They go on the attack, going so far as to lump global warming skeptics in with Holocaust deniers[121] and suggest they be tried in Nuremberg-like fashion.[122] They accept their premises and solutions with blind faith and defend them with a religious fervor. Their behavior is antithetical to the scientific process global warming alarmists claim to revere.

The climate change myth is contradicted by polls indicating a trend away from global warming alarmism. Most Americans do not think man is causing global warming.[123] Polls also indicate[124] that people aren't willing to pay for climate change remedies and don't list it as something they believe should be a top legislative priority.[125]

Tens of thousands of scientists disagree with the premise that global warming is a catastrophic man-made problem.[126] This is in sharp contrast to the so-called consensus of the highly politicized United Nations Inter-governmental Panel on Climate Change, whose reports are often cited by the alarmist camp.[127] In fact, there is a host of peer-reviewed research *countering* the global warming alarmists' claims.[128] Feeling the heat, so to speak, climate alarmists continue to attempt to link every problem of the day to global warming. Nothing is irrelevant: frog reproduction,[129] military strategy,[130] you name it. Meanwhile, Gore and congressional proponents continue to jet around the world in private planes burn-ing up excessive carbon-based fuel for speeches and taxpayer-funded boondoggles.[131]

Why, then, does global warming alarmism abound? As The Heart-land Institute's Jay Lehr explains, "The pressure on scientists to support global warming is huge because there is five billion dollars in research funds available from the federal government annually to all of the uni-versities in America."[132] The federal government has an official posi-tion on a theory of global warming. Thus, to get those federal dollars scientists are highly incentivized to not only take the government's position on global warming, but to cram a global warming link into otherwise irrelevant research. As Dr. Richard Lindzen, the world-renowned MIT physicist states, "If you are questioning global warming you will get bad reviews on your paper. Your proposals will be poorly reviewed. For a young scientist this is crucial. It will affect your funding, it will affect your publication, it will affect your promotion."[133]

One wonders if the politicians espousing global warming hysteria even believe the allegations themselves. During the highly publicized "earth hour," whereby citizens were encouraged to "vote green" and turn off all electricity, Al Gore pulled a Motel 6 and "[left] the light on."[134] This isn't the first example of his hypocrisy. He's known to run up a high electricity bill[135] and jet around the world in private planes and limousines, as he unabashedly shows in his global warming thriller *An Inconvenient Truth*. Don't worry, he offsets this by buying green energy credits.[136] It's like paying for enviro-indulgences!

President Obama isn't much better. He had this to say on the campaign trail: "We can't drive our SUVs and eat as much as we want and keep our homes at 72 degrees at all times."[137] Putting aside the fact that he's saying you can't eat as much as you want, things changed a bit once he got to D.C. Speaking of breaking Bush's protocol of wearing a jacket and tie at all times in the Oval Office, senior advisor David Axelrod said, "He's from Hawaii, okay.... He likes it warm. You could grow orchids in there."[138]

Charity: Our Way or the Highway

Almost immediately upon taking office, the Obama administration declared its intention to reduce the tax deductibility percentage of charitable donations. Just as charities were suffering the most due to hits like the general financial crisis[139] and the Madoff scandal[140] the administration decided to raise revenue by skimming a bit off of charities and philanthropists.

Obama defended this policy stating it would not, in fact, hurt charities. "If it's really a charitable contribution, I'm assuming that that shouldn't be the determining factor as to whether you're giving that $100 to the homeless shelter down the street."[141] But it wasn't the

$100 donor people were worried about, nor the $100 donor Obama officials were targeting. It is the wealthy who donate millions upon millions of dollars who were wrenched shut by Obama. The *Los Angeles Times reported:*

> Using the example of a bus driver who pays income tax at a rate of 28 percent and his own situation as a high-income earner taxed at a higher rate, Obama argued that current law allows him a greater tax benefit than the bus driver would receive for a charitable cash contribution of equal value.
>
> "He gets to write off 28 percent. I get to write off 39 percent. I don't think that's fair," Obama said.[142]

What isn't fair is the higher tax rate of 39 percent. But if that's the rate you're getting taxed at, why wouldn't your charitable contributions be deductible to that percentage? The plan would have reduced the deductions one could itemize and would inevitably lead not to a reduction in donations themselves, necessarily, but to a reduction in the amount of money given to charities. It is very simple: people may still give to charities, but if less of the contribution is going to charities and more is going to the feds, they are given the incentive to give smaller gifts.

Charities were rightly skeptical. As Lisa Hillman of the Association for Healthcare Philanthropy stated, "To put any block between the donor and the charity at this time, I think, is not helpful."[143]

Obama went so far as to cite Reagan as his influence. But as *Barron's* Jim McTague notes, this was a "whopper":

> Reagan's top marginal income-tax rate at the time also was 28 percent. Obama would raise that top marginal rate to 39.6 percent, where it was under Bill Clinton. Thus, under Obama, the tax savings from the charitable deduction for those earning $250,000 or more would be appreciably smaller than under Reagan, when taxpayers got close to a full deduction.[144]

Obama claiming this wouldn't hurt charities shows a frightening lack of basic economic common sense or some serious disingenuousness. His plan was *banking* on the fact that it would hurt charities by redirecting money to the government, as his plan was projected to raise $318 billion over 10 years.[145]

One wonders if the Left would rather have government be the source of charity than individual giving. The more successful America's charities are, the less bureaucrats and politicians are necessary to forcibly redistribute wealth—according to their whims and fancies. It seems as though they want government to determine where monies will be spent or; when they can't, that they skim off as much money as possible. It is a selfish, backward strategy that only helps big government at the expense of the poor.

Obama's Army

Before taking office, Obama spoke of expanding the ranks of the various taxpayer funded volunteer corps.

> [As] president I will expand AmeriCorps to 250,000 slots [from 75,000] and make that increased service a vehicle to meet national goals, like providing health care and education, saving our planet, and restoring our standing in the world, so that citizens see their effort connected to a common purpose.
>
> People of all ages, stations and skills will be asked to serve. Because when it comes to the challenges we face, the American people are not the problem—they are the answer.

Just who is claiming Americans are a problem isn't clear. Obama continued with gushing enthusiasm about creating government jobs to solve our nation's every ailment:

> So we are going to send more college graduates to teach and mentor our young people. We'll call on Americans to join an energy corps, to conduct renewable energy and environmental cleanup projects in their neighborhoods all across the country.
>
> We will enlist our veterans to find jobs and support for other vets and to be there for our military families. And we're going to grow our Foreign Service, open consulates that have been shuttered and double the size of the Peace Corps by 2011 to renew our diplomacy.

It sounds so magical, so perfect. We'll take a job crisis and turn it into a solution for clean energy and veteran care. How? There's no limit to how you accomplish these things in a rhetorical world. Then we'll send liberal college students abroad to consulates and in the Peace Corps to solve the world's problems. What could go wrong?

As if this frightening pie-in-the-sky daydreaming masquerading as leadership wasn't bad enough, Obama had this to say about his future army of volunteers:

> We cannot continue to rely only on our military in order to achieve the national security objectives that we've set. We've got to have a civilian national security force that's just as powerful, just as strong, just as well-funded.[146]

We can't rely on our military for national security objectives? Paired with diplomacy, that's exactly who we can and *do* rely on, and properly so.

"United We Serve"

Within months of taking office, the Obama administration began running ads on serving ones country. The federal government has a web site called "Serve.gov." In a creepy, foreboding twist on "United We Stand," the web site's banner reads "United We Serve."

The mentality of servitude is disturbing, particularly in the context of an eerily idolized head of state calling on the nation's youth to "unite and serve." Just who are they serving? It isn't the nation; they are getting paid and presumably getting put into a government job. Service is done for free, not as an occupation, but as a gift. It plays into the liberal idea that feelings, not results, matter; that intent, not consequences, is the only ingredient for moral action. Give yourself up to the government in service, and good things will happen. This is not to denigrate service. Service is addressing a societal need. Service is the hard work of Americans to move up in the world, to make a living, to have some money to spend as they see fit, to have increased leisure time, time to genuinely serve at a soup kitchen or homeless shelter. To push a generation into a government bureaucratic farm league and to feed them the poison that *this* is the American dream, living off of taxpayer dollars and cleaning up communities through feel-good green initiatives is despicable. The real service here is to the liberal mind's need to justify handouts and to push a radical agenda.

One advertisement for another web site, USAService.org, features President Obama listing off the great accomplishments of the moon landing, saying:

> America's greatness was not crafted in skyscrapers alone . . . but on the ground by those who could see what needed to be done, volunteers who in service stepped forward, on to the dust of the moon, the levee in the heartland, the marble steps of a dream. . . . You may ask yourself where's my moon, my levee, my dream. Well it's here, with you. Step forward, help renew America at USAservice.org.

While service is certainly noble, the driving philosophy behind these advertisements is troubling. In a perversion of John F. Kennedy's "don't ask what your country can do for you," Obama invites the nation's youth to join temporary, taxpayer subsidized jobs. Furthermore, the ad gives the impression that in order to do something great, you must do it in government. Of course, this service ends up buttressing elected officials as much as the poor and needy. Most of what Obama cites was not really service in the sense of community service, like Jimmy Carter's Habitat for Humanity or the type many Americans do part-time in their communities. Astronauts and levee builders weren't working pro bono. Hard work and entrepreneurship made our country great, and are the only characteristics that will sustain our nation. Most of the greatest accomplishments of our nation—of mankind—have been driven by individuals in the private sector. People with vision who took a chance on an idea like electricity, the car, the computer.

Obama's stress on so-called service is a clear throwback and possible payback to his community organizing ACORN roots. Increasingly, we are seeing that ACORN, in particular, is not the Girl Scouts. It should give pause to all Americans that these organizations are actively being promoted to our nation's youth with taxpayer dollars.

AmeriCorps is a grants vehicle crafted from the Corporation for National and Community Service. It started as a pet project of President Bill Clinton that has been widely criticized as ineffective and wasteful.[147] According to its web site, the heavily taxpayer-subsidized AmeriCorp calls on its paid volunteers "to make a big difference in your life and in the lives of those around you. It's a chance to apply your skills and ideals toward helping others and meeting critical needs in the community."[148]

As for their mission, the web site states "Each year, AmeriCorps offers 75,000 opportunities for adults of all ages and backgrounds to serve through a network of partnerships with local and national nonprofit groups. Whether your service makes a community safer, gives a child a second chance, or helps protect the environment, you'll be getting things done through AmeriCorps!"[149]

There's an AmeriCorps advertisement that urges us to "fight poverty with compassion." Compassion, and all the rest of it, are all well and good, and, one could argue, a requisite state of mind to take action to fight poverty and alleviate social ills. But compassion and caring don't pay the bills. Lifting people out of poverty does, enabling and incentivizing people to increase their quality of life through hard work.

The Obama administration hasn't merely hijacked the rhetoric of volunteerism through AmeriCorps and similar government-sponsored volunteer programs, it's thwarted oversight of these organizations, fighting any reform tooth and nail.

Upon taking office, President Obama had Gerald Walpin, Americorps' inspector general fired. As Byron York reported in the *Washington Examiner*:

> Walpin was fired in part because of his aggressive investigation of the misuse of AmeriCorps funds by Sacramento mayor—and prominent Obama supporter—Kevin Johnson. The acting U.S. attorney in Sacramento, Lawrence Brown, took a strongly pro-Johnson position in the matter, even though there's no question that Johnson misused federal money. In the end, Brown played a key role in helping Johnson get off easy and in setting in motion the chain of events that led to Walpin's firing.[150]

You see, service only counts if you are serving yourself. Obama thought he could keep Americans in the dark about his connections to ACORN. Inspector General Walpin was terminated for his zeal to keep Americans informed.

AmeriCorps and many of its volunteer kin are noble ventures. They provide a way for our nation's youth to get involved in our communities in many constructive capacities. But these are not careers, nor should they serve as farm leagues for government bureaucracy. Obama's expansion of these programs and his rhetoric surrounding them are built upon false pretenses, which do a disservice to the genuinely hardworking youth in these programs and other vehicles for genuine community service. Furthermore, there are countless volunteer opportunities in communities throughout the nation that involve no federal bureaucracy. Community service is a wonderful thing. But as with any element of our society, to give government a monopoly—moral or otherwise—on charity is a fatal mistake. To *rely* on government programs for the well-being of our own communities or our nation's future is pure foolishness. To pretend that government-organized volunteerism built our past is a pure fabrication.

The Market Reacts

Ironically, the often-denigrated (semi-free) market reacted to many of these radical policies by implicitly and explicitly adopting the theme of "the government can help" and the Left's cry to blame someone else.

We've long seen this in our overlitigious society, but these specific ads reacting to market signals of perverse government incentives is just amazing. At this writing, you couldn't step on to a bus or train in Chicago without seeing at least one advertisement asking "Are *you* a victim of your mortgage?" A victim of an inanimate object! Ambulance chasers are replaced by deadbeat chasers stating "we fight the bank so you don't have to!" Dancing shadow mortgage ads on the Internet pop up proclaiming "Obama wants to expand homeownership!" and "Obama backs car insurance regulation—think you pay too much?" playing off of the backward priorities of the political climate that brought about the financial crisis to begin with.

Back in the U.S.S.R.

An amazing expansion of government has taken place behind the curtain in the form of "czars." This informal term refers, in most recent history, to the very formal titles of Russia's rulers up until the time of the Russian Revolution in 1917. But the word originates from a Slavic abbreviation of the name of history's most fascistic tyrant: Caesar.

Indeed, history repeats itself. Czar Nicholas II of Russia represented the twentieth century's best example of antidemocratic monarchism, and the end of his political rule was celebrated as a win for democracy. The current administration's use of this vile term to describe the unelected stewards of its regime says less about the inherent notoriety of the title than the unstated goal: to ensure that Russia's unfinished socialist vision is carried out in the United States. The 30-plus czars present a precarious position for the world's greatest liberal democracy. The czars are neither elected nor approved by the Senate and yet are so close to the president that their rules and orders broaden the scope of executive power and threaten the expansion of federal regulation.

This trend of the president nominating czars to serve as his advisors was a notable trademark of Franklin Delano Roosevelt (FDR) who used government largess as a pretense for fighting a corrupt Wall Street. But this political habit was not limited to Democrats—Nixon had czars as well. Nixon's biography is evidence enough to show that anointing ideological advisors with the privilege of executive power is not a sign of good government, regardless of the appointer's political affiliation.

The appointment of czars within the executive branch is a hostile gesture to the constitutional tradition of having one's presidential appointments confirmed by the Senate. Boston College law professor Richard Albert argues that Obama's czar appointments, while "indefensible," are constitutional, for only certain judicial appointments, executive agency commissioners, and inspectors general need Senate confirmation under the Constitution.[151] It has been constitutional custom since FDR for presidents to appoint czars. Given that czar appointments are political questions, the federal courts do not have jurisdiction to test their constitutionality.

But independent of the constitutional argument there is a good government argument that a president should have czars confirmed by the Senate. First, Obama has set a record that neither Stalin nor Mao could beat in terms of czar appointments. Second, for a president who preaches transparency, senatorial confirmation is an act of interbranch coordination and good federalism.

Obama's legal actions have been consistent with his goal to devolve authority away from state and federal legislatures into the executive branch. Obama is much more Machiavellian about federal power than his much criticized predecessor ever was. It has become clear the he and his administration do not respect the principle of federalism.

Tossing Federalism Aside

The most prominent example of how Obama has violated the Constitution in order to expand federal power is the stimulus bill. Every American child learns about the way our countrymen suffered during the Great Depression as well as the enormous aggrandizement of federal power that occurred under the New Deal. But Roosevelt understood an important political principle: surround oneself with advisors who have a diversity of political talents. While law school dropout FDR had to consult others as to the meaning of the Constitution, President Obama, in addition to being the president of the *Harvard Law Review*, was a professor of constitutional law at the University of Chicago. He has no such excuse. Obama understands better than anyone how to use executive prerogative to sidestep the Constitution. The stimulus bill clearly violated the constitutional principle of federalism that has been central to conservative principles of liberty and freedom. America's federalism principle is clearly stated in the Tenth Amendment, which instructs that powers not explicitly directed to the president are reserved to the states or, respectively, to the people.

Division A, Title XVI, Section 1607 of the American Recovery and Reinvestment Act of 2009 (the stimulus bill) provides the following language:

(a) Certification by Governor: Not later than 45 days after the date of enactment of this Act, funds provided to any State or agency thereof, the Governor of the State shall certify that:
1. The State request and use funds provided by this Act; and
2. Funds be used to create jobs and promote economic growth.
(b) Acceptance by State Legislature: If funds provided to any State in any division of this Act are not accepted for use by the Governor, then acceptance by the State legislature, by means of the adoption of a concurrent resolution, shall be sufficient to provide funding to such State.

The stimulus bill does not, on its face, violate the Tenth Amendment rights of states. However, the stimulus bill has been interpreted by several states to mean that stimulus-related programs can be passed without presenting the bill to their respective governors for signature. The stimulus is unconstitutional in states where all resolutions must be presented before the governor, unless such resolutions called for the amending of the state constitution. In states where all resolutions function like bills, §1607 of the American Recovery and Reinvestment Act is unconstitutional because it allows the states to pass bills without the approval of their governors.

The language of the bill allows states to pass concurrent resolutions to circumvent the governor. As stated, the bill does not stand for the proposition that state legislatures can pass stimulus-funded programs into law without approval from the governor of the state. It is important that the states understand that accepting stimulus money through joint resolution does not allow them to pass programs without presenting bills to the governor. If the state constitution interprets resolutions as similar to bills, then §1607(b) either does not apply because the state would still require the governor's signature on the resolution or it is unconstitutional because it conditions money on the state amending its constitution.

Consider Louisiana as an example. Governor Jindal of Louisiana refused stimulus money.[152] Louisiana requires that the governor be presented with all bills.[153] But there is a glaring problem with subpart (b) of Section 1607 because it assumes that a state like Louisiana could pass a joint resolution to accept stimulus funding without the governor's approval. In Louisiana, all resolutions that do not seek to amend the state constitution function as bills and thus require the governor's signature.[154] Article III, §15(a) of the Louisiana Constitution states: "The legislature shall enact no law except by a bill introduced during that session, and propose no constitutional amendment except by a joint resolution introduced during that session, which shall be processed as a bill." Thus, Article III §17(b) of Louisiana's Constitution, which reads, "No joint, concurrent, or other resolution shall require the signature or other action of the Governor to become effective" *only* applies to resolutions for constitutional amendments. Accepting stimulus money is not a resolution to amend a state constitution.

Unless §1607(b) contemplated "resolution" to mean that states should be directly forced into amending their constitutions—which is itself unconstitutional—then resolution in §1607(b) is to be interpreted as being synonymous with a bill. In that case, the American Recovery and Reinvestment Act of 2009 allows the United States federal government to condition funding to a state upon that state's violating its own constitution. This condition violates the U.S. Constitution.

The 2009 American Recovery and Reinvestment Act is unconstitutional in many states where resolutions function as bills. In states like Louisiana, where resolutions function as bills, the stimulus bill would potentially force an unwilling governor to accept funds or would encourage the state to violate its own constitution.[155] *South Dakota v. Dole* held that the spending power "may not be used to induce the States to engage in activities that would themselves be unconstitutional." [483 U.S. 203, 210 (1987)]

In addition to Louisiana, Nevada, Missouri, Alaska, Florida, Texas, Mississippi, West Virginia, North Carolina, Utah, Oregon, and Alabama treat resolutions that do not seek to amend the constitution as bills.[156]

While the stimulus bill, on its face, does not violate the Tenth Amendment, there is concern that the bill, in fact, conditions money upon states violating their constitutions. In any case, the bill might encourage states to pass stimulus-related programs without presenting those bills before their respective governors.

When the federal government induces state legislatures to circumvent their governors, the Tenth Amendment is violated.[157] As Justice Scalia declared in *Printz v. United States*, "Not only do the enactments of the early congresses . . . contain no evidence of an assumption that the federal government may command the states' executive power in the absence of particularized constitutional authorization, they contain . . . precisely the opposite assumption." [521 U.S. 898, 909 (1997)]

Louisiana and at least 11 other states have the Tenth Amendment right to protect their constitutional provisions requiring the governor to be presented with all legislative bills and resolutions. The 2009 American Recovery and Reinvestment Act would violate that right if states adopted specific programs without the signatures of their respective governors. The stimulus bill, like the hundreds of New Deal legislative enactments, threatens to rewrite the constitutional order of our country. It aggrandizes federal power at the expense of the judgment of the individual states, which preceded our national government. This is a country of states united in freedom, not a kingdom united in tyranny.

Changing the Rules

Like President Obama, House Financial Services Committee Chairman Barney Frank is a Harvard-trained lawyer who lacks formal economics training and has negligible experience as a lawyer. But a hubristic Barney Frank has threatened "cram-down" legislation that would allow bankruptcy judges to rewrite mortgage contracts when homeowners file for bankruptcy. President Obama has tried to help at-risk homeowners by pressuring mortgage servicers to modify home loans. The Treasury Department has revealed that only 9 percent of eligible borrowers have received modifications and that the mortgage servicers have had an "uneven" performance. Is it any wonder that government-controlled economic solutions function terribly? In addition to an economically illiterate president and financial services chairman, our country is blessed to have Timothy Geithner, who lacks a degree in either finance or economics, as the point man of the most important economic regulatory body in the world!

Barney Frank's solution will gain momentum as our country's economic dunces continue to try to reinvent the wheel in thinking that loan modification will create economic balances. The idea of judges having the power to rewrite loan agreements, which are legal contracts, gives legislative power—a power granted by hard-working American people—to an unelected judge. Worse, bankruptcy judges are federal judges whose power comes from Congress, not Article III of the Constitution, which lays out the rules governing federal judges. Barney Frank's powerful congressional mandates would functionally rewrite the Constitution and remove the fundamental right to freedom of contract from the pens of individuals to the signature of unelected legislative judges.

Still think Obama and Frank care about distressed homeowners? Obama and his wealthy political allies have never experienced what it means for an individual to declare bankruptcy and go through drawn-out legal proceedings. It is neither a quick nor cheap process. James Lockhart, who oversees government-controlled Fannie Mae and Freddie Mac, told the *Wall Street Journal* that "[w]e shouldn't make people have to go through bankruptcy to get their mortgages modified or refinanced."[158]

Obama's $75 billion Making Home Affordable program gives lenders taxpayer subsidies to lower the mortgage payments of distressed borrowers. However, the *Washington Post* reported that "Of the top 25 participants in the program, at least 21 specialized in servicing or originating subprime loans."[159]

On Regulation

Obama's callous disrespect for the Constitution reflects an overall shift away from individual rights to an organic understanding of humanity. For example, many of the Obama administration's proposed new financial regulations would hold brokers to the same high fiduciary duty that other investment advisers must abide by. As a result, brokers will engage in less costly and more tax-efficient investment recommendations, thus substantially cutting away the risk that allows for market innovation. The Treasury Department's proposed Investor Protection Act of 2009 would allow the U.S. Securities and Exchange Commission to "promulgate rules" establishing a fiduciary duty, thus creating uniform regulation of all securities dealers and investment advisers, destroying the diversity of market participants and negotiators.[160] As of this writing, the suggestions are in legislative draft form.[161]

Citizen Truth Brigade

Obama is so zealous about his polemical agenda that he has breached the Privacy Act of 1974—designed to prevent Nixon-like governmental snooping—by cataloguing information about individuals who have spoken privately against the president's health plan.[162] According to the White House, flag@whitehouse.gov was set up for Obama's supporters to send anything "fishy" about the president's health care plan.[163] Furthermore, they began *accidentally* spamming citizens with their propaganda—citizens who hadn't signed up to receive any e-mail from the White House. This practice is illegal.[164] Both of these functionalities on their web site were scrapped amidst public outcry and media pressure.[165]

Universal Health Care

Next on the Left's docket is the finishing touch on our Utopian society: free, universal health care for all. Who will pick up the bill? It doesn't matter. Liberals believe that top-notch medical care—most of which was not in existence a mere 50 years ago—is a *basic human right*. What's more, they believe it can best be administered by the government that brings us the failures of the Department of Motor Vehicles and the Post Office.

This policy battle would bring out an entirely new wave of protests and controversy as radical politicians and their media allies defended indefensible government expansion and intrusion.

I get into the health care debate in more detail in Chapter 8.

Sliding Down the Slippery Slope

The largest spending spree in history was frightening to say the least. It is one thing to make the case for bailing out large financial institutions in the name of saving millions of innocent bystanders—the unwitting investors and retirees screwed by big bad Wall Street, the lack of government oversight, or bungled government intervention. Putting practical and principled arguments opposing bailouts aside, it is almost as easy to sell the idea of temporary government help to save the underlying foundation of our economy.

But what began as an allegedly critical temporary suspension of principles and common sense became the prevailing thought of the age: Government knows best. Critics of the bailouts were assailed as fanatics or idealists. Just over one year later, the actual damage is clear: The government has strayed far outside the boundaries of its charter and taxpayers in this and future generations will pay for it.

The bailouts did dangerous things to the psychology of the nation as a whole. They numbed officials and the public to the vast sums of money actually being spent and to the consequences of the spending.

The oft-touted, oft-doubted slippery slope is quite apropos here. The (mental) state of the nation and its leaders led to what would have previously been written off as unforeseeable, unbelievable actions. The bailouts, the handouts, the cash for clunkers-type programs, the government's hooks in major financial institutions, and government ownership of a major car manufacturer would have been laughable propositions just a few years earlier. In the pipeline, the nation faced the very real prospect of a cap-and-trade energy Ponzi scheme and government-run health care.

All of a sudden, the outcries of the "unrealistic" capitalistic idealists and fanatics didn't seem too far off the mark. If you give politicians an inch, they push for a mile. Eventually, Americans may find themselves miles off course.

Americans would soon find that the path our country had been directed down was not due to an involuntary slip induced by mere political gravity, but the result of deliberate force by some very powerful, insidious elements.

CHAPTER 7

RADICAL TACTICS

Our tyrants and bandits are more hateful than those of earlier times because, invoking such self-deceptive rhetoric, they pose as intellectuals. Our tyrants write philosophy in the morning and torture in the afternoon.

—Richard Rorty, *Consequences of Pragmatism,*
University of Minnesota Press (June 1982), p. 171

In 1787, the American patriots won a battle for American independence. Those patriots declared their independence in written form, proclaiming a moral vision for liberal democracy throughout history: "that all Men are created equal, that they are endowed by their Creator with certain unalienable Rights, that among these are Life, Liberty, and the Pursuit of Happiness—That to secure these Rights, Governments are instituted among Men, deriving their just Powers from the Consent of the Governed."

The modern Left gets nervous when they see American people organizing to resist government policies that were made without the people's consent. Leftists, who have historically been linked with public activism and protest, cannot possibly understand what is meant by conservative activism. Only the liberal mind would look toward a declaration of the law as a protest simply because such a mind is incapable of understanding why people would fight for the preservation of what is natural or customary or God-given. The Declaration of Independence signaled a declaration—not a protest or an activist campaign—of what was a matter of natural right. One has to declare rights in order for them to be recognized. Conservatives use activism to declare preexisting rights that are being threatened by illegitimate and arbitrary government policies. The modern Left uses activism to protest against policies they view as impeding rights that will likely never come to fruition.

Much recent activism on the left proudly proclaims the mantra of "gimme more" in the name of fairness. In the 1950s and '60s (but starting much earlier with Eleanor Roosevelt and before many progressives actually jumped on the bandwagon), progressives protested segregation and racial inequality. This was a noble battle and led to much needed change in federal, state, and local policies and laws. The protests weren't so much about gimme more as they were about demands that all peoples receive the same, that we not segregate according to color.

In modern times, however, the Left has taken the fight for racial equality to be a Good Housekeeping Seal of Approval for all their protests. They claim to be fighting for equality, but what the nanny-state proponents want is to legislate everything from your car's mileage, despite safety concerns,[1] to whether you can smoke in your own home, allegedly *due* to safety concerns, and much more.[2] Where will it end? What's worse, the Left does not merely want to inhibit others, it wants to enrich itself while manufacturing consent. While the Right wants to be left alone, the Left wants to take, control, and distribute as it sees fit when it sees fit. Leftists are moochers who depend on the fruits of a harvest carved out by secretive, niche legislation, government mandates, and union dues— force and fraud rather than the successes or failures of individual attempts at productivity. Oddly, it is the very state that they want to empower to control everything that once controlled some matters with a heavy, uneven hand. The assumption seems to be that a once unjust government has somehow evolved to a state of inherent goodness—a state only the state, not its citizens, can bring about.

To best combat these societal leeches, it is crucial to understand not just their principles and policy positions, but their playbook as well.

The Playbook

Saul Alinsky's *Rules for Radicals* is considered the playbook for modern community organizing. Alinsky, a University of Chicago dropout and socialist community organizer, influenced both Hillary Clinton and Barack Obama.[3]

In *Rules,* Alinsky's concept of organizing is based on three general principles: (1) win real, immediate, concrete improvement in people's lives; (2) give people a sense of their own power; and (3) alter the relations of power. He emphasized the importance of confrontational tactics to redistribute power. In *Rules for Radicals*, Alisnky begins with the following introduction:

> What follows is for those who want to change the world from what it is to what they believe it should be. *The Prince* was written by Machiavelli for the Haves on how to hold power. *Rules for Radicals* is written for the Have-Nots on how to take it away.

Saul Alinsky outlined his antisocial stance in stating, "There are certain central concepts of action in human politics that operate regardless of the scene or the time. To know these is basic to a pragmatic attack on the system."[4]

Alinsky described the choice of organizing as an effort to fulfill a personal need to promote social change. Social change, for Alinsky, seems to be a selfish, not altruistic, pursuit. Central to Alinsky's ideas was the belief that communities are politicized according to individual self-interest. Indeed, Alinsky argued, "[t]here has always been universal agreement on the part that self-interest plays as a prime moving force in man's behavior. The importance of self-interest has never been challenged; it has been accepted as an inevitable fact of life."[5] For Alinsky's low-income and economically distressed pawns, organizing was a psychological form of ego protection—protest against society instead of working toward individual responsibility.

Rules for Radicals defined the organizer as the driving force in a social action organization. Alinsky viewed organizers as the "highly imaginative and creative architects and engineers"[6] of community organizations. *Rules for Radicals* stressed the importance of arousing public anger about a situation, and Alinsky wrote that organizers must "rub raw the sores of resentment." Moreover, organizers must embrace moral uncertainty: "An organizer working in and for an open society is in an ideological dilemma. To begin with, he does not have a fixed truth—truth to him is relative and changing; everything to him is relative and changing. He is a political relativist."[7]

Alinsky was wary of electoral politics and its ability to create social progress for America's low-income population. Obama and Clinton clearly disagreed. But one student of Alinsky's did not: Wade Rathke.

The Organizers

The Association of Community Organizations for Reform Now (ACORN) is an impressive army of community organizers that liberal politicians can tap to get elected and to promote their agendas. As a taxpayer-subsidized Astroturf force, their operations deserve significant scrutiny.

ACORN was founded by Wade Rathke in 1970 in Little Rock, Arkansas.[8] Rathke came from Students for a Democratic Society, the radical leftist group that spawned Bill Ayers, the co-founder of the terrorist Weather Underground Organization (Weathermen). ACORN now boasts hundreds of affiliates in 41 states and registered 1.3 million people to vote in the 2008 election.[9] The ACORN Council, composed of all ACORN chapters and affiliates, has over 360 organizations throughout the United States.[10]

ACORN has always couched its community organizing as a grass-roots operation. Wade Rathke himself never sought elected office. Despite ACORN's nonelectoral facade, the organization has received millions of dollars in government funding while simultaneously abusing the privileges it receives at the cost of the American taxpayer by engaging in voter registration fraud and other illegal activities.[11]

According to a report issued by the Committee on Oversight and Government Reform of the House of Representatives, released in 2009, "one-third of the 1.3 million voter registration cards turned in by ACORN in 2008 were invalid."[12] The report stated ACORN has been investigated for voter registration fraud in Arkansas (1998), Pennsylvania (1999, 2009), and Nevada (2008, 2009).[13] According to the report, ACORN perpetrates interstate fraud:

- In June 2009, seven ACORN workers in Pennsylvania were charged with forging 51 signatures and violating election laws in advance of the 2008 presidential election.
- In May 2009, two ACORN staff members were prosecuted in Clark County, Nevada, for paying bonuses to workers who registered more than 21 individuals per day.
- In July 2008, three ACORN workers were convicted of voter fraud in Kansas City because they flooded voter registration rolls with over 35,000 false or questionable registration forms.
- In March 2008, an ACORN employee in West Reading, Pennsylvania, was sentenced to up to 23 months in prison for identity theft and tampering with records and forging 29 voter registration forms in order to collect a cash bonus.
- In 2007, three ACORN employees pled guilty, and four more were charged, in the worst case of voter registration fraud in Washington state history.
- In 2007, a man in Reynoldsburg, Ohio, was indicted on two felony counts of illegal voting and false registration after being registered by ACORN to vote in two separate counties.
- In 2006, eight ACORN employees in St. Louis, Missouri, were indicted on federal election fraud charges.
- In 2005, two ex-ACORN employees were convicted in Denver, Colorado, of perjury for submitting false voter registrations.
- In 2004, a grand jury indicted a Columbus, Ohio, ACORN worker for submitting a false signature and false voter registration form.
- In 1998, a contractor with ACORN-affiliated Project Vote was arrested in Arkansas for falsifying 400 voter registration cards.

In addition to Nevada, Missouri, Pennsylvania, Washington, Arkansas, Colorado, Kansas, and Ohio, there have been prosecutions against ACORN workers in Connecticut, Texas, Wisconsin, and Michigan.[14]

ACORN has "evaded taxes, obstructed justice, engaged in self dealing, and aided and abetted a cover-up" of an embezzlement of close to $1 million by founder Wade Rathke's brother, Dale.[15] ACORN treated the $1 million embezzlement as an "internal matter" deciding to neither notify its board nor the federal government.[16] ACORN has received $53 million in federal funds since 1994 and is eligible for $8.5 billion more.[17] ACORN used federal money to engage in political activities, submitted false filings to the Internal Revenue Service and the U.S. Department of Labor, and violated the Employee Retirement Income Security Act of 1974.[18]

ACORN is a national network of groups with community control that reflect Alinsky's intellectualized zeal for social anarchy buried under a lust for power. Wade Rathke learned these rules for radicals well and successfully covered up the embezzlement of nearly $1 million by his brother, Dale, as well as supervised illegal transactions between taxable corporations, tax-exempt nonprofits, labor unions and charitable foundations through a network so vast, complex, and multitentacled that the Department of Justice, Department of Labor, and the Internal Revenue Service have yet to pierce its corrupt veil.[19]

It is important not to underestimate the degree to which liberal elites advocate social change through an imprimatur of cunning to manipulate the masses. In September of 2009, Andrew Breitbart's BigGovernment.com broke an incredible story. Freelance journalists Hannah Giles and James O'Keefe revealed ACORN employees advising the couple on sex trafficking and prostitution best practices in a series of undercover videos recorded at multiple ACORN offices around the country.

ACORN receives money from the federal government and philanthropic U.S. citizens and instead of hiring high-quality employees to advise the poor on taxes and register them to vote, they employ experts to advise individuals on how to perpetrate criminal activities. The Left operates on a declaration of protest of the Constitution—a "Protestution" of Independence. The Left seeks to abide by Protestution, while the Right defines good government through its constitution. A Protestution of Independence would mean that pornographers dumb-down the Constitution while simultaneously robbing the American people. This has unquestionably been the reality of ACORN—our current president's first major employer.

ACORN's leftist elites have created a national corporation that diverts hard-earned taxpayer money to promote a radical antiestablishment agenda often under the radar of the law.[20] ACORN's bright, educated leaders have successfully outmaneuvered several federal laws. Just one example is Jon Kest, the brother of ACORN executive Steven Kest. John Kest is a registered lobbyist for ACORN in the city of New York, yet he is not registered under the Lobbying Disclosure Act in Congress. ACORN is such a successful multimillion dollar corporation because it has strategically planned its political activism to circumvent every conceivable loophole in the federal statutes that ought to trap its tentacles.[21] There is nothing scarier nor more frustrating than a criminal who, by law, cannot be caught.

Concern about ACORN is hardly irrational fear mongering as many in the media and political class proclaim. The September 2009 news regarding ACORN's seeming support of prostitution and underage sex trafficking was hardly surprising and hardly theoretical given ACORN's history. In 2006, ACORN organized its Chicago members to earn money for sex and one ACORN worker was arrested for illegal prostitution and drug charges when she offered her services to an undercover police officer.[22] She stated she was employed by ACORN and a used crack pipe was found on her person.[23] Thus our hard-earned tax dollars are not only funding voter fraud, embezzlement, and partisan lobbying, but sometimes prostitution and drugs as well.

ACORN bashed the tea parties as partisan,[24] yet in typical Chicago fashion they sought to use the census to gather enough information on U.S. citizens to get even with their enemies. Most Americans had been duped into thinking that ACORN has long been a partner with the Census Bureau. In fact, ACORN has never been a national partner of the Census Bureau. It almost was until Republican congressmen pressured Census Director Robert Groves to sever the relationship. ACORN is described by the aforementioned Committee on Oversight and Government Reform Report as having "repeatedly and deliberately engaged in systemic fraud" as well as having a history of hiring convicted felons.[25]

Obama's election threatened to allow ACORN to finally have control over the U.S. census and thus the shaping of political districts.

The census is the most important tool the federal government uses to create congressional districts. How districts are structured determines who wins elections. Obama's administration supported the notion of ACORN employees being hired to determine how districts will be apportioned by population and thus a criminal enterprise would have been given the power to shape the political future of our country.

Due to the investigative reporting of Hannah Giles and James O'Keefe—reporting not done by traditional media outlets—both houses of Congress moved to defund ACORN.[26],[27] The IRS severed ties[28] and the DOJ launched a probe into the organization.[29]

ACORN calls the tea parties partisan because it does not want Americans to believe that social change can occur in nonradical ways. It wants Americans to engage in the liberal process of forgetting—including forgetting that being American was historically identified by those people who protested against British taxation without representation—in order to guarantee the success of their propaganda. What is really radical is having the government replace the role of individual responsibility. The Left wants a world where the government is so big that there is no alternative to the government controlling the choices and lives of individuals. This is slavery. The stimulus bill, cash for clunkers, cap and trade, and universal health care—all steps along the way to a complete upending of the Constitution.

ACORN thrives under these conditions. In 1980, ACORN gave a tour of the Detroit slums to 13 Republican delegates to the Republican National Convention there. Sidney Bass, a tour leader, claimed "[n]eighborhoods are revitalized by a commitment to housing rehabilitation money. . . . Neighborhoods are rebuilt when the people in them have a voice."[30] In 1980, ACORN's answer to the Detroit problem was "more federal public housing money, poor people on the boards of large corporations, and laws forcing banks to lend housing money to the poor."

Thirty years later Detroit is in straits much more dire than it was in the 1980s. Now America's Detroit-based car manufacturers are bankrupt and thousands of hard-working Americans have been laid off. Why has this happened? Poor people—or greedy Democrats—have been on corporate boards. Just think of kingpin Franklin Raines and his $100 million paycheck at Fannie Mae. His corruption and the corruption of Fannie Mae and Freddie Mac were part of a vision that ACORN sought to propagate. The result: a housing crisis and a financial collapse with thousands, if not millions, of Americans now dangerously close to poverty. ACORN has made America's minorities worse off. In 1980, in response to ACORN organizer Sidney Bass, Republican national committeeman Leon Oistad replied, "I believe that tax policies could be used to encourage industry to locate in certain areas, to have training programs for people who need the jobs, but I don't think it's something the government can do by itself for these people."[31] If only ACORN cared enough to listen back then.

Perhaps the scariest trend of all is how community organizers have been positioned within President Obama's cabinet. Van Jones was appointed associate director for Green Jobs at the White House Council on Environmental Quality (CEQ).[32] Jones was the founder and president of Green For All and a long-standing board member of the Apollo Alliance.[33] Wade Rathke, ACORN's founder, was on the board of the Tides Foundation, which is the parent organization of the Apollo Alliance. Apollo put out a draft stimulus bill in 2008, which included nearly everything that ended up being approved in the government's package.[34]

According to the Apollo Alliance's web site, "[t]he Apollo Alliance is a coalition of labor, business, environmental, and community leaders working to catalyze a clean energy revolution that will put millions of Americans to work in a new generation of high-quality, green-collar jobs."[35] Obama's hiring of Jones may corroborate the president's views on the environment but it more readily depicts Obama's understanding of political leadership. Van Jones is a self-identified communist[36] and "rowdy black nationalist"[37] who has twice been arrested for political protests. After Glenn Beck ran a series of candid videos of Van Jones, he was forced to resign. Buried by his own words, he claimed that he was the victim of a smear campaign. The rest of the media was forced to play catch-up and cover the fallout of a major story they'd failed to discover or cover.

ACORN also has labor union affiliates, most notably Service Employees International Union (SEIU) Local 100 in New Orleans and Local

880 in Chicago. SEIU Local 880 lobbied in support of now-disgraced Illinois Gov. Rod Blagojevich.[38]

The trillions of dollars in lost opportunity costs resulting from the stimulus bill and its progeny, cap and trade and national health care, could have been avoided. The loss of millions of dollars to the fraudulent practices of ACORN and its affiliates could have been avoided. Saul Alinsky's antiestablishment psychosis could have been avoided. In 1972, Alan Cranston of *Playboy* magazine interviewed Saul Alinsky.[39] In the interview, Cranston asked Alinsky, "Did you rebel in areas other than religion?" Alinsky responded:

> Yes, in little ways I've been fighting the system ever since I was seven or eight years old. I mean, I was the kind of kid who'd never dream of walking on the grass until I'd see a KEEP OFF THE GRASS sign, and then I'd stomp all over it.

On the one hand, Alinsky's rejection of restrictions on personal liberties seems to be an admirable gem in his philosophy that liberty-minded Americans can agree with. But Alinsky and defenders of liberty live in two separate worlds. Alinsky saw a world of inequality and blamed prosperity and capitalism. Thus anger was central to Alinsky's moral vision. He viewed progress with anxiety and he mistook the existential angst of philosophers and artists as a justification for his political ends. Paralyzed by fear, Alinsky blamed his misanthropy on a corrupt society and its institutions. His solution for freedom was the destruction of the norms that have traditionally guaranteed man's well-being.

Defenders of liberty do not share this vision. Those who defend liberty know well that human history is human progress, and the roots of our civilization and our freedom originate from laws that can never be destroyed. Lovers of liberty are immune to the petty fears of those who find personal responsibility too harsh a burden to be expected of anyone.

Thus Alinsky's desire to stomp on the grass is not an exercise in personal freedom, but a lack of personal restraint and a desire to rebel against rules as an end itself regardless of the consequences. In this case, Alinsky exhibited a lack of respect for property rights, a cornerstone of a civil society.

Alinsky remarked in the interview that his father beat him regularly, most beatings culminating in the statement, "You ever do that again and you know what's going to happen to you!"[40] One day, Alinsky told him no, he didn't know what would happen. He found that his father had no response, to which he inferred, "Power is not in what the establishment has but in what you think it has."[41] Cranston then asked Alinsky, "Was your relationship with your father uniformly hostile?" Alinsky replied, "Yeah, pretty much so." Cranston responded, "A psychoanalytic interpretation of your life might conclude that your subsequent career as a radical was motivated more by hatred of your father than by opposition to the establishment." Perhaps Alinsky should have consulted a therapist instead of concocting a revolution.

The Enforcers

One of the most overlooked influences of labor unions is their role in promoting and financing modern leftist politics. With their radical agendas and exceptionally deep pockets, unions are fundamental to shaping the political landscape of the day. This is neither a secret nor a concocted conspiracy theory. On the campaign trail, Barack Obama told ACORN and its affiliates, including Project Vote, the SEIU, ACORN-affiliate unions Local 100 in New Orleans and Local 880 in Chicago,[42] "You are going to shape the agenda."

Their role goes well beyond the mere difference between two worldviews of protecting your job through hard work versus protecting your job through a union that will defend you against your oppressive employer. Indeed, labor unions are such a minority in today's workplace that many people's understanding of unions' goals is limited to just such an analysis, and it reflects to some extent most of what people know about why unions came to be so many decades ago, albeit in a very simple way. Yet, there is so much more depth to the issue of labor unions' involvement in modern politics that an entire book could be written on the subject. Suffice it to say, freedom loving people—average Americans—need to understand how incredibly corrosive today's union movement has become and how it uses its war chest to fund the most radical leftist agenda in decades.

Investing in Change

Labor unions are the largest contributors to Democratic politicians, and the amount they spend on politics is remarkable. For instance, according to the web site www.opensecrets.org, government unions contributed $181,336,679 since the 1990 election cycle, while building trade unions gave $135,544,030. All told, unions shoveled $673,833,567 toward politics in the last 20 years, and almost all of that money (92 percent) went to Democrats.[43] Given that kind of money, the Democrats are hard-pressed not to do the bidding of their masters in the labor movement. Ensuring common sense regulations on their financial activities is not on unions' priority list.

The end of the nineteenth century ushered in the Industrial Revolution, and with it came a new set of challenges as workers and employers dealt with rapid changes in the workplace. In that context, unions served an important purpose. They allowed large groups of workers to organize and negotiate for better wages and working conditions. Even at their inception, however, unions were rife with problems, hijacked by opportunistic politicians and criminals, and subsequent years have not eliminated the more unsavory aspects of these organizations. More important, though, today's unions have adopted a radical social agenda that extends well beyond simply advocating for a 40-hour workweek, and despite their relatively small numbers, they seek to impose their socialist worldview on the rest of the United States (while, presumably, conscripting everyone to join their ranks), an effort that drives much of the increasingly divisive political disagreements our country is now having. The radical agenda of labor unions is so far at odds with traditional American values that it is difficult for passions not to take over as our mainstream, centrist populace, which generally understands the American political tradition of individual liberty, confronts an angry mob of malcontents who want to destroy the American way of life.

The Rise and Fall of Unions

Perhaps one of the most notable aspects about the labor movement in the United States is that it is seemingly irrelevant to most workers, particularly in the private sector, where unionization rates amount to a paltry 7.6 percent, according to the Bureau of Labor Statistics.[44] Yet, despite their relatively small numbers, unions exert a major influence in the public policy arena. Among their many aims is to reverse a decades-long decline in membership.

At the turn of the twentieth century, when the U.S. economy was transforming and modernizing, the belief that workers should have more control over their working conditions took strong root in labor unions, although there were certainly notable differences between groups like the American Federation of Labor (AFL) and its cousin, the Congress of Industrial Organizations (CIO). In the middle of the Depression, New Deal legislation—much of it unconstitutional[45]—was passed to expand federal control over the nation's economy. With Franklin D. Roosevelt, an avowed liberal who sought more power for the federal government, as president, it is little wonder that labor unions succeeded in passing the National Labor Relations Act of 1935 (also known as the Wagner Act). Interestingly, however, even FDR worried that giving in to the unions might interfere with economic recovery. With the aim of making it easier for unions to organize workers, the law handed them a sledgehammer to use against employers. The law declared that unions could act as the sole representative for employees who were deemed to be part of a collective bargaining unit, thereby stripping workers of their ability to negotiate their own pay and benefits with their employer. The Wagner Act made it far easier for unions to get people to sign up as members through various means, and as a result union membership increased until well after the end of World War II. (See Exhibit 7.1.)

As America adjusted to the post-war years, though, the inherent problems with labor unions started to become apparent as unscrupulous labor leaders used their newfound leverage to intimidate employers. In particular, as these unions consolidated more power for themselves, they engaged in a number of strikes and other public disruptions that often led to violence. With public sentiment sympathetic to labor during the 1930s, unions were able to rapidly sign on workers and in doing so use their power to strike for practically any reason as a bludgeon against employers. Interestingly, the Wagner Act had defined a number of "unfair labor practices," as the term is known, that regulated what employers could or could not do when it came to unions, but the law

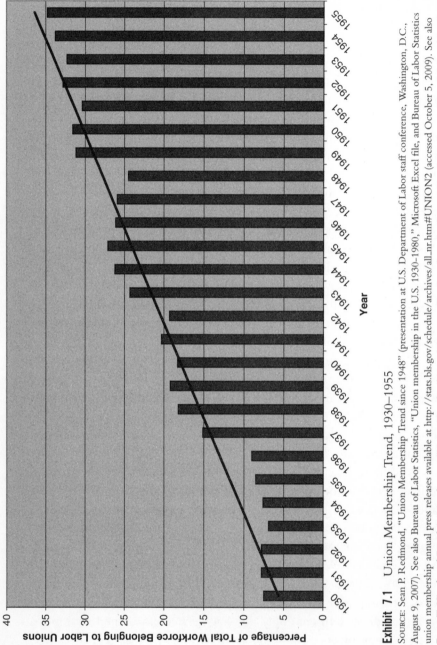

Exhibit 7.1 Union Membership Trend, 1930–1955

SOURCE: Sean P. Redmond, "Union Membership Trend since 1948" (presentation at U.S. Department of Labor staff conference, Washington, D.C., August 9, 2007). See also Bureau of Labor Statistics, "Union membership in the U.S. 1930–1980," Microsoft Excel file, and Bureau of Labor Statistics union membership annual press releases available at http://stats.bls.gov/schedule/archives/all_nr.htm#UNION2 (accessed October 5, 2009). See also Barry T. Hirsch and David A. Macpherson, "Union Membership and Coverage Database from the Current Population Survey: Note," Industrial and Labor Relations Review, Vol. 56, No. 2, January 2003, pp. 349–354, available at www.unionstats.com (accessed October 5, 2009).

did no such thing to limit the behavior of the labor unions, thus opening the door for problems down the road. By the mid 1940s, the country was weary from waging a violent war against fascists. The public's palate for disruptive strikes and violent union thugs began to wane, and in 1947 Congress passed the Labor—Management Relations Act (more commonly known as the Taft-Hartley Act). The law corrected a major loophole that had existed previously when unions enjoyed free rein to engage in virtually any kind of disruptive behavior without fear of unfair labor practice charges, and it outlawed a number of different types of strikes that previously had been used to extort employers. It also permitted states to enact "right to work" laws that permitted employees to decide for themselves whether they wanted to join a union. One of the lesser utilized portions allowed the federal government to intervene in major labor disagreements that threatened to significantly disrupt economic activity. When the Taft-Hartley Act was proposed, Big Labor derided it as the "slave labor" act and complained bitterly that the proposal was "dastardly."[46] They seemed to think that bullying employers (and those who didn't agree with them) was their birthright.

After the Taft-Hartley Act was passed, union intransigence hardly disappeared. Union membership continued to grow until 1955, when almost 35 percent of the American workforce belonged to one. For the next 50 years that percentage steadily declined by about two thirds, and today, just over 12 percent of the workforce in the combined private and public sectors belongs to a union. (See Exhibit 7.2.) Big Labor to this day despises the Taft-Hartley Act and would love nothing more than to get rid of it, which it's trying to do incrementally. First and foremost among the provisions labor unions would change is the ability for workers to freely decide whether they want to join a union, which, of course, is a freedom Big Labor would rather not permit. Unions are "progressive" and thus hard-pressed to believe that anything they do could be wrong. Convinced of the righteousness of their every action, they would rather not be subject to unfair labor practice charges or face federal intervention when their unreasonable demands threaten to shut down portions of the economy, as has happened several times over the years. In the meantime, they ignore their own responsibility for losing members and for the fact that only 9 percent of nonunion workers in the United States say they would want to join a union.[47]

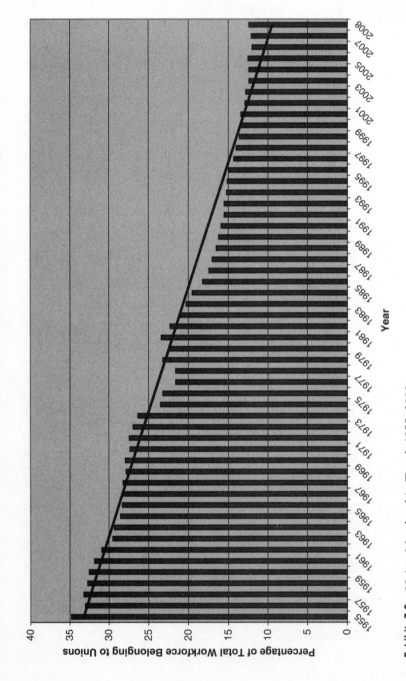

Exhibit 7.2 Union Membership Trend, 1955–2008

SOURCE: Data Bureau of Labor Statistics (www.bls.gov/cps/cpslutabs.htm).

The truth is Big Labor's long decline in membership is due to many factors, not the least of which is a perception of widespread corruption and lack of transparency. Movie lovers will recall the 1954 Academy Award-winning film *On the Waterfront* and its mobbed up union boss Johnny Friendly. Marlon Brando's character, Terry Malloy, worked on the docks where Friendly ruled with an iron fist. When Malloy tried to fight the union's entrenched leadership, he was badly beaten and his brother was murdered. That movie, which was based on a 1949 exposé about the extensive corruption in New York's dock workers union, reinforced a negative public image of labor union leadership that they were hard-pressed to shake. By the late 1950s, Congress was investigating allegations of corruption within the labor movement, and in doing so awakened the public to a network of corrupt, mob-linked unions that stiffed the working man to enrich a handful of fat-cat leaders. In February 1957, Arkansas Sen. John L. McClellan convened a series of hearings, aptly named the McClellan Hearings, to investigate the extent of racketeering and other criminal deeds in Big Labor, particularly within the Teamsters' union led by Jimmy Hoffa. While Hoffa and his merry band of union thugs paraded in and out of the hearings, the public came to realize that giving unbridled power to labor leaders was a serious mistake (thus proving the conservative position that too much power aggregated to any one authority is corrupting, and making the case for the U.S. federalist system of separation of powers between the federal and state governments). In the wake of the hearings, more than 20 individuals were convicted of crimes, and Congress passed yet another law, the Labor-Management Reporting and Disclosure Act (LMRDA, also known as the Landrum-Griffin Act), to prevent crimes like embezzlement and fraud by creating a system of financial reporting for labor unions. Despite Congress' usual flash-in-the-pan interest, the public relations damage was done, and the precipitous decline of union membership began in earnest.

In the face of declining membership and legitimate labor disputes, unions are forced to create problems where they don't exist, and push for ridiculous provisions in the name of progress. The right to a fair wage quickly morphed into the right to a wage under lifetime job security. Yes, lifetime job security. Take, for example, the unions at the *Boston Globe*, which have managed to finagle this extraordinary perk for 430 of

their members.[48] Even while the newspaper was facing massive financial hardship and possible bankruptcy, the unions demanded extravagant
benefits, all in the name of some distorted notion of workers' rights—
as if there were a right to a lifetime job. But it doesn't stop there. As if the
ridiculous belief in lifetime job security weren't enough, this concept
morphed into passing on jobs to the next of kin. Such is the case for longshoremen on the West Coast, who pass along their union membership
from generation to generation.[49] These are just some examples of the
outrageous demands unions make, and often get, by hook or by crook.

Pay for No Work

Notwithstanding intensely corrupt leadership, labor unions have spe-
cialized in bad conduct that ordinary workers understand to be patently
unfair, or at least inimical to the idea of working hard for a living. Take,
for instance, no-show jobs. In this type of scheme, a union boss of some
level will demand from an employer a job, either for himself or maybe
one of his relatives or lieutenants, where the employee collects a paycheck for work neither needed nor performed. The employer gives in,
as if this were a cost of doing business, to keep the peace and avoid either
a strike or, perhaps, violence. If this sounds like something out of *The
Sopranos*, well that's not too far off—these types of arrangements popped
up in the popular television program every once in a while when Tony
Soprano had to reward one of his henchmen. Sadly, this type of corruption still goes on, and when it happens, it can cost businesses millions
of dollars. In one prominent case in New York, members of the International Union of Elevator Constructors were accused of holding two
or three no-show jobs at a time, and when two members who weren't
in on the gig spoke out against the scheme, they were allegedly beaten
and one of them was kicked in the teeth.[50] In addition to those clever
little tricks of the trade, unions have been known to insist on no-work
jobs where the employee actually shows up for work but then doesn't do
any work.

   While these sorts of shenanigans are not widespread, the idea of
unions' promoting inefficiency persists because of similar practices that
defy common sense. Take, for example, the notorious job banks run by
the Detroit automakers. Back in the 1980s, the United Auto Workers'

(UAW) union negotiated these job banks because, like their cousins in the Longshoremen's union, they couldn't stand to sit idly by and let the car companies improve efficiency without extracting something in exchange. No, in the union mind-set, employers' efforts to run businesses like businesses, rather than charitable paycheck production enterprises, must be met with resistance. So, the union demanded the jobs bank program so that members who lost their jobs due to automation and other improvements could sit idly by and work crossword puzzles all day while still getting paid most of their salaries. In 2005, some 12,000 workers were reported to have been participating in these jobs banks—12,000 people doing absolutely nothing of value to the car companies but who were still getting paid.[51] That such an idea could make sense to anyone is truly a curious phenomenon, but of course to unions, hamstringing the employer and saddling it with needless costs seems to be the objective, even if it means killing the goose that lays the golden eggs. For the rest of us, it is little wonder that the car companies were doomed to go bankrupt and beg for bailouts. With Government Motors on the dole, we all get to contribute part of our paychecks to someone else's sweetheart deals.

The unions highlight fundamental differences between the liberal mind and the rest of the nation. Most Americans view effort as valuable in terms of how the free market prices such work. Liberals view effort as valuable in itself—the steel worker who produces hundreds of metal bolts in a day is more productive than the scientist who spends a lifetime working on a cure for a world-threatening disease. Unions operate from the assumption that labor—independent of whether it is valuable or necessary—ought always be paid for.

"Work" Rules

There is no limit to unions' desire to reject all things efficient and productive. Unions have implemented and vehemently defend work rules to keep employees from working one iota more than their collective bargaining agreement permits or, God forbid, from foraying out of their area of defined expertise to pitch in and get a job done. These rules, widely practiced in union shops from factories to office buildings, not only prohibit employees from doing something outside their jurisdiction, but can also result in a written complaint against someone who violates them. So, a perfectly intelligent and capable electrician working on a union project might need to tap something in with a hammer, a 15-second job, but instead he would be forced to place a work order to get a carpenter to do the job or face a reprimand for using a carpenter's tool. In fact, jurisdictional lines are so detailed that they dictate things as trivial as which union members get to unload computers and which ones get to unload audio-visual equipment at the Philadelphia Convention Center. Even more bizarrely, disputes between competing labor unions can occur when they fight over who gets to handle PowerPoint presentations. The situation in Philadelphia actually got so bad at one point, with workers openly fighting and sabotaging convention setups, that convention business started going to other cities. Who wants to deal with infantile disputes over who does what? Not surprisingly, situations like this jeopardize business, but also reinforce the public's impression that unions are out in left field because normal, common sense people simply don't understand such juvenile behavior.[52]

On the other side of these kinds of disputes engendered by labor unions are the use of work rules to avoid lifting a finger more than what is required by collective bargaining agreements. Whereas successful, nonunion workplaces—that is, ones that value the American tradition of hard work—won't tolerate people who refuse to be team players, unions specialize in telling people that they don't have to—indeed, should not—go the extra mile for the employer or the enterprise, even if it wouldn't be that much more work and it would be more efficient or helpful to realizing an objective. The old retort, "That's not in my job description," summarizes this attitude, and it pervades the union mind-set. A perfectly rational response for an employer who hears an employee say that would be to respond, "You don't have a job description; you're fired." But in the union mind-set, this harsh treatment of insubordination is viewed as oppression by the employer. It is upside-down logic that rewards laziness and a poor work ethic, leading to justifiable scorn of the organizations. It's also insidious. If your colleagues act this way, then you end up acting similarly because there is no incentive to be a team player.

Seniority Rules

Most Americans understand that in order to maintain a job, they need to keep up their skills and avoid complacency at work. Jobs, after all, are not a birthright, and paychecks represent payment for providing something of value to the employer. Unions seem to detest judgments that might reward some but penalize others, thus they love the concept of seniority, a mechanism by which longevity enjoys primacy over such trifling things as skill or ability. In the union world, people are interchangeable: a teacher is a teacher, a pilot is a pilot, a laborer is a laborer; the idea of assessing performance and telling someone they're outstanding or substandard is anathema to the union mentality.

Nowhere is the obscene philosophy more unpalatable than in schools, for obvious reasons: The kids are the ones who suffer when teachers aren't up to the task. Teachers' unions have long enjoyed a stranglehold over the public school system, and school boards often timidly accept the demands of these politically potent unions—after all, who wants to be against teachers? Yet, many people look to the lack of progress in places like Washington, D.C., and intuitively understand that it is the teachers' unions, certainly not a lack of funding, that keep children stuck in a quagmire of poverty, because these teachers' unions refuse to help students succeed if it means putting a teacher's job at risk. Instead, they negotiate labor contracts that ensure that teaching assignments are directed on the basis of seniority rather than ability. Even if a younger teacher is roundly loved and valued by students and parents for his or her exceptional traits, union rules often dictate that the more senior teacher be given preference.

In New York City this problem was illustrated profoundly when an exceptionally popular teacher was removed after another teacher with more seniority claimed her job teaching fourth grade gifted and talented students. Lorraine Uhlmann was revered by parents and pupils alike for her ability to inspire her mostly low-income students to work hard in school, but when another instructor gunned for her job, the union backed his claim despite what parents and their children wanted. As one frustrated parent complained, "The teachers have rights, but the children don't. These kids don't want to lose their teacher."[53] In the perverse union world, the last thing that matters is whether or not a teacher is popular or has made a significant impact on his or her classroom. Instead, the emphasis is placed on seniority while avoiding any judgments about performance, whether by principals or parents, even though anyone with common sense knows that two people with the same diploma in a frame could have wildly divergent teaching abilities.

Teachers' unions defend their members at all costs, sometimes even when teachers are accused of heinous malfeasance such as sexual abuse, and have made firing poorly performing employees a Herculean task.[54] In Los Angeles, as in many other cities, most school administrators are loathe to try and remove teachers who cannot teach because they know they will have to navigate an insanely bureaucratic system put in place by teachers' unions to keep even the worst teachers from being let go. It often takes the most serious of allegations to trigger action against teachers and even then, sometimes in the face of allegations of sexual abuse, teachers can be protected from discipline and left free to prey on their students. Take the example of Gary C. Lindsey who got fired from his Iowa teaching job for inappropriately touching a student. As Martha Irvine and Robert Tanner reported, "it didn't end his career. He taught for decades in Illinois and Iowa, fending off at least a half-dozen more abuse accusations." Forty years after that first little girl came forward—it wasn't a principal or a state agency that ended his career. It was one persistent victim and her parents.[55]

This is hardly an isolated example of abuse or school systems' failures to protect children. As the Associated Press reported in 2004: "More than 4.5 million children are forced to endure sexual misconduct by school employees...according to an exhaustive review of research that reads like a parent's worst nightmare.[56] In another instance, Tanner writes of teacher Chad Maughan who got caught viewing pornography twice at the school where he taught and was allowed to continue teaching. Within two years, he was convicted of rapping an underage girl.

How does this happen? Strong teacher's unions and perverse legal loopholes they carve out for themselves and vehemently protect. Reports Tanner, "State efforts to strengthen laws against sex abuse by teachers have run into opposition from school boards and teachers' unions."[57] All of this is done in the name of protecting teachers and comes at the expense of children. It is like protecting the "F" student from the stigma of failure, even if he is the class bully and never does his homework.

This condemnable philosophy is best summed up by the former president of the American Federation of Teachers, Albert Shanker, who famously stated in 1985: "When schoolchildren start paying dues, that's when I'll start representing the interests of schoolchildren."[58]

After decades of celebrating mediocrity and undermining excellence, American unions have suffered continuing losses because people have come to understand that unions are more interested in protecting themselves than anything else. Parents and other observers understand what Kathleen Collins, associate general counsel for the Los Angeles Unified School District, was trying to say when she lamented that "Kids don't have a union." Most of us know that kids shouldn't need one.

Outrageous Demands

Perhaps one of the most radical labor unions in the country is the relatively small International Longshore and Warehouse Union (ILWU), but it provides one example of how a union's efforts to win concessions for its members can seriously damage the rest of the nation. With just 10,500 members working on the West Coast ports, the ILWU's disagreement with port operators cost the U.S. economy nearly $50 billion (over $2 billion a day) back in 2002 when it ultimately caused a work stoppage all along the West Coast from San Diego to Seattle.[59] Even as the economy faltered just months after the 9/11 terrorist attacks on the United States, from July to October that year, the ILWU wrestled with the Pacific Maritime Association, which represented the port operators, to increase pay and benefits for its members. The union's contract called for full-time longshoremen to be paid an average of $80,000 a year, though some earned up to $340,000 and even part-timers earned around $70,000, hardly slave wages by any stretch of the imagination.[60]

Nevertheless, the ILWU insisted on more, even if it meant shutting down commerce across the country. On top of that, the port operators wanted to upgrade their system of tracking cargo and use twenty-first century technology to automate inventory tracking—like other industrialized ports were already doing. The employers also wanted to automate hiring and abandon the practice of having job seekers show up at a union hall to be assigned work on a chalkboard (a la *On the Waterfront* back in the 1950s). But all of this was too much for the union, which imagined itself in another century's labor dispute. It was afraid the new technology would replace its workers (and the clipboards and pencils they used to track cargo) or make it look like the employer had the power to assign people work. Perish the thought. So, the ILWU engaged in a work slowdown that ultimately forced the ports shut, costing U.S. businesses money at a time when the country was struggling to regain its footing. When President Bush invoked the Taft-Hartley Act, which permitted the use of government mediators to help settle significant labor disputes, Big Labor howled in protest.[61] In the end, with the new negotiated contract, an average longshoreman would be paid approximately $100,000 and Americans were treated to yet another spectacle of labor unions demanding concessions that hardly any right-minded person could believe were reasonable and posturing as if robber barons were around every corner.[62]

Right to Work

The modern workforce is vastly different from that of the Industrial Revolution, and the benefits of the early union struggles remain and are largely kept in place by a more informed electorate and consumer base and the 24-hour news cycle. In addition, watchdog groups, investigative reporting and generally easy access to news bring much quicker attention to bad actors on the employer side. Despite the economic merits (or lack thereof) of the minimum wage and workplace safety regulations, at some level those things are a part of the landscape and will remain regardless of unions. The problem is, even with so few legitimate battles to pick, unions won't simply disband and congratulate themselves for a job well done. Like career politicians and government bureaucrats, they are in the business of staying in business. Notwithstanding the vastly different modern workplace and the fact that American workers are seemingly ambivalent toward unions, Big Labor tends to believe that people share its beliefs and would join a union if they could.[63] It is little wonder that union leaders want to strip away basic democratic rights so they can force more people to join their ranks.

The prevailing union attitude toward the decline in its membership has been that public policy has been stacked against unions for decades, at least since the passage of the Taft–Hartley Act. Derisively known at the time as the Slave Labor bill, labor leaders constantly complain about many of its provisions, including the states' ability to pass Right to Work laws (which the unions call Right to Freeload laws). This particular part of the law infuriates unions because the individual states were allowed to decide for themselves whether to allow unions the practically unchecked authority they had enjoyed under the Wagner Act to make people join them. In the years since the Taft–Hartley Act was passed, 22 states decided that their citizens should not be forced to join a union as a condition of employment. In terms of the constitutional protection of freedom of assembly, it stands to reason that if you have the right to join an organization you believe in without the government's interference, you ought to have the right not to join one with which you wish to have no affiliation. In the union view, however, Right to Work laws are the enemy because unions covet hardly anything more than the right to compel people to join them in order to have a job. It is about as antithetical to the idea of freedom as anything one could imagine.

Card Check: Redefining Democracy

Another reason unions dislike the Taft–Hartley Act is that it helped level the rules for establishing union representation so that employers could have an opportunity to express their views and seek an election supervised by the National Labor Relations Board (NLRB). Giving employers any kind of leverage to resist being unionized apparently made union leaders sick, as demonstrated by United Mine Workers of America leader John L. Lewis: "Every day, I have a matutinal indisposition that emanates from the nauseous effluvia of that oppressive slave statute."[64] Before Taft–Hartley, while representation elections were one option, unions had a giant loophole in the law that allowed them to organize workers through a process by which they could simply get people to sign a card saying they wanted to join. Once the union collected enough of these cards, they could go to the NLRB and demand to be certified as the workers' bargaining representative. With the deck stacked in their favor, the unions could intimidate workers into signing cards or even falsify cards, and it got to the point where the NLRB finally decided that secret ballot elections run by the government were the only fair way to determine what workers truly wanted. This position was codified by the Taft-Hartley Act, stirring the scorn of labor leaders, whose unfettered ability to force people into unions was largely reduced.

Because of the many drawbacks associated with labor unions and workers' reluctance to join them, unions lose secret ballot elections anywhere from a third to half the time.[65] Often, union organizers will spend considerable time trying to win an election, and with pressure to organize a constant, winning these representation elections is vital to them. One way that they have tried to avoid the often lengthy and unsure election process has been to revive the old card check process by getting the employer to agree to recognize the union once 50 percent of employees sign a card. In recent years, the card check campaigns have generally occurred in the context of a neutrality agreement whereby the employer in question agrees to remain silent on the issue of union representation and allow the union to pursue this method of organizing. In doing so, the employer strips itself of its leverage to resist an organizing campaign and allows the union control over the discussion of pros and cons surrounding unions. Employers are frequently pressured into accepting these types of arrangements because unions know exactly how to exact their revenge on those who do not capitulate.

Now that liberal Democrats are in charge of Washington, unions are desperately trying to pass legislation called—in an affront to honesty by any stretch of the imagination—the Employee Free Choice Act, which would strip workers of their right to secret ballot elections and mandate government control over collective bargaining contracts if employers will not accede to union demands.

Corporate Campaigns

As it stands today, employers that resist the card check method of organizing (by insisting on their right to an NLRB election) frequently become the targets of very intense campaigns that often involve bad publicity, pressure against third-party vendors doing business with the employer in question, and other methods designed to force them to accept union demands. It is the sort of thuggish behavior that long has given unions a bad reputation. In one particularly outrageous example, Unite-Here, a union representing hotel and textile workers, found itself in trouble for defaming a client of one of its targets.[66] In that campaign, Unite-Here was trying to pressure Angelica Textile Services, a laundry cleaning company that provides cleaning services for a variety of clients, including several Sutter Health hospitals in California. While it was trying to win benefit concessions from Angelica for existing contracts as well as pressure the company not to resist efforts to organize other workers, the union sent postcards to customers of Sutter Health. Designed to bring pressure from one of Angelica's major clients in the hopes Angelica would cave sooner, these postcards were sent to thousands of expecting mothers warning them that the company did not properly clean laundry and that "blood, feces and harmful pathogens" might contaminate sheets used at the Sutter Health hospitals because they were cleaned by Angelica. For this outrageous lie, Sutter won a defamation lawsuit against Unite-Here for $17.3 million, but at the end of the day, the corporate campaign succeeded in forcing Angelica to settle with the union.

Sutter Health was an innocent bystander in Unite-Here's dispute with Angelica, but the health provider notes that it has had its own experiences with union misinformation campaigns in its dealings with the SEIU.[67] That union has a long history of participating in these types of campaigns, and at least two of its locals (100 and 880) reportedly were listed as partner organizations on ACORN's web site and provided extensive funding for a controversial program called "Muscle for Money."[68] This effort amounts to little more than an extortion scheme whereby ACORN and the SEIU essentially shake down a company by protesting on the lawns of corporate leaders. The idea is to make life so miserable for company officials that they give in to the union's demands, no matter how insane. According to a very informative exposé on this subject, yet another tactic is to shake down company and government officials for donations in exchange for protection against the ACORN's goon squads.[69] In one example highlighted by the article, a bus of homeless people organized by ACORN invaded the headquarters of a company called Liberty Tax when the company refused to give in to ACORN's demands. The ensuing melee sent at least two Liberty Tax employees to the hospital with bite and scratch wounds. Rather than pursue expensive legal action against ACORN, Liberty Tax instead contributed $50,000 to one of the group's affiliates, presumably in the hope that this would buy some peace. Unfortunately, the rest of us have bullies like these shaking down our government and trying to do little more than undermine the freedom and liberty that our country has known for so long.

Violence and Intimidation

No strangers to intimidating employers, unions like the SEIU won't hesitate to turn against their own when someone dares to speak out against Big Labor leaders. In California, SEIU's Andy Stern has been locked in a battle with the head of one of their biggest affiliates who doesn't want to tow the party line. This leader, Sal Roselli, has resisted Stern's efforts to take over the United Health Workers-West, and to undermine Roselli, the SEIU allegedly hired a security firm to infiltrate UHW-W meetings and follow, videotape, and photograph union officials coming and going to work.[70] Beyond these kinds of tactics, union members also have a long tradition of promoting violence against nonbelievers.

Needless to say, with a militant philosophy and legal loophole so large, it should come as no surprise that violence in the labor movement is a constant problem. The National Labor Relations Board routinely hears cases involving threats and actual instances of violence. In one infamous case, the International Brotherhood of Teamsters was locked in a battle with the trucking company Overnite for three years, and the union took a no-holds-barred approach in its fight. After continued accusations of violence against people who did not sympathize with the union, the NLRB forced it to settle and post a four-page notice to its members outlining the things it would no longer do. As part of the settlement, the Teamsters had to concede, "We will not use or threaten to use a weapon of any kind, including but not limited to guns, knives, slingshots, rocks, ball bearings, liquid-filled balloons or other projectiles, picket signs, sticks, sledgehammers, bricks, hot coffee, bottles, two by fours, lit cigarettes, eggs, or bags or balloons filled with excrement..."[71] When the government has to force an outfit like the Teamsters to make those kinds of concessions, maybe, just maybe, there is a problem with unions in the United States.

A Culture of Corruption

More and more, union leadership is stocked with professional union organizers with community college degrees on the subject, not rank and file working men and women who have risen up to leadership from the front lines. These opportunistic bureaucrats thrive off the often forcibly-taken union wages of their members, who by force of law are required to forfeit their money whether they want anything to do with the union or not. What is truly a shame is what happens with the money once it is collected. With the major battles of reasonable workplace conditions and wages behind them, union officials are free to gallivant around the world with huge salaries, to golf courses, to ski chalets, with gifts like Cadillacs awaiting their retirement.[72] For hard-working union members who are supposed to be paying dues for some economic security, it is hard to match the behavior of union management once you look past the facade they put up about protecting workers. In one illustrative case, the Plumbers and Pipefitters Union's pension fund stood accused of squandering hundreds of millions of dollars of pension money to build a resort in Florida. At the same time that union leaders were wailing about Ken Lay and Enron (and how that company's failure was George W. Bush's fault), the plumbers' pension fund spent $800 million building the Westin Diplomat Resort & Spa, doubling the estimated budget of $400 million. The U.S. Department of Labor ultimately sued the fund, alleging its leaders steered sweetheart deals toward friends and associates and failed to have a sound financial plan to build the resort.[73]

Not surprisingly, the lifestyles of the union bosses often breed corruption and a violent protection of the status quo. Favoritism, conflicts of interest, and outright fraud permeate much of the major unions' activities. In the highly regulated private sector, Sarbanes-Oxley and a host of regulations and regulatory bodies aim to protect consumers. Businesses spend millions upon millions of dollars a year complying with onerous regulations for transparency for shareholders and the general public from conflict of interest statements to workplace regulations to the verbal-numeric labyrinth that is the tax code. The government's own Small Business Administration concluded that businesses in the United States are forced to spend nearly $103 billion for tax compliance alone, while spending an astounding $1.1 trillion to comply with the myriad government regulations imposed on them.[74]

Yet, unions, some of them large multibillion dollar, multinational organizations in their own right, don't have a fraction of the regulatory oversight corporations have, and they fight any attempts at transparency tooth and nail. In other words, they don't hold themselves accountable to the same standards as the companies with which they fight to burden with work rules and lifetime job guarantees. While corporations have been required to spend an average of $2.92 million each year to comply with Sarbanes-Oxley audit requirements, the U.S. Department of Labor at one point estimated that given its resources the average labor union (which, mind you, does not have to have outside audits like private sector corporations do) would be audited by the government once every 133 years.[75] That level of accountability is laughable.

Political Contributions

For the unlucky workers in the 28 "right to steal wages" states, there is no option. These states allow unions to enforce a street tax. In return for a chunk of each pay check, workers are protected from their employers, given aforementioned benefits like work rules and pay, and won't likely be harassed. Workers can opt out of contributions not related to collective bargaining (e.g., political expenses) under a Supreme Court ruling referred to as the Beck Decision—an option known as "agency fee" payments, though many are not aware of this option, and unions are not really interested in telling them about it. By collecting money from people who do not wish to join them, unions are in theory supposedly being compensated for the collective bargaining they do that benefits all employees, union members or not. But, unions have expanded their politics well beyond the issues most salient to workers (e.g., work conditions) and now take sides on things that have nothing to do with work, such as promoting homosexual marriage and abortion rights.

Not surprisingly, many workers object to these stances, regardless of their opinions about the unions themselves, but their voices are ignored by blithe union leaders who are part of a massive leftist political machine that has no room for dissenters. In Washington, the voters finally got fed up with this situation and passed a law that required unions to obtain permission from agency-fee payers before using money on political issues. The Washington Education Association sued, arguing in typical upside-down logic that its First Amendment rights were being violated. In a sign that there might still be some hope for freedom yet, the U.S. Supreme Court ruled against the unions. It would be foolish, however, to think that unions will not try to think of other ways to force dues money to fund their radical leftist political agenda.[76]

Steps toward Accountability

For every positive step made forward toward financial transparency, like those made in the Bush administration, reform can quickly be repealed by the next Democratic administration. The organization responsible for overseeing union financial disclosure and investigating much of unions' criminal activities is the U.S. Department of Labor's Office of Labor-Management Standards (OLMS). Because unions are the Democrats' biggest piggybank, it is not surprising that this law enforcement office went largely neglected during the Clinton years. To kill a government agency is nearly impossible—it would lead to lost bureaucratic jobs and Democratic voters. To do a job half-assed and to starve the functionality of all effective portions of an agency is not only doable, but to the delight of lazy bureaucrats, it is a Democratic politician's specialty.

When Elaine L. Chao took the reins of the U.S. Department of Labor in the early days of the Bush administration, OLMS was in sad shape, even by federal bureaucratic standards. OLMS was placed as far as physically possible away from the Office of the Secretary in the Department's Francis Perkins Building on Constitution Avenue in Washington, D.C. When incoming political appointees asked for union officers' conflict of interest records, they were directed to a series of bookshelves with unlabeled, unorganized files. The annual financial disclosure forms filed by giant labor unions were laughable when compared to the many different filing forms used by private sector companies. Line items on union reports had totally obscure labels such as the National Education Association's $74.5 million for Contributions, Gifts & Grants with no underlying data to show union members (or anyone else) where dues money was being channeled.[77] The staffing for OLMS had been gutted, not that it was ever that big to begin with. At its prime in the early 1990s, OLMS had only 400 or so investigators and staff members nationwide. By the time the Bush administration was in charge, OLMS had been slashed to 260 employees—roughly a 35 percent decrease. Until Elaine Chao came along as Secretary of Labor, hardly anyone noticed or cared much about the fairly obscure OLMS and union financial disclosure, but she knew that union members across the country had long been denied a full accounting of their unions' financial dealings. Much to the chagrin of labor leaders, she often would remind them that the Department of Labor represented all workers, not just organized labor, and she undertook a massive reform effort to bring more sunlight to the dark world of unions. Significant changes were made in a number of disclosure forms, with unions fighting every step of the way.

For all of Chao's efforts and the ground gained under her leadership, OLMS never was able to restore all of the positions lost during the Clinton administration. Today, under Solis, things are only looking worse for the oversight agency.

Investments Pay Off

As SEIU President Andy Stern put it, "We spent a fortune to elect Barack Obama—$60.7 million to be exact—and we're proud of it."[78] To be sure, unions knew what they wanted in electing a key sympathizer to the White House, and they did not waste any time getting started on their wish list. The new Labor secretary, Hilda Solis, is the daughter of a Teamsters Union shop steward from Mexico, and, to no big surprise, when she served in Congress, some 60 percent of her political contributions came from unions.[79] Thus, she is hardly in a position to be objective about labor unions while she facilitates the dismantling of the Chao-era transparency reforms. With the new administration, funding and staffing for OLMS is back on the chopping block—at a time when the rest of government is exploding in size, they have already cut OLMS's tiny budget by nearly 10 percent in 2009, and more cuts are sure to come.[80] Likewise, the Democrats have installed one of their shills to head OLMS to spearhead the effort to reverse all of the transparency reforms accomplished under Secretary Chao's leadership. John Lund, the new deputy assistant secretary in charge of OLMS, is a leftist professor on a leave of absence from the School for Workers at the University of Wisconsin who repeatedly submitted comments in opposition to OLMS's reforms during the Bush years. As an avowed opponent of those long-needed changes, Lund will lead the way toward restoring the obscurity and lack of financial accountability that union officials enjoyed for many decades. And, this brazen crippling of the government's only union oversight agency takes place while Secretary Solis is adding a whopping 670 new investigators elsewhere in the department to go after employers.[81]

While Big Labor no doubt is elated that a veil on financial transparency is returning, gutting OLMS is surely not the only way unions are cashing in on electing one of their own to the White House. Within the first few months of Obama's presidency, and with a Democratic Congress to conspire with them, unions have accomplished several other of their goals. One little-noticed law, but one long-sought by unions, was the Lilly Ledbetter Fair Pay Act, which made suing employers for alleged discrimination much easier by removing time limitations for filing such claims. In doing so, employers will now have to stand ready to produce evidence of their innocence in case someone conjures a complaint against them somewhere down the road, and this kind of torment for employers is precisely what unions (and their allies the trial lawyers, who will get the legal fees from these cases) wanted. Big Labor's biggest success in 2009 was the auto company bailout. As the U.S. car industry has languished for years and given way to foreign competitors who were smart enough to build their plants in right-to-work states like other unions, the UAW has steadfastly refused to accept the proposition that their philosophy contributed to (much less was a major reason for) the car company failures. With their excessive pay and benefits packages and indefensible programs like the massive jobs banks, union-negotiated deals saddled employers with massive costs that were bound to doom them. In the new America though, with Barack Obama's sympathetic ear in the White House, labor unions were able to get a much better deal for themselves than they would have if the car companies had gone bankrupt.[82]

Sharp Distinctions

Political movements on the Left and Right can be distinguished on characteristics ranging from funding to motivating factors to their general tenor of discourse. One camp consists of a powerful, rent-seeking few while the other is made up of a broad base of concerned citizens. One relies on shouting, emotions, and scores of instances of outright intimidation and violence, while the other wields genuine concern supported by lawful action. One consists of a heavily funded, highly motivated minority while the other a broad cross-section of America with principle-based concerns.

As was seen throughout the tea party movement, the labels don't fit quite as many on the Left as the media would have you believe. More often than not, it is the modern Left that employs bullying tactics to promote radical policies that protect and enrich the interests of the concentrated few who bankroll their activities. For what they lack in millions of dollars from leftist billionaires, activist enterprises on the Left rely heavily on funds received by force or fraud in the form of extorted union dues, outright embezzlement, and—worst of all—from government subsidies and handouts funded from the pocket of the American taxpayer.

This is in sharp contrast to the organizations on the Right, often maligned as Astroturf. Funded primarily by private donations from concerned citizens, these organizations consist of hundreds of thousands of genuinely concerned citizens. They aren't looking for bailouts, handouts, or special treatment. In contrast to the union bosses and political hacks on the Left, they aren't protecting a taxpayer-funded, legal loophole-protected source of income. They do not receive, seek, or desire government grants and taxpayer money. Their only skin in the game is concern for the direction of this country.

Thus, tea party protestors reject the notion of handouts and bailouts for entrenched partisan interest groups. But it is not merely the financial scope of these actions—as mind-boggling as the spending of billions of dollars is to the average American—but the backward principles behind the justifications for the spending and the expansion of government. Most notably, the sense of entitlement many interest groups have and many politicians protect. Paired with the idea that government has all the answers, the threat to individual liberty is hardly theoretical. This became crystal clear to millions of Americans as the health care debate heated up in the summer of 2009.

CHAPTER 8

THE TEAPOT BOILS OVER

HEALTH CARE TAKES CENTER STAGE

If you think health care is expensive now, wait until you see what it costs when it's free.

—P.J. O'Rourke, remarks delivered at Cato
gala dinner in Washington D.C., May 1993

The tea parties of April 2009 led to positive permutations of political activism beyond anyone's imagination. The powerful grassroots movement many believed had culminated in the tax day tea parties was only the beginning. The power and underlying principles of the tea parties were harnessed and turned against specific legislative proposals like cap and trade, and most notably, health care reform. The frustration, the call to action boiled over into the major policy battle of health care in a way that had significant political repercussions.

The Health Care Policy Debate

Following the tax day tea parties, Americans continued to tighten their belts while politicians in Washington continued to defy both fiscal and public relations logic. One proposal earmarked millions of dollars be spent on luxury jets to shuttle them around on their domestic and foreign taxpayer-funded boondoggles. Eventually that was chalked up as a "miscommunication" and the plan to drastically expand the number of military jets for Congress was set to be scrapped.[1]

As the August recess drew near, Congress was under pressure to meet an end-of-year deadline set by the audacious new president for health care reform.[2] As five bills floated around both houses of the legislature, it was clear that no comprehensive health care reform would happen before the August recess.[3] Instead, congressional Democrats went back to their districts to sell a plan that seemed less and less appealing to Americans the more they scrutinized it.

The minority party is often criticized for nay-saying without presenting viable options, and the Right is not immune from this. One of the great myths surrounding the health care debate is that opposition to so-called universal health care—dubbed "ObamaCare"—is opposed to reform itself of any kind. This couldn't be further from the truth. To better understand political and popular opposition to this major policy proposal, it is important to cut through the political spin and see what is actually being proposed, and what real reform would actually look like.

No one can argue that the United States isn't at a crossroads where health care is or at least should be a top domestic priority. The health care system in this nation has been suffering for some time. The problem with our health care system is highlighted by the fact that the United States spent about $7,400 per person on health care in 2007, up from $4,700 in 2000.[4]

Liberals are reluctant to admit it, but the Right has been far from antireform, having put innovative reform ideas forward for years. They have argued for leveling the tax treatment of health care to make it fair for everyone, no matter if you buy it from your employer or you get it as an individual. They have pushed for the expansion of Health Savings Accounts (HSAs). They have pushed to allow state insurance markets to compete against each other by allowing for the cross-state purchasing of health insurance, much like the life insurance industry. Republicans and conservatives continue to push for reforms that would give small businesses the power to band together to create larger risk pools through their trade associations. Thanks to bad tax policy, frivolous lawsuits, government price fixing, and overregulation, access to quality care is on the decline and drastically increasing health care costs have left us with 45.7 million Americans without basic health insurance.[5]

Health care is not a separate, distinct part of our economy. It is a network of participants in both the private and public sectors who are constantly interacting and readjusting to one another. Further complicating this arrangement are the federal tax code; Medicare and Medicaid (the government's large and costly health programs for the elderly and poor, respectively); and the lack of transparency in the cost of medical services. Because the components of health care range so widely, addressing the problems in only one or two areas while leaving the others unchanged will yield only limited, temporary short-term benefits. In order to ensure that health care reform will truly be lasting and truly be reform, we need to take a step back and look at the broader picture.

President Obama called on Congress to act quickly. He is correct, but quick action must be the right action. The status quo, if left unchanged will eventually force more and more employers to either not offer health insurance or ask their workers to pay an even larger portion of the bill. Without the right fixes, waiting times for doctors and hospitals will continue to grow as the cost of health insurance and health care continues to increase, and America's best and brightest will no longer consider medicine as a career.

In the U.S. Congress, we have been presented with two schools of thought on health care reform. One approach assumes that government-controlled health care is the only practical solution to solving our crisis. The other is a free-market approach where the focus is on fundamental reform in access, quality, innovation, and prevention.

The Government "Solutions"

The health care debate has been building for an entire generation. The last time a debate of this size and scale was seen was during the creation of Medicare and Medicaid in 1965. Much like then, this debate has centered a lot on what is fair and what is right. As with most policy matters, the Left's definition of fair and right is divorced from what most Americans believe.

The current debate is centered on two very distinct questions: How do we cover America's 45.7 million uninsured and how do we contain skyrocketing health care costs? These two questions have ignited a debate where Republicans and Democrats, liberals and conservatives, and yuppies and hippies are at each other's throats. The problem is enhanced and exacerbated by the fact that hard left liberals believe no market should exist in health care other than the government. They are convinced that the only way to achieve true health care reform is through a single-payer, government-run health care system where the federal government is the one paying all the bills. This concept is the holy grail of liberal health care policy.

On June 15, 2009, President Obama laid out a staggering claim for his health care reform proposal. He said, "No matter how we reform health care, we will keep this promise to the American people. If you like your doctor, you will be able to keep your doctor, period. If you like your health care plan, you'll be able to keep your health care plan, period. No one will take it away, no matter what."[6]

This promise, which has become the one constant and unchanged message to come from the president, has served as the basis for his reform effort. However, just a few short years ago in 2004, Obama laid out his vision for a single-payer health care system paid for and administered by the federal government. He acknowledged that "it will take time" and that "we will get there eventually," but one day we would achieve a single-payer health care system.[7]

Is he right? Will Americans be able to keep their plan and doctor? The answer: probably not. President Obama must understand that health care is not a separate part of our economy, but a highly complicated, integrated network of participants. When the president proposes enacting drastic public policy changes that will ultimately change that dynamic, the entire marketplace will have to readjust and adapt. You cannot wave a magic wand and insure 47 million people with an already strained hospital and provider network. Simply put, care from doctors and hospitals will necessarily change in drastic ways and nobody can guarantee that

Americans will be able to keep the care they are accustomed to. Things like employer mandates could have immediate negative effects. Employers, burdened with the possibility of fines for not providing insurance, may lay people off to make ends meet. They may even drop insurance coverage for employees altogether if the mandated coverage fine is less than their current cost of providing health insurance.

Democrats push a public option plan as the cornerstone of health care reform. The more appropriately named "government option" plan is meant to serve as a government-provided health insurance plan that will operate in competition with private health insurance plans. How is this new government plan going to compete on a level playing field while providing insurance to the under-insured and the uninsurable? In short, it can't.

In the early stages of selling the public option to the public, the president and Democrats in Congress pointed out that the plan was necessary to keep private insurance companies honest. As George Will pointed out in one of his opinion-editorials for the *Washington Post*, "Presumably, being 'honest' means not colluding to set prices, and evidently he [President Obama] thinks that, absent competition from government, there will not be a competitive market for insurance."[8] Will goes on to point out that there are currently 1,300 competing health insurance providers in the marketplace today, which begs the question: what will one more plan on an allegedly equal playing field do to help? Nothing, unless it puts private health insurance providers at an unfair competitive disadvantage—a claim Democrats quickly dismiss to disarm claims that the government plan would crowd out private health insurance.

If we have learned anything from the Medicare Prescription Drug Benefit, also known as "Part D," the evidence clearly shows that in a robust marketplace where government intervention is minimal, competition works well. When Part D was created with the Medicare Modernization Act of 2003, the Bush administration caused a huge uproar when it estimated the program's cost at $534 billion over a 10-year period (2004–2013). But thanks to competition, the Medicare Trustees Report revised that same 10-year estimate to $378 billion—almost 30 percent *lower* than expected. Furthermore, in 2006, the Congressional Budget Office (CBO) estimated that the 2007–2016 cost of the program would be $1.2 trillion, but that estimate has dropped every year since and stands at $520.7 billion or 43 percent lower than expected.[9]

There is still considerable debate among conservatives and libertarians regarding whether Congress should have created a new entitlement program without actually reforming the Medicare program first, but the fact remains that the truly competitive Medicare Part D has resulted in premiums that are 40 percent lower than projected in 2004 and a satisfaction rate of 87 percent among beneficiaries.[10]

The results, however, seem to be irrelevant to today's debate on health care reform because President Obama and congressional Democrats would like to model the public option plan after Medicare. However, they are more interested in the parts of Medicare that do not offer choice and competition, Medicare Part A and Part B. These parts of Medicare handle hospital insurance (Part A) and medical insurance (Part B). Using traditional Medicare as a model for reforming our entire health care system should worry us all. Not only is the government bureaucracy ineffective, but it is also extremely expensive.

By using Medicare as the model for designing the public option plan, we can see more clearly how government-run health care is going to look. Medicare fixes prices using statutory and regulatory schemes and when Medicare's prices do not cover the full provider cost, shortfalls are then shifted to private payers who end up subsidizing the public program. This means that private plans will continue to get expensive while the public plan will stay the same.

Even if the public option attempts to control costs by paying less for services, drugs, and technology—as with Medicare—there is no guarantee that premiums under the public plan will be any cheaper. In fact, the CBO has said in a preliminary report, absent subsidies from the federal government, the public option will not have lower premiums than those charged by private insurers.[11]

While Medicare was created with the best of intentions, the program has reduced access to doctors due to a poor reimbursement rate (Medicare reimburses physicians at an average of 81 percent of private rates), deteriorated the standard of care, and is in danger of collapse due to an uncontained cost structure. Consider this: When Medicare was created in 1965, the long-term budget projected that the program would cost $9 billion in 1990 but the program cost taxpayers $67 billion in Part A alone. This year, the program will cost $450 billion which is equal to almost 12.5 percent of our federal budget.[12]

Medicare Part A already takes in less tax revenue than is paid out in benefits, which has put the entire program on a schedule to go bankrupt in 2019. The current unfunded liability for Medicare—benefits owed, but that cannot be paid—stands at $37.8 trillion, or in simpler terms, $333,585 per household.[13]

With all of that in mind, we don't need to guess or speculate or consult crystal balls to tell us what a government-run health care system would eventually result in for health care consumers. It is hardly a theoretical policy exercise. We know what will happen. As similar programs in Great Britain and Canada have shown, a government-run health care system would lead us down a path where the relationship between the doctor and patient will suffer. Bureaucrats in Washington will control the delivery of care. Individual taxpayers will end up footing the bill for so-called free universal health care through increased taxes.

Universal health care, in theory, has considerable appeal. But universal care doesn't mean consistent, quality care. In fact, it encourages just the opposite. Where it has been enacted, socialized medicine is hampering the development of new medical technology (the U.S. has five times as many MRI units per million people and three times as many CT scanners as Canada),[14] fostering poor quality (surveys indicate that 60 percent of Canadians believe their system requires fundamental changes and 12 percent say it should be scrapped),[15] long waiting times (the Fraser Institute says there are over 750,000 Canadians waiting for treatment at any given time),[16] and the rationing of care in ways that put patients at risk. Furthermore, countries like Canada have seen a sharp increase in those who also carry private insurance.[17]

Real Reform

The free market approach to reforming health care is one that is built on the principle of individual ownership. Personal responsibility, a tenant of the tea parties, has long been a central component of America's prosperity. Yet this principle still does not apply to how most of us deal with health care. One reason is the federal tax code, which creates a bias in favor of third-party payers of health insurance and against individual purchasers. As a result, health insurance is owned by employers or the government. This means that patients don't really control their own health care choices. Thus, the most efficient, equitable health care solutions must involve health insurance being owned more by the individuals who use it and less by detached third parties.

Empowering individuals as health care consumers does a number of things. It restores the most important relationship in health care—between the patient and the doctor. Rather than the patient speaking with a doctor being paid by a distant insurance company who is in turn being paid by an employer, a patient would be sitting across from someone with whom they have a significantly more direct consumer-provider relationship. Furthermore, as more consumers interact with insurers, insurers would be given the incentive to develop a greater variety of coverage options, making the health insurance market itself more effective and efficient.

There is no question that any free-market reform plan must provide a sustainable safety net for low-income people or those with health problems that put affordable coverage out of their reach. A number of state governments have established high-risk insurance pools for such individuals—proving once again that state governments often are more responsive to their individual populations. We should encourage more of this state-based creativity through grants and waivers, and at the same time arm individuals with the resources to buy across state lines if necessary.

Now or Never

There is little doubt that President Obama took on the biggest domestic issue in a generation. However, he increased the gamble by pushing for quick passage of health care reform. Health care accounts for one-sixth of the U.S. economy,[18] which means any piece of legislation that is designed to have an impact on a major part of our economy, not to mention 300 million people, should be debated thoroughly.

Obviously, President Obama sought to avoid the mistakes that President Bill Clinton and then-First Lady Hillary Clinton made when they pushed for comprehensive health care reform in 1993 and 1994. Much of that bill was written by the White House and behind closed doors. The public was forced to sit and wonder how their lives were going to be changed by the sweeping legislation. This left open the door for opponents to mobilize and begin denouncing the effort by the Clinton administration.

In trying to avoid the mistakes of the Clinton administration's health care push, President Obama made things worse. Originally, he wanted to be the pitchman for the Democratic agenda for health care reform while the Congress would have the burden of actually owning the legislation. This would afford him the ability to discuss health care reform *principles* from a 50,000-foot-level using sound bites like "cost containment," "access for the uninsured," "private insurance companies run amok," and "overly expensive prescription drugs." However, this means that Congress is writing the legislation—and releasing bits and pieces of several bills that become moving targets. Thus, going into the 2009 August recess, there were *five* pieces of legislation being considered in the United States Congress—two in the Senate and three in the House of Representatives.

This—and the effective messaging strategy used by opponents—has caused enormous confusion within the general public. An inconsistent message and the president's general lack of knowledge of what Democrats in Congress have been writing has forced President Obama to sell a plan he did not write but the public believes to be his plan.

In a September 9 speech to the joint session of Congress, President Obama laid out three principles that any health reform legislation must adhere to: (1) It will provide security and stability to those who already have health insurance; (2) It will provide insurance to people who do not have insurance; and (3) It will slow the growth in health care costs.[19] These are basic and very vague goals by any standard and Republicans have introduced plans that would achieve these ideals. However, the president has never had an interest in Republican ideas on health care reform.

Filling the void of Democrats not having a plan that met President Obama's three principles, Sen. Max Baucus (D-MT) proposed a bill that would cost an estimated $880 billion. It would offer the option of lower cost insurance, with protection only against the costs of catastrophic illnesses, to those 25 and younger. In addition, it would provide basic

Medicaid coverage to millions of low-income people who are currently ineligible for the program, but the benefits would be less comprehensive than standard Medicaid. The plan includes a proposal for a co-op instead of a full-fledged government plan. To help pay for his plan, Sen. Baucus would impose fees on insurance companies, on manufacturers of medical devices, and on clinical laboratories. The Baucus proposal also would levy a tax on insurance companies that offer the most expensive insurance plans, a move that would raise around $180 billion over 10 years. In addition to the fee on high-cost plans, the proposal also would extract about $400 billion in cost savings from Medicare, cuts that are stirring unease among lawmakers in both parties because of the potential backlash among senior citizens and Medicare's precarious fiscal state.[20]

This legislation could look very different once it is finally voted out of the Senate Finance Committee, but the fact remains that the bill will be enormously expensive, seniors will be pushed out of popular Medicare plans, and it will not address the rising cost of health care for American families.

Something's Fishy

Following the tax day tea parties and the retracted right-winger DHS report, the Obama administration did everything possible to undermine all protests, because if people disagree with you, they must not only be slandered, but they should be identified and tracked. The White House started suggesting that people report false (read critical) claims about ObamaCare to the White House via a special e-mail address.

The web site, which was launched by the White House on August 4, 2009, was introduced by Macon Phillips, the White House Director of New Media. He suggested in a blog post on the White House web site that, "There is a lot of disinformation about heath insurance reform out there, spanning from control of personal finances to end of life care. These rumors often travel just below the surface via chain e-mails or through casual conversation. Since we can't keep track of all of them here at the White House, we're asking for your help. If you get an e-mail or see something on the Web about health insurance reform that seems fishy, send it to flag@whitehouse.gov."[21]

Once the public found out about the White House's attempt to establish a citizen reporting system, Press Secretary Robert Gibbs was quick to do some damage control. He sought to assure people that the White House was not collecting names for the purpose of discrediting Americans who disagreed with President Obama's policies.

When this story broke, several legal questions arose asking if it is permissible for the White House to collect *any* data on private American citizens. FOX News legal analyst, Judge Andrew Napolitano summed it up best when he said, "The White House is in a bit of a conundrum because of this privacy statute that prohibits the White House from collecting data and storing it on people who disagree with it. . . . There's also a statute that requires the White House to retain all communications that it receives. It can't try to rewrite history by pretending it didn't receive anything. . . . If the White House deletes anything, it violates one statute. If the White House collects data on the free speech, it violates another statute."[22]

FOX News went on to explain that Napolitano was referring to the Privacy Act of 1974, which was passed after the Nixon administration used federal agencies to illegally investigate individuals for political purposes. This law was enacted after Richard Nixon's resignation in the wake of the Watergate scandal. It clearly prohibits any federal agency from maintaining records on individuals exercising their right to free speech.

The White House realized its blunder and moved to discontinue the e-mail account as of August 17, 2009. The damage was already done, however. The move was amateurish and reeked of down in the mud campaign politics, not presidential governance, further tainting a White House already criticized for importing the "Chicago way." At a time when many Americans were already concerned about Orwellian policies involving the health care of millions, the White House reinforced the sentiment that it intended to push for its way—a government takeover of health care—at any cost and by any means necessary.

Dems Feel the Heat

During the August recess, Obama allies in Congress were given marching orders to hold town halls and push the health care plan.

Americans turned out district by district during the August recess to confront their elected officials at local town hall meetings. This is a fantastic example of taking the ideas and frustration that drove the rallies and channeling it at the people who make the decisions in Washington that affect our lives.

Many times elected officials betrayed their disdain for even speaking with constituents, particularly those that disagree with them. YouTube videos of confrontations spread like wildfire. One notable one was Congressman Tim Bishop of New York. When questioned, he grew frustrated, pausing and looking visibly irritated as if he were just suffering through his ignorant constituents' questions.

Soon after this town hall, Congressman Bishop decided to suspend his town halls because he thought they were "pointless."[23] Eventually, under pressure from his constituents, he resumed the meetings, but how much trust had been lost as a result of his refusal to listen to people who voted him into Congress?

Overwhelming Public Response

Evidence that the general public has become concerned about Obama Care is not limited to the town halls. It was reported that the e-mail system at the House of Representatives became so overwhelmed by e-mails that it crashed. A spokesman for the House's chief administrative officer was quoted saying, "it is clearly health reform," and that "there's no doubt about it."[24] The spokesman continued by highlighting the fact that the last time the e-mail system had been so bogged down was during the debate on the $787 billion stimulus plan.[25]

The overwhelming response was not just limited to the House e-mail system; it was prevalent at the town halls. Sen. Arlen Specter bore most of the brunt of the anger early on in August. Constituents in his state of Pennsylvania were visibly frustrated and shaken in Internet videos. One constituent went so far as to accuse Sen. Specter of being beholden to lobbyists in Washington.[26]

Another much viewed interaction was one between Sen. Specter and Health and Human Services Secretary Kathleen Sebelius. In a similar town hall meeting, Specter was confronted about whether Congress was actually reading the bills it was passing. Specter made the point that decisions have to be made fast and action needed to be taken—an answer the crowd was certainly not looking for—while Secretary Sebelius tried to deflect the crowd by saying she was not a member of Congress.[27] In the same video, Sen. Specter attempts to explain the legislative process to justify why it is not necessary to read the whole health care reform bill. Not only did this upset the crowd even further, it fueled the sentiment that members of Congress just do not care about the thoughts of their constituents.

Also, these stories put a spotlight on the fact that the general public had become distrustful of our congressional leadership in Washington. Senator Claire McCaskill encountered a similar situation where she very bluntly asked attendees at her health care town hall if they trusted her. The answer from the crowd was a resounding "no."[28] It seems that this kind of thing was not an isolated incident, but common at most of the town halls.

Town Halls

Politicians respond to constituents' mail, e-mail, and phone calls, and host town hall forums where they talk and constituents speak and ask questions, for one simple reason: The more people feel that they have say in the political process, the less likely they are to get riled up and insist on policy or personnel changes in the form of electing someone else. This basic premise is often incorporated into private institutions. Mid-level managers in a given company have no *right* to speak their minds and insist that the CEO respect their views and incorporate them and count on job security. However, if all managers meet once a week and give input, there is buy-in to the direction the organization is headed, even if it isn't what each individual would like.

The problem from the perspective of the taxpayer, though, is that this paradigm favors politicians. They field questions, give half-answers filled with half-truths, and you are supposed to sit down and let the next person talk. Some politicians go beyond this, insisting on tightly controlled venues, prescreened, approved questions, and outright planting of individuals asking questions. Obama got a lot of heat for such stunts.

At town halls, fund-raisers posed as regular citizens asking questions.[29] An Internet press conference only allowed for prescreened questions.[30] At press conferences, friendly press were given precedence to ask prear-ranged questions.[31]

Given the media and political response to the tea parties, many constituents could not and would not operate within this traditional paradigm. This refusal is a good thing, because citizens need to remember Congress *works for us*. We are not corporate employees; we are the board of directors they report to.

If there is one thing the town hall protests and the reactions of Democrats has shown, it is these politicians' disregard and often outright resentment for their own constituents and their concerns. The events elucidated a fundamental issue behind the tea parties that so many in the media failed to capture: Government's power comes from the people, and its charter is to work at the behest of the people for their best interest, in accordance with the United States Constitution. Simply put by many protestors at these events, "You work for us."

The frustration can be summed up best by the *Wall Street Journal's* Peggy Noonan. As she writes, people get suspicious of things they don't understand, odd phrases like "public option" and "single payer."

> ... when normal people don't know what the words mean, they don't say to themselves, "I may not understand, but my trusty government surely does, and will treat me and mine with respect." They think, "I can't get what these people are talking about. They must be trying to get one past me."[32]

Thus the Democrats' strategy of pulling a fast one backfired. Their blatant attempts to jam legislation down the throats of the opposition and their constituents triggered another gut reaction in Americans, one similar to the one seen in the tea parties: This isn't right.

What Happened to "Democracy in Action"?

In a series of half-truths and outright lies, liberal activist enterprises and politicians attempted to marginalize the health care protestors for two reasons. For one, bad press is bad press. Their universal health care utopia may not happen if people see protestors as legitimate citizens concerned about the future of their nation. Secondly, should protests be seen as mainstream, not extreme corporate-funded staging events, politicians may cave. Plenty of Democrats in formerly GOP-represented areas would waiver. Remember, a politician's main currency is votes. If they believe town halls erupting in their state or their district are representative of the people who elected them and who determine their job security, the most loyal liberal Democrat can be swayed out of rational self interest. Thus it was crucial for supporters of ObamaCare to undermine them in every way possible.

In an outright attempt to have it both ways, House Speaker Nancy Pelosi has led the charge to discredit any American who raises questions in town hall meetings. In 2006, during the Bush administration when tensions were particularly high due to the war in Iraq, Speaker Pelosi said she was a "fan" of antiwar protestors, no matter how vocal or aggressive.[33]

Speaker Pelosi even thought that antiwar protestors disrupting meetings was exciting. "It's always exciting," she said of protesters who interrupted a meeting in January 2006, according to an account in the *San Francisco Chronicle*. "This is democracy in action. I'm energized by it, frankly." At another event in 2007, she said, "just go for it, I respect your enthusiasm."[34]

It wasn't until the country turned its focus to President Obama's plans for health reform that Pelosi changed her tune about critics. On August 10, 2009, she and Congressman Steny Hoyer, the Democratic Majority Leader in the House, published a column in *USA Today* where they called those that questioned ObamaCare "un-American."[35] Almost immediately, President Obama's Deputy Press Secretary Bill Burton said, "the president thinks that if people want to come and have a spirited debate about health care, a real vigorous conversation about it, that's a part of the American tradition and he encourages that, because people do have questions and concerns. . . . And so if people want to come and have their concerns and their questions answered, the president thinks that's important."[36] But it wasn't long before Democratic leadership in the United States Senate began to denounce ObamaCare critics. Senate Majority Leader Harry Reid of Nevada joined Pelosi in denouncing ObamaCare critics by calling them "evil-mongers."[37]

Other members of Congress began canceling events.[38] Many charged a fee for their constituents to attend.[39] Some were criticized for avoiding the issue all together.[40] Some held a town hall but found it more interesting to take a cell phone call while a constituent, who happened to be a cancer survivor, was trying to ask a question.[41] The health care town halls showed a stark contrast between everyday Americans and their representatives in Washington, as they treated their constituents' basic right to be heard as an inconvenience instead of their due.

Pay No Attention to the Doctors!

Several news outlets have covered the growing shortage of physicians, especially those who practice primary care—the front line of basic medical care. The *Washington Post* reported in June that "50 years ago, half of the nation's doctors practiced what has come to be known as primary care. Today, almost 70 percent of doctors work in higher-paid specialties, driven in part by medical school debts that can reach $200,000."[42]

The same report goes on to say that "fixing the [uninsured] problem will require fundamental changes in medical education and compensation to lure more doctors into primary-care offices, which already receive 215 million visits each year."[43]

The Obama administration's answer to this problem is to increase reimbursement levels for primary care physicians at the expense of physicians who practice specialties. This has triggered an enormous lobbying effort pitting doctors against each other.

Many physicians took to attending the town hall meetings. One such physician attended the town hall of Congressman David Scott of Georgia. Scott, a Democrat who represents part of Atlanta, held his town hall to discuss transportation issues. Transportation issues. The federal government was actively pushing the most significant overhaul of health care ever, and he held a town hall on transportation. How can *any* member of Congress expect constituents to sit on their hands and *not* ask about the future of health care?

This particular physician, named Dr. Brian Hill, patiently waited until the end of the program when the floor was opened up for questions. Naturally, Dr. Hill inquired as to how Congressman Scott was planning on voting on the health care legislation pending before the House of Representatives—a question that is not particularly inflammatory—at which point Rep. Scott accused Dr. Hill of "hijacking" his town hall meeting. Scott embarked on a tirade in which he felt it would be appropriate to infer that Dr. Hill was not a resident of his district and that only residents of the district would be allowed to ask questions. As it turns out, Dr. Hill *was* a resident of Rep. Scott's congressional district.[44] Based on Scott's behavior, though, that probably doesn't hold much weight.

Don't Anger the Trial Lawyers!

Many would argue that one of the major issues facing doctors in the United States is skyrocketing medical malpractice insurance premiums. But relief from this problem is absent from President Obama's health care agenda and Democrats in Congress are not willing to include it in ObamaCare. At a town hall meeting held by Congressman Jim Moran, Democrat of Virginia, former Democratic National Committee Chairman Howard Dean, himself a physician, was asked why such an important component of health care reform was left out of all of the bills being considered by Congress. His answer was remarkable. He said, "the reason tort reform is not in the [health care] bill is because the people who wrote it did not want to take on the trial lawyers in addition to everybody else they were taking on. And that's the plain and simple truth."[45]

According to the American Medical Association (AMA), defensive medicine—the practice of diagnostic or therapeutic measures conducted primarily not to ensure the health of the patient but as a safeguard against malpractice liability—costs our health care system between $84 and $151 billion every year.[46] Most of this is for naught when you consider that 60 percent of claims against physicians are dropped or withdrawn. These situations still cost an average of almost $19,000 per case.[47] When the claims do go to trial, physicians are found not negligent in over 90 percent of cases, but more than $100,000 is spent on each case defending those claims.[48]

It's not all about the money. This is about patient access. In another AMA study, 45 percent of hospitals reported that concerns over liability resulted in the loss of physicians or reduced coverage in emergency departments.[49] Whether we like it or not, emergency rooms are the first place most people go when they are sick or need care. Medical students are no longer willing to practice medicine in areas with adverse liability climates.

During his September speech to a joint session of Congress, President Obama finally acknowledged—to a certain degree—that malpractice premiums were having a negative effect on U.S. doctors and that the problem needs to be addressed.[50] However, the trial lawyer lobby would not allow President Obama to pursue caps on noneconomic damages, which is the preferred policy of the American Medical Association and doctors around the country. The policy he did advocate for was a series of state "demonstration projects" where medical courts would be used to determined liability cases. In reform legislation written by Sen. Max Baucus (D-MT), $25 million is set aside to fund these courts. The U.S. Chamber of Commerce quickly argued that amount is 1/40,000th of 1 percent of what is actually needed to fund the courts.[51] Furthermore, the coalition of health care providers at the Health Coalition for Liability and Access added that the Baucus bill would do almost nothing to reduce health care costs as it relates to defensive medicine.[52]

Trial lawyers are a very powerful lobby in Washington. From 2003 to 2004, trial lawyers gave $182 million dollars to congressional candidates.[53] In that same timeframe, trial lawyers were paid $18.2 billion for their services in medical malpractice lawsuits[54]—a 10,000 percent return on their investment. And the power keeps on growing. During the 2008 election cycle, lawyers gave Democrats a whopping $179 million in campaign contributions compared with $54 million to Republican candidates.[55] No wonder true medical liability reform is not part of *any* of the plans being considered by Congress. While medical liability premiums continue to stabilize in many states, those rates are stabilizing at near or all-time highs.

White House Spin and Spam

The White House was actively part of the effort to marginalize protestors. The administration, too, realized it was critical to buck up congressmen who could determine the success or failure of this legislation. The White House told its rank-and-file that "if you get hit, we will punch back twice as hard."[56] They told senators to zero in on the insured, because that's who needs the convincing.[57]

There is a fundamental flaw in this sort of thinking. According to a September 23, 2009, Gallup Poll, 80 percent of this country's insured population is satisfied with its health insurance coverage.[58] By selling ObamaCare to the public in such a confrontational and pushy manner, the administration risks the wheels coming off of the train. To put it another way, for generations we have spoken about change when it comes to our government, but most people are unsure about what that means. They may want change, but that doesn't necessarily mean they want changes in *their* lives.

Michael Kinsley of the *Washington Post* put it best:

> Despite protestations to the contrary, Americans don't like change . . . as soon as it seems that change might actually happen—as soon as we leave the abstract for the particular—we panic. We suddenly develop nostalgia for the comforts of the status quo.[59]

Americans do want change in the abstract, which is why we elected an arguably inexperienced senator from Illinois to be President of the United States. American *were* tired after eight years of the Bush administration and it is only natural for the let's-kick-the-bums-out mentality to kick in.

Consider this: Polling has been trending back to Republicans ever since President Obama and congressional Democrats began taking on the health care issue. And now change is coming in the form of a Republican resurgence. Political analyst Charlie Cook released an analysis of the 2010 midterm election that shows congressional Democrats—and, by default, President Obama—are digging themselves into a deep political hole. The report reviews all recent polling data and shows "a scenario in which Democratic House losses could exceed 20 seats."[60]

In the case of health care reform, President Obama clearly did not take the town hall attendees seriously. He blamed the media for causing the "ruckus" at town halls and warned that Americans have "got to be careful about those cable networks."[61]

Rather than respecting the right of people to disagree, the White House went after millions of Americans skeptical about its plans and genuinely concerned with the direction of the country. Press Secretary Robert Gibbs came out swinging again, calling the protests "manufactured anger."[62] Unfortunately, the anger and concern were quite real. What should be frightening to all Americans is that Gibbs and the rest of them either don't see it or simply refuse to.

Axelrod's Turf

The proverbial witch-hunt torch of fake activism—referred to as Astroturf—was reignited during the 2009 congressional August recess. Confronted with constituents angry about runaway spending, the threat of cap and trade to their wallets, and universal health care to their families, many in Congress blew off protestors as Brooks Brothers protestors, implying that they were wealthy or well financed—neither of which are true—and that that made their arguments irrelevant—a fallacy of logic. One was Sen. Barbara Boxer from California, most recently in the news for revealing her apparent disdain for those in uniform when she chided a military man for referring to her as "ma'am."[63] Of course this doesn't make sense. As Peggy Noonan aptly pointed out: People don't just go out because some right-wing organization tells them to. They do it because they *care* about the issue.[64]

Liberal politicos assume protests from anything but their adoring fans are disingenuous Astroturf. We know just the opposite to be true. More often than not, the Left taps paid provocateurs for causes from cap and trade to health care to war protests. In July and August 2009, online advertisements for jobs that paid people hundreds of dollars a week to push ObamaCare and the president's progressive agenda popped up on Craigslist.[65]

Ironically, the original Astroturfer is part of the Obama team. David Axelrod, who served as the chief strategist on President Obama's campaign, developed the concepts of Astroturfing while he was a partner in ASK Public Strategies. ASK is well known in Chicago for developing advertising campaigns that shift public opinion for corporate clients. In a testament to ASK's talent, Chicago Alderman Brendan Reilly was quoted in 2008 saying that ASK is "the gold standard in Astroturf organizing. This is an emerging industry, and ASK has made a name for itself in shaping public opinion and manufacturing public support."[66]

The experience at ASK certainly carried over to the White House. The Obama machine looked to its list of 13 million e-mail addresses to mobilize in favor of ObamaCare. The e-mail sent via the president's political arm, Organizing for America, was authored by Executive Director Mitch Stewart. It read:

> As you've probably seen in the news, special interest attack groups are stirring up partisan mobs with lies about health reform, and it's getting ugly. Across the country, members of Congress who support reform are being shouted down, physically assaulted, hung in effigy, and receiving death threats. We can't let extremists hijack this debate, or confuse Congress about where the people stand.[67]

This e-mail message went on to invite its recipients to participate in a bus tour across the country to show support at 2,000 events throughout the country.[68]

Mobilizing Union Muscle

As we've seen, unions are often used as foot soldiers for the Democratic Party to push through—sometimes quite literally—their policy planks. There was little doubt that unions would once again be called upon to exert that force in the ObamaCare debate.

In early August 2009, it was reported that HHS Secretary Sebelius, held a conference call where she encouraged her "brothers and sisters" in the SEIU to show up in support of congressional town halls espousing the benefits of ObamaCare.[69] As Congress pimped the idea of universal health care to constituents, it used union soldiers to help hammer home the message. In St. Louis, a conservative activist—who was also black—was attacked by another black man while attending a town hall meeting held by Democratic Congressman Russ Carnahan.[70] Video shows the attacker, who used racial slurs and caused injury to the man's knee, back, shoulder, and face, wearing a purple SEIU shirt.[71]

As Michelle Malkin wrote in her book *Culture of Corruption*, such tactics aren't aberrations but explicit union policy. Just listen to Andy Stern, SEIU's president:

> Asked about his organizing philosophy, Andy Stern summed it up this way: "[W]e prefer to use the power of persuasion, but if that doesn't work we use the persuasion of power."[72]

The SEIU loves propaganda and sexual slander. It created a video entitled "Tea Baggers against Health Care" and claims that it will "continue to elevate" the conversation.[73] It is pretty well established that the term "tea bagger" is as derogatory as they can get without calling them racists. The SEIU could possibly use a refresher course in civil disposition.

The AFL-CIO is another union group that didn't want to miss out on the action. AFL-CIO President John Sweeney sent out a memo outlining his thoughts on how best to combat the tea party patriots. He said:

> The principal battleground in the campaign will be town hall meetings and other gatherings with members of Congress in their home districts. . . . We want your help to organize major union participation to counter the right wing "tea party patriots" who will try to disrupt those meetings, as they've been trying to do to meetings for the last month.[74]

The Huffington Post touted the memo saying, "A showdown between unions and grassroots conservative organizations could make for an August full of fireworks, with even more dysfunctional town hall meetings."[75] This quote should give great pause to anyone with a level head. Are the unions there to participate constructively in the process, or are they there to intimidate those who disagree with them?

Lying to Grandma

There are about 43 million Americans on Medicare[76] and, understandably, those Americans are worried about how ObamaCare is going to affect them. President Obama and Congressional Democrats expect to obtain more than $150 billion in savings by cutting payments to Medicare Advantage plans. Medicare Advantage plans—in which more than 10 million seniors participate[77]—are a private option that offer more comprehensive benefits than traditional Medicare. The group that is charged with protecting America's seniors from such a catastrophic cut is the Association for the Advancement of Retired People (AARP).

AARP has run into a good deal of trouble since the push for ObamaCare began. Since July 1, 2009, more than 60,000 seniors have cancelled their membership in AARP.[78] Members became uneasy when President Obama incorrectly stated that AARP had endorsed his plan.[79] It came as a relief to the membership when AARP issued a statement saying, "While the president was correct that AARP will not endorse a health care reform bill that would reduce Medicare benefits, indications that we have endorsed any of the major health care reform bills currently under consideration in Congress are inaccurate."[80] However, the exodus came when AARP began airing ads in favor of the president's agenda.[81] This classic case of doublespeak had AARP members scratching their heads and wondering if they had been duped by the organization they thought would protect their interests.

One former member wrote on why she cancelled her AARP membership in a piece for the *American Thinker*, "Imagine my surprise when, a few days after seeing AARP's CEO claim that the organization had not decided whether to endorse Obama's health reform bill, an AARP commercial appeared on TV urging members to contact their representatives in support of it."[82]

Free-Range or Free-Market?

Many Americans have weighed in on the health care reform debate, but people usually take more notice when CEOs of large corporations decide to voice their opinion. Even more people notice when the CEO in question is the co-founder of one of the most popular, progressive retail food stores in the country. That CEO is John Mackey of Whole Foods.

On August 11, 2009, Mackey took to the pages of the *Wall Street Journal* to voice his opinion on the health reform debate in a piece called:

"The Whole Food Alternative to ObamaCare."[83] He explained in his piece that, "health care is a service that we all need, but just like food and shelter it is best provided through voluntary and mutually beneficial market exchanges." And he declared, "there is no intrinsic right to health care."[84]

Many praised Mackey for his honesty and for taking the initiative to come up with innovative health care solutions for his employees. The Left, on the other hand, assailed him for it. Almost immediately, a Facebook page calling for a boycott of Whole Foods was launched and within 12 days of Mackey's *Wall Street Journal* piece, the page had over 22,000 members.[85] Protests at various Whole Foods stores throughout the nation were organized and scores of shoppers expressed sentiments of feeling betrayed. One person said, "It is an absolute slap in the face to the millions of progressive-minded consumers that have made [Whole Foods] what it is today."[86] An organizer for the United Food and Commercial Workers union advocated for the dismissal of Mackey as the Whole Foods CEO by saying, "you need a compassionate person who's for reform."[87]

What kind of reform are these people talking about?

In his editorial, Mackey proposed eight individual reform proposals on how the free-market can tackle rising health care costs and increase access to care. He wrote about the virtues of Health Savings Accounts (HSAs), equalizing the tax treatment of health care, removing state barriers to allow for cross-state purchasing of health insurance, repealing government benefit mandates, enacting tort reform, increasing transparency, enacting Medicare reform, and allowing for charitable donations for those who have no affordable health care options. All of these ideas would point the United States in a better direction than we are headed now.

The problem with the progressive-minded people who are pushing for the boycott of Whole Foods is that they *thought* that they had an ally in John Mackey. Mackey uses phrases like "community," "shared fate," and "sustainable living" and, therefore, he must believe in a government takeover of health care, right? Isn't he *progressive*?

Consider this: Whole Foods allows *all* team members to vote on what health care benefits they most want the company to fund. Whole Foods pays 100 percent of the premiums for all team members who work 30 hours or more per week.[88] It provides up to $1,800 per year to employees in additional money for health and wellness.[89] The company has a salary cap that limits the compensation (wages plus profit incentive bonuses) of any executive to 19 times the average total compensation of all full-time team members in the company.[90] Finally, each store has the power to create policies that reflect the will and understanding of its employees.[91] Now *that* is progressive thinking.

When we hear about John Mackey's now famous editorial, we rarely hear about his closing paragraph. Regarding the general principles of reform, Mackey writes:

> . . . it is essential that they be financially responsible, and that we have the freedom to choose doctors and the health care services that best suit our own unique set of lifestyle choices. We are all responsible for our own lives and our own health. We should take that responsibility very seriously and use our freedom to make wise lifestyle choices that will protect our health. [92]

Mackey sums it up nicely that patient choice, personal responsibility, and freedoms are the three pillars of any health care reform effort.

Fannie Med?

U.S. senators have taken notice of the political beating their House colleagues have been taking in the polls and at town hall meetings. Some senators are looking for another way to achieve the president's goals without incorporating the public option plan into their legislation. One idea is creating health insurance cooperatives. The Cato Institute highlights cooperatives as "member-run health plans that already exist in many areas of the country."[93] Cato specifically mentions Group Health Cooperative, which covers 580,000 Americans in Idaho and Washington.

This particular idea is being pushed most aggressively by Chairman of the Senate Budget Committee Senator Kent Conrad (D-ND). In a June 30, 2009, press release, Sen. Conrad laid out his vision to forge a bipartisan deal based on regional or state-based cooperatives.[94] In that same release, Sen. Conrad admits that it would be necessary for the health insurance cooperatives to receive federal subsidies in order to operate. Most estimates put the seed money anywhere from $4 billion to $6 billion dollars, which begins to put private health insurers at a competitive disadvantage in a way similar to the public option plan. It gets worse. Sen. Conrad's plan calls for the establishment of a federal board to oversee the operation of the cooperatives. This board would be granted the power to institute Medicare-like price controls on everything from physician and hospital reimbursement to the price of prescription drugs. The *Wall Street Journal* points out that these requirements make cooperatives "sound a lot like a health care Fannie Mae and Freddie Mac, which Congress created because there was supposedly no secondary mortgage market. The duo proceeded to use their government subsidy to dominate the market and drive out private competitors."[95] And then they had to be bailed out.

A Civics Lesson for Congressmen

If there is one thing the town hall events revealed it is that many politicians view constituents as means toward ends. Members of Congress suffer through their constituents' questions and don't take them seriously. And when the constituents can't be persuaded, they are attacked.

Health care is an emotional issue. It touches every life. Compassion and patience is paramount when talking about it. We have seen over the course of the last six months that President Obama and congressional Democrats do not have compassion or patience. What they *do* have is distain and suspicion that average citizens attending their meetings are really henchmen loyal to the vast right-wing conspiracy.

Make no mistake; democracy is in action and the current health care debate is the center of the universe. The tea parties, town halls, and other rallies are perfect examples of public unrest. A quick scan of YouTube shows that Americans are concerned and they want answers. They want to know if the country can afford to spend over $1 trillion on health care reform and more important, can our children and grandchildren afford to pay that money. They also want to know how ObamaCare is going to affect them. As of this writing, the primary House bill is over 1,000 pages long[96] and not surprisingly, most members of the House of

Representatives have no idea what the bill says. The most recent parallel is the Patriot Act. Members were assailed for not reading the entire bill and are receiving the same heat on the health care bill. Most laugh it off and say it is unrealistic to read the entire bill.[97] They had better read the bill because *if* it passes, they are going to need to know how to explain why their constituents no longer have access to their preferred doctor or their preferred health insurance plan.

Just as the tea parties were not only bailout or tax protests, the town hall protests were about much more than health care. They were about the government taking over too much, too quickly. As Janet Adamy and Jonathan Weisman of the *Wall Street Journal* noted:

> ... voters often started with complaints about health care, only to shift to frustrations about all the other things President Barack Obama and the Democrats have done or tried to do since January. The $787 billion economic-stimulus package, the government-led rescue of General Motors Corp., and climate-change legislation all came in for criticism. ...[98]

If elections have consequences, as they say, so do town halls. Rep. Chris Van Hollen (D–MD.), chairman of the Democratic Congressional Campaign Committee, stated, "I've warned our colleagues from day one back in January, this is going to be a very challenging cycle. You just have to look historically. ... We're pleased people are being shaken out of their complacency."[99]

These events did much more than shake people out of complacency. The health care debates brought to head the same larger, broader philosophical issues that sparked the tea parties. As William McInturff summed it up, this was a "larger debate about what the role of government is. ... The health care debate is at that fault line."[100] A line millions of Americans believe the Left has crossed.

CHAPTER 9

THE TEA PARTY MANIFESTO

Once the nature of revolution is understood . . . we lose our monoview of a revolution and see it coupled with its inevitable counterrevolution.

—Saul Alinsky, *Rules for Radicals: A Pragmatic Primer for Realistic Radicals*, Vintage (1989), p. 17–18

The tea parties were in large part a gut reaction to very radical government action. This is a healthy thing. Despite the watering down of American history in our public schools, it is ingrained in millions of Americans that when the government oversteps its bounds, you must exercise your rights to keep it in check. The Founders counted on this self-correcting mechanism of democracy as inherent in all free people and relied on elected politicians to faithfully ensure that implied freedoms, like the freedom of speech, were constitutionally protected.

Thus, the movement is not and never was a revolution but a counterrevolution. This is a crucial distinction. To revolt is an attempt to break free from and overthrow a long-standing political structure.

The tea parties do the opposite by opposing the radical policies of bailouts, handouts, wealth redistribution, and intrusion into our lives that can only be described as radically revolutionary. Big spending and a nanny state government is radical. Saul Alinsky wrote, "I will argue that the failure to use power for a more equitable distribution of the means of life for all people signals the end of the revolution and the start of the counterrevolution."[1]

The tea party backlash is the counterrevolution of which Alinsky warns. It is about *protecting* individual liberty and the documents and institutions that have made it possible. Thus we must reject lingo like "radical conservatives" as playful takes on Alinsky's terminology. The tea parties and the movement they ignited aren't about a radical right-wing agenda but an American agenda. Our values are the values of the mainstream. The only radicalism involved in this movement is the preservation of the once radical ideas defended by the Founders that people should have a right to life, liberty, and the pursuit of happiness.

The counterrevolutionary must reject the false dichotomy of two radical wings—one conservative, one liberal—battling for the heart of a centrist nation. It is inaccurate and strategically perilous. We are mainstream; we defend the founding principles of this nation and the rule of law. That is not radical. Attempts to undermine our free, democratic society are radical. Defending that system is not radical, it is *right*, and polls following the tea parties indicated that most Americans agree.[2]

As the tea party movement progressed and the town hall movement took off, participants and speakers at rallies and town halls sought not only to combat radicalism, but also to assert their rights in sharp contrast to the underlying philosophical premises of recent government actions and the politicians who enabled these actions with reckless, unconstitutional disregard for their constituents.

As the historical record has been substantially perverted, redacted, ignored, or muddied with what the tea parties were not, here I offer my humble view of what they *were*.

Not Our Turf

The claim that the tea party movement is Astroturf can be handily dismissed when one looks at the facts of how they were actually organized.

The Left, through various organizations like ACORN and unions like the SEIU, engages in highly organized fake activism by a concentrated, rant-seeking few. These paid provocateurs are vested in policy because they are looking for special exceptions and handouts. On the Right, citizens organized alone, through the Internet, or with the aid of loose, bottom-up networks that facilitate activism.

Two of those groups that have drawn criticism more appropriately directed at the Left are Americans for Prosperity and FreedomWorks. As Americans for Prosperity's Phil Kerpen remarked to me:

> The Left's obsession with exposing the secret AstroTurf structure of the tea parties was pure projection. Labor unions, environmentalists, community organizers like ACORN, and other elements of the political Left see the large, passionate, angry crowds and they know how they would have done it: tens or hundreds of millions of dollars to pay vast armies of union workers, organizers, and environmentally-inclined college kids to show up and read off a script. Thus the left operates on these principles, so it isn't far-fetched that they would assume that everyone does as well. Their paid protestors speak to not only their methodologies, but the philosophy of leftist organizers and participants. They are principally looking for handouts from the government to protect their share of the pie. It is no surprise that they assess that Craigslist-advertised cash is both an effective and appropriate way to organize.

The idea that this would occur to tea party protestors or be effective is laughable. For one, it doesn't happen. The Right does not advertise for paid protesting positions as the Left did on Craigslist to support ObamaCare.[3] Nor does it have an army of disgruntled union members that can be called up at a moment's notice to bus to a town hall three counties away.[4]

Secondly, it doesn't fit the profile. Millions of Americans will not participate in tea parties and town halls because someone tells them they should. They are there *protesting* commands and handouts, not looking for them. They do it because *they care*. The Astroturf model exhibited by the Left doesn't principally or in reality hold up to this crowd. As Kerpen said, "Conservatives can't organize that way, even if we tried. . . . Most conservatives have jobs and busy family lives. Offering them $10 to show up at a rally would insult them. It's a sacrifice for them to go to a tea party or other event, and they are doing it in huge numbers because they are scared and angry about the direction of the country."

Brendan Steinhauser of FreedomWorks reiterates this point:

> The left gets paid to protest. The unions spend millions upon millions of dollars to wage their campaigns. And Organizing for America has a huge paid staff throughout the country and is run by the political hacks at the DNC. ACORN takes taxpayer dollars and stages protests or extorts money and other things from people. People that believe in limited government are always outspent and out-organized. But true believers find a way to make their own signs, communicate with each other, and take time off of work to show up at tea parties and town hall meetings to make a real difference in the debate.[5]

Who They Are and What They Believe

Tea party participants and organizers ran the gamut of the political and socio-economic spectrum. They are successful corporate leaders and small business owners. They are stay-at-home moms, traders, electricians, tradesmen, real estate brokers, and veterans. As Megan Barth noted about her tax day tea party in California, she spotted her dry cleaner, Edmund, in the crowd at the rally, holding a sign. When I got home on tax day, my building manager noted seeing me on TV. "Good job. Somebody's got to tell those guys how to run things right," he remarked. As FoxNews.com reported, participants and their reasons for attending varied:

> I have two little kids and I know we are mortgaging their futures away, one protester at a rally in Austin, Texas, told FOX News. It makes me sick to my stomach.
>
> Frankly, I'm mad as hell, said businessman Doug Burnett at a rally at the Iowa Capitol, where many of the about 1,000 people wore red shirts declaring "revolution is brewing." Burnett added: This country has been on a spending spree for decades, a spending spree we can't afford.
>
> In Washington, D.C., Joe Hollinger said he took the day off to attend the protest with his 11-year-old daughter. I'm concerned about the incredible amount of debt Congress is going to put on our children,

Hollinger said, pointing to his daughter's sign, which read, "Congress get your hand off my piggy bank."[6]

CNN echoed the diversity of background and opinions, reporting:

"If you look at these nine little beautiful grandbabies, I'm here for them. Our government's out of control with spending and their future's being robbed," said Mary Wojnas, whose sign had a photo of her grandchildren next to the phrase, Stop Generational Theft.

"Stop out-of-control spending and stop government takeover and intrusion in our lives. They're here to protect us and beyond that, get out of our way," said Wojnas, who attended a rally in front of the Georgia state capitol in Atlanta.

"The importance of these tea parties is to let our elected officials know that there's a lot of people out there who are unhappy. They're not Republicans, they're not Democrats, they're everyday Americans who are concerned about our taxes," said T.J. Welsh, an organizer of a protest attended by thousands in Jacksonville, Florida.

We need to rein in the size of government, and once having done so, we can cut taxes responsibly, he said.[7]

Many of the groups born out of the tea party movement—like Tea Party Patriots—emphasize broad principles of fiscal responsibility and limited government as pillars of the movement. While these are policy issues in line with the principles of the movement, they don't necessarily explain the mass frustration on a person-by-person level evidenced by those who participated in the tax day tea party protests. What does limited government really mean and why should we embrace it? It comes down to a fundamental difference in philosophy. Tea party participants, like most Americans, reject the idea that individuals are more likely to prosper in a highly controlled nanny state. They instead embrace a state where the government acts as a referee, stepping in only when absolutely necessary.

The tea party protestors represent the flip side to the revolutionary ideas that sparked the tea party counterrevolution. They believe that age-old philosophical principles of individual liberty, the pursuit of happiness, and basic property rights, as enshrined in law through the United States Constitution, are the fundamental building blocks of our civil society. More simply put, they believe that government does not and should not claim to have the answer for everything. They reject the idea that big government—at the hands of liberals or conservatives—should be used to solve problems. They see it as unrealistic and they resent the encroachment on their ability to exercise their intellect and free will.

These individuals, on the whole, subscribe to a live-and-let-live philosophy. They believe in free markets and small government. They are Democrats, Republicans, Libertarians, independents, and everything in between. While their opinions on gay marriage, foreign military intervention, or the legalization of drugs may differ, they agree that government is not always the answer. They want to be free to start an honest business, take home most of their paycheck, school their kids how they please, drive an SUV if they so choose, enjoy an adult beverage or even (gasp) the leisure of a tobacco product.

They are hardworking taxpayers who were driven by nothing more than the principles at stake: the protection of a representative democracy that supports the individual right to the pursuit of happiness against egregious, if not unlawful, government intervention.

As Steinhauser states, "The people protesting across the country are typically proponents of the free market and individual freedom. They are hardworking Americans that are tired of seeing big business and big government working together at the expense of the taxpayers and small businesses. They are fed up with the two major political parties and angry about the bailouts, debt, and growing government control over their lives."[8]

Protestors such as those at the tea parties merely ask to be left alone—whether it is their tax dollars, the cars they drive, the food they eat, their guns, how they educate their children, or their relationships with their doctors. They make up what Grover Norquist describes as the Leave Us Alone Coalition. "They do not want the government to give them something. Or take something from others. On the key issue that motivates their vote, they want one simple thing from the government: They just want to be left alone."[9]

A New Avenue

The tea parties and the protests that followed open up an entirely new way for citizens to become involved and engaged in important policy matters that affect them and their families and future generations to come. It was a way to get involved *without* the tainted labels of "Republican" and "Democrat." Steinhauser's experience reinforces what I observed in my own organizing efforts: "Most of these protesters have never demonstrated before, and most of them had to be pushed up against a wall before they would push back. But now that they have seen the power of mass protest and community organizing, they have been able to make a real difference in the national and local policy debates. This new, loosely confederated network of activists is committed to defending the free market and protecting individual liberty. They will make a long-lasting difference in the politics of this country by shifting the debate and halting this lurch to the left under presidents Bush and Obama." Thus the tea parties allowed people to shed these superficial labels that hold no inherent philosophical meaning and unite under principles, not parties.

The people who make up this movement were driven not only by the principles, but by the opportunity to get involved in public policy debates. They took the opportunity to step up and get involved in something exciting and engaging, which spoke to American beliefs in ways the Republican and Democratic parties could not. Jean Nickel of Arlington Heights, Illinois, attended the Chicago tax day tea party. As Jean put it:

> This was the first time that I had ever participated in an event like this . . . but I feel that our nation is at a tipping point and people like myself have to stand up and start being counted. Our elected officials are mortgaging the future of this great nation. The tax burden that we and our children will face as a result of unchecked spending and increased entitlement programs will doom us to low growth, high unemployment, and high taxes for years to come.

Megan Barth, from California, got involved through Facebook. She flew east to D.C. on her own dime for the February 27th White House tea party where she volunteered to help plan and execute the event. Megan got involved not only because she believed in the principles, but because she felt the burgeoning movement was the best vehicle for her to get involved in the political process:

> The tea party movement allowed me to find and connect with like-minded people, to engage in politics with "boots on the ground"

activism as opposed to taking action at the voting booth or blogging. I had been unhappy with my political party for quite some time and it was a relief to know that I was not alone and that there were thousands of others.

Virginia Crossland-Macha was another unlikely activist who felt the call to duty:

> For the last six years I have worked to get out the vote and supported candidates that are fiscally responsible. I live in a small town, Iola, Kansas, and until the election of 2008, I could have retreated to my nice home and managed to keep most of what we have earned over the [years]. . . . After an election of disappointment, a marine son who ended up wounded in Iraq in December, a severely depressed economy for our part of Kansas, and a steady stream of veterans at my door asking me to help them voice their worries for our country, I finally saw what opportunity was before me. Since April, I have organized many tea parties.
>
> . . . This is not about me or my generation, it is about the future generations. These students are enthusiastic, so the spin has been a positive event that will empower people to think outside the box. Just when you pose that inevitable question of "Was it worth the effort and will I continue?" you cross the path of someone who has attended your events. Not until then do you realize the power of small action making big impacts on lives that otherwise may have lost hope.

Reports Heather Liggett of Austin, Texas, "I am a stay-at-home mom and wife of a small business owner with a voice and the determination to come together with other like-minded individuals to take back America."

Like thousands of people across the country, these volunteers served as energetic, inexhaustible organizers driven neither by a union or party boss, nor the goal of seeking anything in return, but merely protecting the existing principles this nation was founded upon.

Popular, Not Populist

The tea parties were simultaneously couched by the liberal media and politicians as small and insignificant but out of control, populist mobs.

They were neither. On close inspection, the tea parties were popular and widespread. Exact numbers are difficult to come by given the sheer number of tea parties. There were over 700 events posted on taxdaytea-party.com and other sites by April 15th. The site administrators of many of them had to stop posting events taking place in small cities and towns due to the sheer volume of submissions. By most estimates, there were a quarter to half a million people in the streets on April 15th, 2009.[10] All things considered, it was an impressive turnout. Even compared to other high-profile protests and marches, the tea parties ranked well. The highly contested numbers of the alleged million-man march of 1995 were reported to be as low as 400,000.[11]

Despite their widespread popularity, I would argue the tea parties were not populist, per se. Populism is often used to describe the tea parties, particularly their anger directed at corporations.[12] This is in many ways an anachronism. Populism as a political ideology is a ploy used to get progressives elected. "Vote for me, man of the people, and I'll represent you and yours amongst the elitists in Washington." It is, in essence, class warfare that depends on defining society as two classes pitted against each other: the elites and the rest of us. It is often invoked *by* the elites to get elected by the rest of us. This is not to say that political elitists don't rightfully draw the ire of the public. It is not their status, however, that draws criticism, but their belief that their status alone justifies their warped view of reality and the misguided and often malicious policies that follow. Take corporations. Unlike the populism of the past, the tea parties are not about redistributing wealth and taking on corporate leaders. They are not about asking for welfare from successful businesses and their executives, but rather against welfare *for* them. Corporations can and should seek to maximize profit; this is right and good. What angers people is when their hard-earned tax dollars are used to cushion the fall of irresponsible corporate decisions.

Populism as a philosophy is the idea that the common man has more wisdom than any senator or scholar can offer. This may sometimes be the case, but it is not universally true. There are scholars with more wisdom than most men, and those who can't tie their own shoes. We must judge people on their merits, not their social status or profession. It is the blind acceptance of the aforementioned elite politicians as knowledgeable and trustworthy that got us into this mess in the first place.

The tea parties were a rejection of this categorizing, superficial, and frivolous methodology of perverse value judgments. The tea parties were an assertion of individualism and personal responsibility. The point is not to criticize politicians and corporations for existing. It is the substance of the discussion that is important to the tea party protestors. They're more than happy to give the senator a fancy office in a marble building with security and staff galore. What disgusts Americans is the junk that often leaves that office, garners just enough "yays," and with a flick of a pen, becomes another shackle on an already overregulated and overtaxed populace.

Dispelling False Dichotomies

The Left often presents us with the false dichotomy of progressive versus regressive, and this is exactly how they see the world. For every two steps forward progressives make, those pesky regressive conservatives are pushing back one step, always hindering progress and change for the greater good.[13]

This elucidates fundamental differences between two competing visions for civil society. Liberals, self-described progressives, are so sure that their way is the right way, that they believe it is empirical progress. Think about that for a minute. They see the world in terms of problems, they believe they have the solutions, and they believe these solutions should be codified by government and imposed upon society. Once one accepts the false premise of any leftist concoction being progressive and thus good, no methodology is too Machiavellian and no law too Orwellian to meet said "progressive" ends. This is quite dangerous. Saul Alinsky, the founder of modern community organizing, wrote, "The practical revolutionary will understand Goethe's 'conscience is the virtue of observers and not of agents of action'; in action, one does not always enjoy the luxury of a decision that is consistent both with one's individual conscience and the good of mankind. The choice must always be for the later."[14]

Yet, blinded by the perceived righteousness of their actions, results are often irrelevant to the Left. Their unions reject calls for efficiency and their politicians reject calls for transparency and accountability.

The progressive's world is one of good intentions. Progressives, lulled into the self-hypnosis of the goodness of their every deed, become immune to a reality of nefarious means and unattained ends. They are more dangerous than overtly selfish power mongers. The liberal mind can see no internal contradiction for all intentions and outcomes are presumed as good regardless of reality. They are true believers whose conviction blinds them to the real consequences of their actions.

The rest of us, the Right included, live in a world not only of intent, but of action and result. We grew up hearing and heeding the phrase "the road to hell is paved with good intentions." We know at work that intentions don't translate into raises, promotions, and bonuses—results do. We know that feelings don't pay the rent, the mortgage, or the electric bill—hard-earned money does. This is the mind-set of the tea party protester. Hard work pays off, and hard work and prudence should not be punished. This is not old-fashioned "regressive" conservatism. As Rick Santelli proclaimed, "This is America!" You can pull yourself up by your bootstraps and your family can go from working class to upper class in a generation. A family can go from immigrants to assimilated millionaires in a decade. This is a beautiful thing, and something that should be cherished, not watered down under the false pretenses of diversity and equality. The road to mediocrity is paved with these homogenizing platitudes.

On the Role of Government

From smoking bans to payday loan regulations, the Left is quite fond of telling us what's best. This is out of sync with our nation's laws and guiding philosophy. And practically speaking, their plans don't often work out as anticipated. Exhibit A: the recent cash for clunkers program.

Government is explicitly intended to be *for and by* the people. It is meant to be a necessary evil. Congress, the presidency, the Supreme Court, the mayor, the state senator, city hall—we give up part of our freedom to these individuals and institutions. These institutions are not intended to be ends in and of themselves. They are necessary institutions, run by a democratically elected few, whose power to make large-scale social decisions is authorized by individual Americans. As a citizen of this nation or a guest within its borders, you have either explicitly or implicitly entered into a contract with your fellow man. We give up some freedom to others to make many decisions that will impact us. This is necessary for making broad-stroke decisions that impact us as a society.

One also gives up some of his income in the form of taxes to fund governmental activities. It is the case both practically, in fairness, and under law that the tax burden should not be excessive. If too much is taken from you, you will be disincentivized to earn more. If more is taken from some over others, merely because they worked harder and enjoyed success, the governmental action is unjust. These concepts aren't merely vague philosophical musings—they are hard and fast rules enshrined in our Constitution, but rules that have been long forgotten in many facets of public policy and public discourse. Taxes are intended to be a way for us to pitch in for absolutely necessary items: no more, no less.

The Founding Fathers saw and the average Joe can see that it is both philosophically right and practically sustainable for people to enjoy the maximum fruits of their labors, with the government skimming off as little as possible. Furthermore, it is intuitive to most people that one should be able to enjoy those fruits with minimal intervention from the government.

This much makes sense to most Americans. They recognize that the litany of handouts and entitlements promulgated by the Left like free health care, free houses, guaranteed jobs, and free cars aren't what the framers had in mind. They reject the notion that government exists to tell them what is best or that government has the right to tell them what to do in any category of their lives.

This is a key difference between the Left and everybody else. The Left piously believes that it knows what's best and how best to do it. From human behavior and health care to the complex workings of the world economy or the Earth's climate, the Left has the hubris to believe that they can control everything and that they know best how to determine every possible outcome.

Once one accepts the Left's premises, founded on the perversions of the philosophical principles that founded our nation, no cost—literal or figurative—no forced measure of control, and no statist intervention is too egregious or too great for the citizenry to bear in the name of the "common good."

This myth has allowed the Left to succeed under the aegis of offering new ideas. The Right, which has preserved the ideas that have worked—that is, constitutional ideas—has been challenged in finding ways to apply these ideas to contemporary politics. It is difficult to conceive of universal health care without government intervention or cap and trade without taxation. The liberal mind tells the American people that government is necessary if everyone is to have health care or if corporations are to stop polluting. But the liberal mind assumes that better health or cleaner environments are something best obtained through governmental means. Universal health care or cap-and-trade are not necessarily the best programs for the United States. But they are excellent goals for a stronger and more powerful government bureaucracy.

The Left prefers an uninformed, unquestioning electorate. Common sense is stripped away and all that's left is a mass of helpless, homogenous zombies looking to government for every answer. They see this as a win-win: a tamer, more easily led electorate, and more government jobs.

The tea parties reject this premise. They embrace government as a necessary evil in constant need of being trimmed back like weeds in the spring. They want their highways, cops, firefighters, and military well-funded so they can go about their lives in a free society with basic guidelines within which they can live their lives as they see fit.

Not Anti-Tax

While the Olbermanns and Maddows of the world had fun making sex jokes, the truly damaging coverage came from the more reputable media outlets that carried a nuanced bias. They referred to the tea parties as "anti-tax." This was repeated over and over again in reports by the media from all angles—including friendly networks. This is a major mischaracterization of free-market folks in general. With the exception of the minority of compound conservatives, this is hardly the case. There are two, simple components to so-called anti-tax movements. For one, it is about *equitable* taxes—be it a flat tax or a sales tax versus the progressive redistribution of wealth. Think about it: You are taxed when you earn money (through payroll taxes), when you spend (through sales taxes), when you give money[15] and even when you die.[16] In Massachusetts, you can't sell a car that you've already paid taxes on to someone else without the government wetting its beak. The buyer must pay taxes not on the amount paid for the car but on the amount the government thinks should have been paid for the car.[17]

The burden to small business owners did come up a good deal at rallies. Many small business owners like Joe the Plumber and others fall into an unfortunate sector of society. They are big enough that they don't fit into liberals' schemes of redistributive wealth and they are eyed for taxes. Unfortunately, they are also small enough not to have lobbyists to pay street tax to money-grabbing politicians.

Secondly, the fiscal concerns of this crowd were not merely current taxes—as unreasonable as they are—but spending. To shift the conversation from reckless spending to selfish concerns over taxation gives cover to the politicians spending like drunken sailors. These protests were mainly concerned with the unbearable taxes of tomorrow that will be needed to pay for the reckless spending decisions of today.

Many protestors were concerned not with their taxes or spending in and of itself, but with the debt that would inevitably be passed on to subsequent generations following the spending spree coming out of D.C. Remember Norm from the Chicago tax day tea party? He got accosted by the CNN reporter because he was there with his child who held a sign that read "I'm two years old and already in debt." This wasn't about selfish rich people—these were citizens worried about the state of the nation they would pass on to their kids and grandkids. As the AP's Shannon McCaffrey reported, Ben and Bree Finegan, two small business owners, brought their two-year-old daughter, Kate, to the Indianapolis tea party rally with a sign hanging from her stroller that said, "In diapers & in debt."[18] In Carson City, Nevada, a young boy sported a sign reading "My Share of the National Debt is $36,500."[19] CNN.com echoed the concern for future generations expressed at the tea parties citing signs like: "Stop Generational Theft."[20]

Rejection of Bailouts, Handouts, and Wealth Redistribution

The tea parties were in large part a reaction to the mind-boggling figures being spent by Washington on bailouts and handouts. They were also a rejection of the backward principles behind the spending. The phrase "too big to fail" was often floated. But who decides? The government intervened to save Bear Stearns, essentially acting as insurer in a sweetheart deal with JPMorgan Chase but let Lehman Brothers fail. Was that the right decision, for instance?

Inevitably, such policies result in a situation where, if you screw up badly enough, Uncle Sam will help you out (maybe). If you are smaller and don't screw up or only screw up a little, you are out of luck and just too small to succeed.

The billions and billions poured into failing businesses like GM and AIG rightfully irked the nation. Particularly in tough economic times, to see recklessness—incentivized by the government no less—*rewarded* spits in the face of the American dream so many politicians claim to stand for.

The large bailouts are easy targets for criticism. The underlying philosophy behind them is of most concern, however. The signals and incentives given to everyday citizens can and will have much deeper, more lasting effects than the high-publicity handouts will have.

Revolutionary ideas like cap-and-trade, universal health care and the cash for clunkers program are radical tactics geared toward creating a system of mob rule where wealth and power is redistributed to the weak and unproductive. By redistributing wealth under the guise of empowering the poor, the Left seeks to foment a revolution. The thought behind causes of such a revolution goes back farther than either Alinsky or Marx. Alexis de Tocqueville, in *The Old Regime and the Revolution*, understood the catalyst of the French Revolution to be a confusion of wealth with power:

> Wealth has become power, there is equality before the law, equal taxation, a free press, open debate; all these new principles of which medieval society was ignorant. But these new things are exactly what, gradually and skillfully introduced into the old feudal order, reanimated

it, without risking its dissolution, and filled it with fresh strength while leaving the ancient forms intact. Seventeenth-century England was already a completely modern nation which had merely preserved within itself, as if embalmed, a few medieval relics. This brief glance outside France was necessary in order to understand what follows; for whoever had seen and studied only France will never understand anything about the French Revolution.[21]

By redistributing wealth, the Left hopes to sow the seeds for revolution. Except they have failed to learn the lesson of Tocqueville—the aftermath of Obama's revolution will be a system of inequality much more severe than what currently exists. Wealth does not create power, value does. The wealthy were powerful before they became rich. Their hard work to add economic value and produce wealth for consumers defines their value; those who lack a character of productivity or an ability to add value for others will always be valueless. Tocqueville warned that the obsession with wealth over economic value was the same fallacy of medieval monarchs who conflated title with authority. ACORN, Obama, and the core of modern liberalism talk about the haves and the have-nots, the wealthy and the poor, but fail to recognize that these terms do not embody the capitalist ethic of added value, productivity, and comparative advantage. Liberal elitism is the most dangerous kind because those who gain wealth through its redistribution can hold onto a form of power completely divorced from a responsibility to create goods and services that improve the lives of others. This is the same ethic that informed feudalism, which kept the world unproductive for centuries.

The tea parties are an attempt to ensure that Tocqueville's warning is not forgotten. While Obama's revolutionaries tote a theory of "gimme more" it is the "leave me alone" mentality of the tea party protesters that will preserve our policy against faction and revolution. Conservatives have stood for the rights that preserve a culture and society of freedom. These rights, either express or implied in the Constitution, include the right to privacy, the right to be left alone, and the right to be free from unreasonable searches and seizures. These rights embody an ethic of personal responsibility because they give meaning to the concept of an individual unencumbered by government. Thus individual rights become a privilege; a privilege that must be jealously guarded.

Personal Responsibility

Fundamental to understanding the heated debate over everything from bailouts to universal health care is the fact that society today does not value personal responsibility. This mentality is most commonly exhibited by the Left. It is the foundation of many of the policies that they hold dear and it is the philosophical premise of many of their proposals for progressive legislation, including welfare, equal opportunity employment laws, and affirmative action, to name a few. What infuriates Americans is to see personal responsibility thrown aside not only *in* the policies coming out of Washington but regarding the very implications of these policies.

Millions of Americans put common sense aside and, prodded by government policies that encourage everyone to own a home, bought homes they could not afford. Millions of dollars of these mortgages were packaged into exotic securities and bought and sold by private entities outside of Fannie and Freddie. Out of this, we are meant to believe it is not the home buyers' fault, nor the fault of the lawmakers that actively pushed these policies that backfired. It isn't even the fault of the organizations that packaged these risky securities whose market value was distorted by government tinkering. No, it is the fault of the mortgage brokers that did perfectly legal business with these consenting adults. It is speculators that "bet against the American people," like that jerk racking up chips on the "Don't Pass" line at the end of the craps table. It was unregulated hedge funds! It is the insidious mind-set that anyone but the grown adults who made poor decisions is to blame.

Why should people pay for things evil speculators did or for mortgages tricky salespeople sold them? Our nation has become so obsessed with blaming others for every problem. It is reflected in our excessively litigious society from the burned McDonald's coffee victim to the "get out of your debt to the IRS" and "are you a victim of your mortgage?" ads. Once you accept the premise that all bad things can and should be blamed on someone else, mediocrity is the threshold for any performance and reckless behavior abounds.

The peddlers and enablers of this philosophy have started to believe it themselves.

On April 7, 2009, Representative Barney Frank was questioned by law student Joel Pollak during a lecture at Harvard University on the financial crisis. Pollak asked, "How much responsibility, if any, do you have for the financial crisis?"[22] Frank, the chairman of the House Financial Services Committee, proceeded to avoid the question thoroughly, turning around and attacking the student:

Frank: I think you're being disingenuous....

...So I do want to ask you, when you suggest that I should apologize for something or take responsibility, what is it you think I should have done that I didn't do?

Pollak: Well, after spending the entire speech blaming conservatives— I happen to think of myself as of as a conservative, and I rent, and I think of myself as someone who cares about poor people—I'm just interested in whether you think you have any responsibility...

Frank: Well, I've answered the question. Sir, I think you're not being fully honest with us. You clearly are implying that I do. And I'm asking you—I have given you my record...

He has, and the record demonstrates that Frank and his congressional colleagues had plenty of blame to bear for the failures of Fannie and Freddie. Frank has served on the House Financial Services Committee since 1981.[23] Frank was a staunch supporter of Fannie Mae and Freddie Mac. On July 14, 2008, on CNBC, Frank had this to say on the two mortgage giants:

Frank: I think this is a case where Fannie and Freddie are fundamentally sound, that they are not in danger of going under. They're not the best investments these days from the long-term standpoint going back. I think they are in good shape going forward.

They're in a housing market. I do think their prospects going forward are very solid. And in fact, we're going to do some things that are going to improve them.

Three months later, Bill O'Reilly questioned the congressman regarding this statement. After Frank shared a muddled and mumbled timeline regarding his track record of "reform" and the GOP's alleged attempts to block it, O'Reilly pushed further:

O'Reilly:	All right, that's swell. But you still went out in July and said everything was great. And off that, a lot of people bought stock and lost everything they had.
Frank:	Oh, no.
O'Reilly:	And—yes, oh yes. Oh, yes.
Frank:	I said it wasn't a good investment. Please stop yelling.
O'Reilly:	Don't give me any of that, we just heard the words. What are you . . .
Frank:	That's wrong.
O'Reilly:	You didn't say that? You want me to play it again for you?

The conversation spiraled into a hilarious shouting match that ended with O'Reilly calling Frank a coward and Frank retorting that O'Reilly was just too "dumb."

Franks' alleged reform notwithstanding, Fannie and Freddie were in trouble, and it happened under his watch and with more than one conflict of interest. Frank had a romantic relationship with a Fannie Mae executive, Herb Moses. This was vastly underreported by the media, save for a number of fluff pieces on the subject. Such as one on July 21, 1991, where Moses wrote in the *Washington Post*, "I am the only member of the congressional gay spouse caucus . . . on Capitol Hill, Barney always introduces me as his lover."

Frank's relationship with Moses sheds some light on why his reform attitude preceded a decade of deregulatory fervor. Bill Sammon wrote:

> Although Frank now blames Republicans for the failure of Fannie and Freddie, he spent years blocking GOP lawmakers from imposing tougher regulations on the mortgage giants. In 1991, the year Moses was hired by Fannie, the *Boston Globe* reported that Frank pushed the agency to loosen regulations on mortgages for two- and three-family homes, even though they were defaulting at twice and five times the rate of single homes, respectively.[24]

Of course the November 22, 1991, *Boston Globe* article did not mention Frank's conflict of interest.[25] Despite devoting an entire article three months earlier not only to the story of the two lovers, but to the reactions of boredom and questions regarding the relevance of the story in Boston and the perceived homophobia these reactions allegedly represented, the *Boston Globe* nonchalantly decided not to report Frank's egregious conflict.[26]

Sammon continues by reporting Bill Clinton's take on Frank's role in the crisis:

> Three years later, President Clinton's Department of Housing and Urban Development tried to impose a new regulation on Fannie but was thwarted by Frank. Clinton now blames such Democrats for planting the seeds of today's economic crisis. "I think the responsibility that the Democrats have may rest more in resisting any efforts by Republicans in the Congress or by me when I was president, to put some standards and tighten up a little on Fannie Mae and Freddie Mac," Clinton said recently.

Frank had several personal connections to the GSEs Fannie Mae and Freddie Mac. Since 1989, he had received over $40,000 in contributions. Frank wasn't the only congressman receiving good money from Fannie and Freddie. Since 1989, some well-known Democrats racked in significantly more than their Republican colleagues. Some highlights include over $51,000 to Congressman turned Obama White House Chief of Staff Rahm Emanuel, over $75,000 to Senator turned Obama-appointed Secretary of State Hillary Clinton, and over $125,000 to Senator turned President Barack Obama. The all-time recipient, however, was Senate Banking Committee Chairman Chris Dodd with more than $165,000 in contributions.[27]

Frank's on-again, off-again relationship with regulation of Fannie and Freddie continued as the mortgage giants were just beginning to be reined in. In June of 2009, he began pushing for further deregulation, citing recent restrictions as possibly "too onerous."[28]

This type of finger-pointing, flip-flopping nonsense from elected officials is what infuriates Americans. Lies and excuses don't fly in their workplace, and they expect more from the people they elect when making decisions in Washington and state capitols around the nation. The tea parties were in large part a mandate for personal responsibility—taking responsibility for past actions but also taking responsibility for forging a path forward.

As Thomas Sowell aptly put it, "Human beings are going to make mistakes, whether in the market or in the government. The difference is that survival in the market requires recognizing mistakes and changing course before you go bankrupt. But survival in politics requires denying mistakes and sticking with the policies you advocated, while blaming others for the bad results."[29]

"The Ideology of Change"

You see, Dr. Stadler, people don't want to think. And the deeper they get into trouble, the less they want to think. But by some sort of instinct, they feel that they ought to and it makes them feel guilty. So they'll bless and follow anyone who gives them a justification for not thinking. Anyone who makes a virtue—a highly intellectual virtue—out of what they know to be their sin, their weakness, and their guilt.

And you propose to pander to that?

That is the road to popularity.

—Ayn Rand, *Atlas Shrugged*

A critical section of Saul Alinsky's manifesto advocates for adopting the empty mantra of change as the activist's sole ideology: "The prerequisite of an ideology is possession of a basic truth.... An organizer working in and for an open society is in an ideological dilemma. To begin with, he does not have a fixed truth —truth to him is relative and changing; *everything* to him is relative and changing. He is a political relativist."[30]

But what exactly does change really mean, and where did it come from? Change for its own sake is empty and meaningless. Change is not a worthwhile end in itself. "Anyone but this guy" is irrational, because there could always be a worse option. Donald Trump could don a leotard and compete in *Dancing with the Stars*. That is not desirable change. To call for change for change's sake is to say that you do not have the answers, but whatever you do, they can't be worse than what's happening right now.

Yet change fits perfectly into the progressive sales pitch. The status quo is bad, change would be good, and *we* represent change. Change does not need to be defined, and it can't be. Otherwise a politician would have to answer to a specific, promised deliverable. It doesn't matter, because, fed the ever-appealing slogans of "change" and "hope," the eager ears of the masses will fill in the blanks.

It should surprise no one that the Obama team employed the slogan "change we can believe in" almost exclusively—and quite effectively. Following the unpopularity of George W. Bush, it turned out to be a particularly great play.

The tea party served as a rejection of this mentality. Millions of Americans' eyes were quickly opened to the realization that the change they voted for was not for a new breed of post-partisan politicians, but more sophisticated sophists—smooth talkers armed with guerilla intellectual tactics and numbed to spending inordinate amounts of their hard-earned labor in the name of change.

They wanted a change in political rhetoric and more change in their pockets. Americans yearned for a different kind of political sportsmanship and a few wins for the public. What they got was a completely new kind of game where the rules were scraped and the odds were stacked for them to come out the loser.

A Rejection of Class Warfare: The Unholy Trinity

In an excellent, unintentional mockery of the Left's desire to categorize and control every aspect of life, Alinsky offers his view of the socioeconomic landscape: the Haves, the Have-Nots, and the Have-a-Little, Want Mores:

> On top are the Haves with power, money, food, security and luxury. They suffocate in their surpluses while the Have-Nots starve. Numerically, the Haves have always been the fewest.

In a continuation of the progressive versus regressive or static distinction, Alinsky writes:

> The Haves want to keep things as they are as opposed to change. Thermopolitically they are cold and determined to freeze the status quo.

The poor, writes Alinsky, are the Have-Nots:

> They are chained together by the common misery of poverty... the cry of the Have-Nots has never been "give us your hearts" but

always "get off our backs"; they ask not for love but for breathing space. Then there is the great middle class to whom all politicians pander. Torn between upholding the status quo to protect the little they have, yet wanting change so they can get more, they become split personalities.[31]

Alinsky's categories are vaguely familiar to us, but they don't hold up against the social and political realities of our nation nor the principles upon which it was founded. The Have Mores should be held up as examples of success, of something to strive for. Instead, Alinsky, like many on the Left, proffers that they are suffocating in their existential and material excesses. The poor are couched as merely wanting to have space to thrive. The former mirrors the immigrant mentality that has brought Jews, the Irish, Greeks, Italians, Mexicans and others to this country and catapulting into the so-called middle and upper classes. This represents the American dream—a poor man with a good work ethic, if given the opportunity, can thrive. It is not, however, the reality of the picture painted by politicians. They do, in fact, actively advocate for handouts in the name of pity and love. This is not to say that society should not have pity on and help the helpless. But to mask charity as the cutting of Haves-imposed shackles is particularly insidious.

What's more, Alinsky and his political offspring of today often speak of this "wealthy few," just a handful of elites who make up a small group of billionaires we should all resent. Obama played this quite effectively. In virtually every domestic policy discussion, when it came time to talk about who would pay for the radical expansion of government he proposed, the answer was *not you*. From health care to energy taxes, the number 95 percent was trotted out to assuage the fear of the Have-Nots and the Have-A-Little, Want Mores. Don't worry about deficits and taxes. You won't be paying that. It will be that 5 percent you and I don't know. They are up in their penthouses and limousines and won't even miss the money. After all, they'd be paying their fair share. Obama's use of the phrase "95 percent" to state, for instance, that 95 percent of small businesses make under $250,000, is a perfect example of the bait-and-switch tactics of the Left's political rhetoric. It would be okay to tax the top 5 percent without harming 95 percent of the wealth producers in the United States. But therein lies the fallacy: Merely because a substantial number of businesses make under a certain amount of profit does not mean that they contribute the majority of wealth in the United States. The greatest wealth producers in the United States are those top 5 percent that constantly strive for innovation and excellence. But the Left's rhetoric gently softens the American mind into a state of naïveté so that individualism is slowly worn off and the collective mind-set captures the mood of the masses. Obama is neither the first nor will he be the last to peddle the ideology of class warfare. Politicians seize on these distinctions.

The great middle class is always touted as the main concern of politicians. Why? Because the middle class makes up the majority of the electorate. Political worship of the middle class is so transparent, politicians don't speak of making things fair and equitable, not even of helping the poor, but of assisting the middle class. Politicians explicitly state their desire to help the median voter. But the median voter is not in need of help. The middle class median voter is the most necessary vote; and, indeed, there are more of them than there are rich or poor people. The rich will pay their taxes, while the poor can't voice their complaints.

The political focus on the median, the common denominator is an intelligent business strategy. Products are marketed to the median consumer and price and quality are balanced such as to maximize profits based on the most common consumer. Empowering the middle class means giving them more purchasing power for consumption of luxury goods.

The tea parties stand for the rejection of class warfare and the psychic divide between the haves and the have-nots. They embrace the idea that we are all Americans and that success should be held up and praised not diminished or punished.

The Rejection of False Prophets

A light will shine down from somewhere. It will light upon you. You experience an epiphany and you will say to yourself, "I have to vote for Barack. I have to do it."

—Barack Obama, "On Deadline: Obama Walks Arrogance Line" by Ron Fournier, *Seattle Times*, March 16, 2008

Barack Obama . . . is going to demand that you shed your cynicism.
That you put down your divisions. That you come out of your iso-
lation, that you move out of your comfort zones. That you push
yourselves to be better. And that you engage. Barack will never allow
you to go back to your lives as usual, uninvolved, uninformed.

—Michelle Obama, "It's All about Him"
by William Kristol, *New York Times*,
February 25, 2008

Part of why Americans have been slow to come up with alternatives
to government control of our livelihood is because we have become
accustomed to political hero worship. Americans worship great athletes,
great actors, and great preachers. Those individuals are paid for their
popularity and valued for it. But we would never want to grant these
public figures the responsibility of running a country.

We must reject these false prophets—individuals who lack the hu-
mility to realize that neither politicians nor the government drive social
change—and instead suck the resources of hard-working Americans for
the sake of political profit. They do not hold all the answers, and they
typically don't mirror the gilded image they project. While many Obama
policies are radical and rightly protested, the practice of making icons
out of politicians must be scrutinized, as blind acceptance of these heroes
can quickly lead to a bound populace.

President Obama employed quite effectively the empty mantra of
change and the poison of class warfare. He positioned himself as a post-
politician, different from anyone before him. A very bright, educated
man, he posed as an everyman who came of age on the tough streets of
Chicago as a community organizer. He and his wife's lives were, in fact,
quite blessed with a level of opportunity and education most Americans
will never reach.

On peripheral inspection, Obama's book, *The Audacity of Hope*, is just
that: audacious. And America will be its victim. The president grew up
in an upper-middle-class white suburb in Honolulu, Hawaii. His father
was a Harvard graduate and Kenyan native who knew nothing about the
"lived-out experience" of black America. His father had multiple wives
and left Obama's mother to raise their son on her own. Obama's mother
was lucky enough to come from wealth and had earned a Ph.D. so that

she could support herself. Obama attended the prestigious Punahou School in Honolulu. Add Harvard and Columbia to that list. He is an elitist leftist, but a more nefarious one, claiming to be one of the underprivileged to whom he panders. Most of America is unaware that Barack Obama, the community organizer from Chicago, spent most of his educational life in expensive, selective, and elite private schools that survive through the generosity of millions of dollars of—gasp—wealthy individual and corporate donations.

To say that Obama is disassociated from the experiences of black Americans is an understatement. President Obama was an academic who wanted to be a preacher but became a politician instead. Obama's approach to race has often been an intellectual one. Yet when Henry Louis Gates, Jr., a Harvard professor, was arrested for race-baiting, Obama jumped to his defense to denounce the arrest as a sign of racism.[32] Where was President Obama during Katrina, where hundreds of black families were suffering? Before and after taking the presidency, he did very little.[33]

The Obama administration is a shining example of how superficial and disingenuous attempts at affirmative action really are. How many racial minorities has Obama hired who came from backgrounds different from his own? Attorney General Eric Holder grew up in a financially well-off home, attended the prestigious Stuyvesant High School, and received two degrees from Columbia University—an ivy-league school. Sonia Sotomayor, despite her depiction as suffering from a rough childhood, grew up middle-class, attended private Catholic college preparatory schools, and received a bachelor' degree from Princeton and a law degree from Yale. Wise Latina woman, indeed. Ironically, the only conspicuous member of Obama's cabinet who seemed to grow up in rough conditions is his white vice president, Joe Biden, who nearly flunked out of college at the University of Delaware and graduated in the bottom of his class at Syracuse law school—after being caught cheating during his first semester there.

What does this mean? The Left's understanding of racial diversity, still seen only through the lens of academic standards, reveals just how dangerous a false sense of identity is when accepted by the electorate. Too often politicians link racial identity to struggle—real or embellished—rather than to the potential for success. What may have started as a noble goal of improving the lives of the poor is too often lost in the race for votes.

Many find it difficult to believe that Alinsky's socialist theories could actually *hurt* the underprivileged the most. Helping the poor and fighting against racial inequality are good things. But why make the jump to a conclusion that it is the government's job to fix the lives of the disenfranchised? Has the government historically been the most effective form of rectification? Has the government sufficient staff, resources, and administrative energy to guarantee productive social change? Of course not. Besides our military, the government can't get much right at all. Then what is the real goal of the Left in expanding government? To help the less fortunate or to increase the Left's scope of influence?

The tea party movement represents an alternative to a blind reliance on government for social change. The movement rejects the notion that the less fortunate should be made to be perpetually dependent on the government. As the movement showed, real social change comes from the people not from the stuffy, bureaucratic halls of Capitol Hill.

Rejection of the Entitlement Ethic

Most Americans believe that you have the right to work hard and keep as much of your earnings as possible to do with what you see fit. The Left is different. Theirs is a philosophy of entitlement. People on the Left don't believe you are free to pursue happiness as you please (except in matters of sexual conduct). Rather, they believe you are entitled to the happiness that they determine is best for you. Philosophically, this notion is incompatible with the founding principles of our nation. Our founders protested against a state that would guarantee every luxury of life through the forced redistribution of wealth.

The Left promises free education for all, and is the primary protector of the teachers' unions that are stunting the success of millions of American students. They believe in lifetime job protection, regardless of results. Welfare, despite its pitfalls, is intended as a way to help the truly helpless get on their feet. People understand that. What's truly despicable to most Americans is welfare for corporations, for underperforming teachers, and for lazy and corrupt bureaucrats and politicians.

A right to a living wage has become a right to a home through government market manipulation, a right to a car,[34] and a right to broadband Internet access.[35] Those who advocate these rights, have the audacity to think that they can determine what "basic rights" should be. Of course, they know who should pay for them, too—anyone who falls above the economic standard that they have arbitrarily set.

There is no shortage of people who remain perpetually helpless by choice, constantly seeking solutions from someone else, like the government. Whether it is a regulatory authority to deal with their consumer issues or an alderman to call a plumber for them, they look externally for answers. Thus, the liberal mind believes that the state is the basis of the law. Whatever the government does is prima facie lawful. There will always be people like this. This fact of life presents an excellent opportunity for (typically liberal) politicians. They can be the man with the plan. They can offer the elixir to solve all your problems, and who doesn't have problems? The status quo can always be improved upon, and there will always be individuals looking to politicians to do it. Speaking at an Obama/Biden rally in October, Peggy Joseph was gushing with enthusiasm:

> This is the most memorable time of my life. It was a touching moment.... I never thought this day would happen. I won't have to worry about putting gas in my car, I won't have to worry about paying my mortgage, you know. If I help him [Obama], he's gonna help me.[36]

This is incredible. This woman, like millions of Obama supporters, believed that her candidate was going to solve all of her problems. What's more, she had no concern about who would be footing the bill. That, ladies and gentlemen, is the liberal politicians' promise. You scratch my back and I'll scratch yours. What could be worse than politicians peddling this political snake oil? The fact that *it works*.

The tea parties stand against the moral sphere of the Left: They reject the entitlement ethic and the morality of mediocrity, which holds that the underprivileged are also incompetent. It is not a movement of the rich defending their turf, but of the poor, the middle class, the upper class—Americans, defending the right to succeed and the right to fail and try again. Government policies that give handouts without strings attached don't respect the intellect and free will of individuals.

Common Sense over Regulation

The failures of government from Enron to Madoff to the financial crisis are hardly controlled experiments where lack of regulation can be pinpointed as the culprit. The only consistency in these cases is human nature. We are presented with the false dichotomy of more regulation or more mischief. It never occurs to many commentators and politicians that stealing money is already illegal. The private sector actually caught Madoff first, the SEC just happened to ignore it.[37] Why? Because the private sector tipster knew Madoff's earnings were impossible, and the SEC was in the business of following procedure, not common sense.

Basing laws on sound political principles informed by a realistic view of human nature will do far more than creating another commission or another czar.

The tea parties were a referendum for common sense. Why? "No job? No credit? No problem!" mortgages and government incentivized failures like Freddie and Fannie all came to roost at once. Taxpayers were left watching the mess unfold before them, thinking, "hey I don't quite understand GSEs and mortgage-backed derivatives, but I know that I didn't buy this house until I had enough money and I don't drive a late model car." The nuances of the financial terms and the (intentionally) convoluted policy jargon spewing from the talking heads and career politicians is difficult to understand, but Americans know in their gut when things just don't add up. Here's what anyone can understand: You can't spend money you don't have; you shouldn't encourage bad behavior; and it isn't right to take from responsible people to bail out irresponsible people, companies, or government agencies.

Rejection of the Mediocrity Ethic

A fundamental issue between the conservative/libertarian and liberal worldview is that of opportunity. Americans are all guaranteed the equal opportunity to live life as they so choose, to apply for a license, to apply to college, to apply for a job. One has a right to purchase stock, the right to get rich and the right to fail. It is the point of action of doing these things—not the actions' results—that is protected for all. This respects the liberty and free will of every human being and the necessary reality that no two decisions made by two different people in two unique circumstances can be expected, let alone enforced, to turn out the same. It is here where liberals get it wrong. They confuse equal opportunity with equal results. This perverted philosophy is the basis for a host of bad laws including, but not limited to, affirmative action and job quotas. The necessary result of these policies is the mediocritization of America. Thus it is not dramatic or right wing to call these policies communist in their nature and fascist in their enforcement. A central part of the tea parties was a rejection of this mediocrity ethic. The mediocrity ethic is an incidental if not intentional tenant of those on the Left.

The Left's obsession with equality is ultimately an obsession with a homogenized culture and an ethic of indifference. If we are all the same, there can be no discrimination or inequality. But if we are all the same, there can be no appreciation of the degrees of difference that reflect the importance of free thought and free action. The Left anticipates a dystopia where freedom is a dirty word.

The Declaration of Independence states that all men are created equal. It does not say that all men are created equally. This means that individuals must discover their talents, develop their skills, and add productively to their society. It means that individual responsibility matters. All people are capable of individual responsibility. We are all equal in that capability. But to say that people were created equally is to replace individual responsibility with social responsibility. Instead of individuals taking responsibility for their lives, the state has that responsibility. Instead of individual innovation—whether the scientist who makes a groundbreaking discovery or the musician who creates an original album—the state will decide what is valuable and what is not. If all men are created equally, it must be possible to assign values for ensuring that no one individual has more than any other. Innovation is impossible if everyone values things equally precisely because there is no incentive to create something new. A plasma television would cost the same as a black-and-white portable. And everyone would be measured by a prefabricated blueprint for life. The American Founders had it in their blood to know that such a world was the endpoint of tyranny.

In a world of absolute equality, the natural result is homogeneity. Diversity is impossible because individuals will fail to recognize difference and thus fail to discern the value of free choice. Without free choice we lose our sense of priorities and our sense of self.

This is fairly intuitive to Americans. As we all learned very early on, be it in gym class or at the spelling bee, we are not all equal at all things, nor should we be. I will never be a professional football player, a math genius, or a matador. For the government to set the standard of acceptance for anyone's life—be it the food we eat or the wages we earn—is fundamentally wrong. The entitlement and equality mentality of the Left dulls the human spirit. It is an impractical, unsustainable form of tyranny that removes the spice of life, that edge to work hard, to do your best, and to take pride in your accomplishments.

The Counterrevolution: From Theory to Practice

The tea parties represent an instinctive philosophical backlash on the part of the American people. The movement is both a backlash to radical ideas, policies, and tactics, and an assertion of positive natural rights. These rights are guaranteed to us as individuals with intellect and free will, as enshrined in our Constitution. We must not, however, be so short-sighted as to simply assert natural rights without ensuring their long-term protection.

To reject policies that inhibit individual liberty is crucial. While absolutely necessary, it is not sufficient, however, to merely hold the line on policy battles. In other words, we know what we believe; now we have to make the political reality reflect our philosophical reality. We must keep the momentum going beyond the rallies and protests to make real, positive steps toward getting our nation and its leaders back on track.

CHAPTER 10

RULES FOR COUNTERRADICALS

When bad men combine, the good must associate; else they will fall one by one, an unpitied sacrifice in a contemptible struggle.

—Edmund Burke, *Thoughts on the Causes of the Present Discontents,* 1770

There is no question the tea party movement and the rallies and town hall protests that followed have made a significant impact on recent history and the public policy debate. It reached out and spoke to millions of Americans, many of whom never before participated in rallies or the political process in general. It revived interest in our nation's founding principles—including individual liberty, small government, personal responsibility, and fiscal conservatism—and brought them back into the mainstream political dialogue. And it has been a wake-up call to politicians on the local, state, and federal level. They've seen the power of an informed, driven citizenry and have begun to grasp the consequences of ignoring it.

Tea parties can be directly linked to the fact that they've brought fiscal responsibility to the forefront of not only the minds of the taxpayers and media but politicians, as well. Blue Dog Democrats and Democrats in historically GOP states and districts, concerned about losing their seats in 2010, began to oppose both health care plans that increase the deficit and cap-and-trade proposals.[1]

In January of 2009, an ABC/Washington Post poll asked respondents what they thought was more important: increasing federal spending to help the economy, regardless of an increase in the federal deficit, or avoiding deficit spending even if it were at the expense of economic stimulation. Fifty-one percent of respondents preferred increased spending, 44 percent indicated it should be avoided, and 4 percent indicated that they were not sure. Just six months later, the trend reversed drastically, with 40 percent favoring increased spending, 55 percent opposing it, and 5 percent unsure. By July, the disparity increased, with 7 percent still unsure, but a mere 35 percent in favor of alleged stimulus spending, and a whopping 58 percent opposed.[2]

By August of 2009, general job approval of Congress was at 31 percent, with 62 percent disapproving and 6 percent of respondents citing "no opinion."[3] At the same time, President Obama began seeing declining job approval ratings of 50 percent, down from his 67 percent January 2009 rating, right between predecessor George W. Bush's first-term August rating of 56 percent and Bill Clinton's August 1993 rating of 44 percent.[4] By September 1, 2009, that number slipped to 45 percent.[5]

In August, Rasmussen Reports came out with the following encouraging numbers:[6]

- Seventy percent of likely voters favor a government that offers fewer services and imposes lower taxes over one that provides more services with higher taxes, the highest level measured in nearly three years.
- Only 19 percent of likely voters prefer a government that provides more services in exchange for higher taxes, the lowest level in over two years. This marks the first time the percentage of voters who prefer this type of government has fallen below 20 percent.
- Fifty-three percent of Americans opposed congressional attempts at a health care overhaul. Support at the time of this writing was at 44 percent, down from 50 percent only two months prior.

What's more, a majority (55 percent) of Americans began to become more concerned about the effect health care legislation would have on the deficit than its chances of passing.[7]

According to an ABC/Washington Post poll, in March 2009 (just weeks before the tea parties) the majority of Americans (52 percent) approved of how President Obama was handling the budget deficit. Only 43 percent of individuals disapproved, with 7 percent unsure. By August 2009, those numbers had reversed with only 41 percent approving, 5 percent unsure, and 53 percent disapproving of his handling of the federal deficit. The same poll revealed that Americans' support for his handling of health care sat at 49 percent.[8]

Tangible policy victories ranged from the likely defeat of the public option in the health care debate to the disabling of the Orwellian flag@whitehouse.gov.[9]

What does this really mean? It means that the tea party protestors, the counterradicals, can and will win in the public policy arena and the court of public opinion on the strength of their ideas.

We cannot, however, stop and sit on our laurels, congratulating ourselves for a job well done. We must continue to keep politicians in check through a variety of means to correct the drastic path our country has gone down and minimize the chances of it happening again.

The 9/12 Taxpayer March

On September 12, 2009, hundreds of thousands of Americans took to the streets in front of the United States Capitol for a taxpayer march on Washington. Organized by FreedomWorks, a broad coalition of citizens descended on the Capitol for a day to make their voices heard. As Brendan Steinhauser of FreedomWorks remarked to me, "people took to the streets because they had shut down the Capitol switchboard and district office phone lines, and so protest was the only way they could speak their minds."

I had the pleasure and honor of speaking at the beginning of the march. What I saw was families, high school kids, seniors and veterans—the faces of the tea party movement—coming together as a unified voice. People chartered buses from every state in the union.

I had never seen so many people in one place. It was absolutely incredible to see and to be a part of.

Total numbers, as with any rally, are hard to come by. Given the contentious numbers surrounding the Million Man March, police in the various agencies with jurisdiction in D.C. are reluctant to go on the record. As Joe Markman pens in the *LA Times*:

> Confusion and anger over crowd estimates are as much a part of Washington as its marble monuments. Organizers of the Million Man March in 1995 threatened to sue the National Park Service over its crowd estimate of 400,000, when their own number was 1.5 million to 2 million.[10]

Although even MSNBC conceded tens of thousands of attendees, the media coverage was more disappointing than expected. As could be expected, many media reports couched it as a racist gathering of extremists.

Various time-lapse traffic cameras, photographs of the mall, and public transportation records of the three-million-person crowd at the recent Obama inauguration put the 9/12 march numbers anywhere from half a million to two million participants.

Regardless of the exact numbers, the march was an unqualified success, and it will go down in history as the largest limited government march in history.

Arguing from an Imperfect Status Quo

One of the challenges in this debate, much like debates over health care or school reform, is that free-market folks find themselves, intentionally or otherwise, defending an imperfect status quo. A pertinent example is the so-called free-market in the U.S. Jonathan Hoenig, a hedge fund manager, dispels the myth of the unregulated hedge fund:

> A hedge fund is simply a pool of money funded by profit-seeking investors and managed by a professional money manager, not unlike a mutual fund. While most people assume that hedge funds make

leveraged bets on risky financial esoterica, the truth is a hedge fund is a legal structure, not an investment technique. Some trade frequently and use leverage, others simply buy and hold stocks for months or years at a time.

So while the media routinely characterize hedge funds as "risky" or "highly leveraged," the reality is hedge fund strategies, just like mutual fund strategies, run the gamut from the ultra-conservative to the highly volatile. What matters are the strategies, positions and discipline that the manager uses to maximize the money.

Lawmakers love to demonize hedge funds as unregulated bandits, running rampant through the capital markets and creating havoc at every turn, a patently untrue perception that fuels the conspiracy theorists who claim that a secret cabal of investors is always behind the scenes pulling the markets' strings.

The fact is that hedge funds are already exceedingly regulated. SEC rules limit those who may invest to wealthy investors and limits the number of customers any one fund can serve. And while mutual funds and brokers spend hundreds of millions of dollars a year on advertising, hedge funds aren't allowed to promote or publicly solicit business in any fashion. Can you think of any other industry that is subject to such oppressive constraints? Yes, hedge funds are exclusive and elitist, not by choice, however, but by government edict.[11]

In reality, we operate in a mixed economy where the financial sector is *heavily* regulated. Holding up its failures as Exhibit A in the case against free-market capitalism is both disingenuous and fundamentally a nonstarter in any economic or political conversation. Most of these exhibits are actually proof of the failure of heavy-handed regulation.

Unfortunately myths and half-truths abound in the media coverage of the financial sector and beyond. Thus, the case must be made not merely for denying the Left's policy goals, but for presenting better solutions to the underlying problems they claim to address. When possible, with issues from health care to the financial sector where the status quo is not ideal, the case must be made crystal clear that reform is necessary, and free markets and policies that empower individuals, not bureaucrats, are more often than not a step in the right direction.

Honing the Message

There is a lesson for us in the rejection of the empty rhetoric of hope and change. A candidate, a party, or an organization must present positive options—not just reject opposition proposals or promote change for change's sake. These kinds of rallying cries may work in the short term to win an election, but it won't take long for people to realize they've been shortchanged. Likewise, "Just say no" rhetoric must be rejected as a useless mantra that only serves to give ammunition to the other side ready to offer a solution.

Another issue is the perceived lack of empathy. Sign after sign at tea party protests read "Your mortgage is not my problem." Most people, on both sides of the fence, probably agree with the sentiment, particularly those who rent because they acknowledge that they cannot afford to own, didn't take out mortgages and home equity lines of credit to buy late model cars, flat screen TVs, and the like. Santelli's rant was spurred by the prospect of the U.S. government buying up bad mortgages—a prospect suggested foolishly by John McCain during a presidential debate in 2008—and that may have been one more reason he lost the election.

The sentiment that rewarding bad behavior is not only crazy but morally wrong is often written off as callous, selfish, and greedy. In fact, many Americans do want to help, and they do. It is the profit motive and America's prosperity that has allowed it to be the most generous, charitable country and people in the history of mankind. The UN's World Food program, like the UN itself, is propped up by the United States and a handful of Western nations.[12] Individual giving is quite generous, as well. In 2008, despite an economic downturn, Americans gave over $300 billion to charity—that's 2.2 percent of GDP.[13] What's more, conservatives give more than liberals across economic lines.[14] What Americans truly resent is being forced to help not the needy, not the helpless, but those who won't help themselves or want to help themselves to a subsidized, excessive lifestyle. What Americans don't want to do is run their charitable dollars, taken by force, through the inefficient, lecherous pipeline of the federal government.[15]

The issue here comes down to a fundamental difference in world-views. Liberals believe that government not only should allocate charitable dollars but that government is best suited to do this. Plus, they argue, it creates jobs in the process. Think of all the paper-pushers necessary to administer a community grant.

Rather than arguing against altruism in its own right and for the legal and philosophical groundings of ethical egoism, we must argue first for the practical sustainability of such a system, and then emphasize our nation's grounding in conservative philosophy and natural law, pointing to their eternal wisdom. Subtle differences in messaging go a long way. A shift from "I don't want to pay my neighbor's mortgage" to "I've lived within my means and cannot and should not subsidize someone who has not" goes a long way. This is not to say that we should make a concession on the point that Norm in Chicago made, that people should be able to work hard and enjoy the fruits of their labor.

These are not contradictory ideas. Showcasing a responsible home-owner or an overregulated, overtaxed small business owner shows that a system where success is punished is unsustainable and morally wrong. One may say that I am conceding the point that the wealthy should be taxed—quite the contrary. The point is that not only is it morally reprehensible to punish prudence at the level of a responsible home-owner, it is equally wrong and impractical to punish success at the level of the multimillionaire. If you successfully make the argument that average, prudent taxpayers should subsidize the foolish few, then defense of wildly successful wealth necessarily follows.

Why be financially responsible unless there is a chance of having increased financial stability down the road if not for you, then for your children and their children? To rile up the lower and middle class against "those wealthy few" can quickly become an impotent argument if we make the case that those wealthy few aren't a distant, selfish minority, but the cream of the crop, what we could all be some day if we work hard, and save up. The other side encourages the idea that to be responsible is foolish and to succeed is suicide.

This is what I referred to as the mediocrity ethic. Everything from the tax code to welfare stipulations actually encourages bad behavior. As Sean Masaki Flynn of Forbes.com illustrates, examples abound in

our everyday lives. Take health care, where the government attempts to
insert itself on everything from coverage specifics to pricing. Doctors
often spend little time with patients, but a lot of time dolling out test
requests. As Flynn writes:

> It's because Medicare and Medicaid set relatively high reimbursement
> rates for diagnostic tests but relatively low reimbursement rates for time
> spent talking with patients . . .
>
> . . . This incentive scheme also stymies the practice of preventative
> medicine. . . .
>
> . . . Instead, the government only pays doctors to treat patients after
> they have fallen ill.[16]

Of course, the Left will never admit that taxes and government policy
drive behavior unless the tax is a so-called sin tax meant to discourage
smoking, drinking, or gambling (or eating chocolate or drinking soda).
Thus we must frame the argument as more than a mere rejection of big
government that doesn't work but a rejection of a big government that
is morally reprehensible, disrespectful to the individual liberty of every
citizen, and out of line with the founding principles of our nation.

Every aspect of public policy must be couched in terms of how it
affects individual liberty and thus citizens. For example, why should the
chocolate eater or soda drinker be punished? And who do higher taxes
on chocolate hurt more? The wealthy, middle class, or the poor kid with
a paper route who wants a treat? Who is the government to decide that
chocolate is bad for you or that any luxury that should be taxed at a
higher rate? Policy cannot be discussed merely in terms of being unfair
or impractical in principle. It must be brought to the individual level:
This tax increase hurts the working class—you and your neighbor. Lack
of school choice isn't just principally unfair and bad for society; it hurts
you and *your kids*.

Mastering the Art of Rallies

Protesting has long been seen as antithetical to libertarianism and conservatism. Most of us would rather engage in a substantive discussion
with a neighbor or read or author an insightful article or Op-Ed.

Or we would rather spend our time on our jobs or with our families and friends. People protesting are just spinning their wheels. You can't fight city hall, right? Besides, who has the time? Somebody has to work to pay the bills and to pay taxpayer-funded liberal protestors.

The Left mastered long ago the art of protesting as a way to get attention for an issue and pressure elected officials. Vietnam War protests are a great example. Like the original Boston Tea Party, the protests events are not ends in themselves. The events are, however, quite useful, as we've seen from the tangible successes of the movement. They draw attention from the media and with the solidarity of a movement, they apply necessary pressure on the professional politicians in state capitals across the country and in Washington. For too long, the Right has been impotent in this field.

Fortunately, some effective groups have formed to address this. A handful of grassroots organizations exist with the sole mission of supporting grassroots activists with rallies, public relations, logistics, letter writing, and call campaigns to their elected officials, and more. Not until the tea parties, however, has a nationwide series of protests of the size and scope of the tea parties ever been accomplished. The amazing thing was that it was a pure grassroots effort, many times organized by citizens who had never protested before nor belonged to a political-type organization or group. Once the ball got moving, some grassroots groups did help facilitate the protests, but even then, the power of the protests came from local, citizen organizers.

We must resist the temptation of many on the Left to succumb to rallies as ends in and of themselves. They are a means for accomplishing public policy change. Thus any rally, march, or protest should be held to the following three crucial, though not exhaustive, conditions: publicity, solidarity, and pressure.

Publicity

Publicity is a key component of any successful movement. If 1,000 angry taxpayers yell in the plaza and no video cameras are there to hear it, did they make a noise? No. The point behind gathering hundreds or thousands of people is to gain publicity, which shows solidarity of some constituency behind an issue, which in turn results in pressure on elected officials. It is often difficult to break through well-documented media bias when it comes to coverage of these ideas. However, if the event is big enough, the media will cover it, if only to marginalize it. Thus, care should be taken to ensure you get boots on the ground and media attention by providing plenty of advance notice and planning. The more signs, the bigger the stage, the bigger the speakers' names, the better. Involve a giant pig to symbolize pork, show what a trillion dollars looks like with a trillion dollars worth of Monopoly money—get your point across loud and clear in a way that attracts numbers and attention.

Solidarity

Solidarity sounds like touchy-feely pointless nonsense to the hardened-heart fact-based reader. It is, however, very important, because for every person who was able to take a lunch break or time off to come out to a tea party, there were a dozen or more at home who could not make it, or did not feel as though their frustration was justified or widely felt. Think of the lone conservative whose neighbors all sport signs carrying the empty message of hope and change. Or my father behind enemy lines in Massachusetts. Getting an e-mail or Facebook message showing there are thousands of people who are on the same page as you regarding the nonsense coming out of Washington can turn thousands upon thousands of people from sympathetic sideliners to players on the front lines. Seeing thousands of people marching on television or folks from all walks of life giving an interview about why they went to a march or protest can give people at home the inspiration they need to get involved in one way or another—through letter writing, calling their elected officials, and of course, getting out and voting.

Pressure

Pressure is necessary because most politicians, with precious few exceptions, are in the business of getting reelected. To do that, they need votes. It is a brilliant market mechanism that the founders enshrined in the Constitution. How do you make sure that those who govern do so for the people? Make their jobs contingent on the will of the people. Not just every two or four years, but all the time. When a politician turns on the TV or picks up the newspaper to see hundreds or thousands of voters protesting policies in his district, in his state, that is a powerful message.

Only when these three components come together can we effectively harness this strategy to bring about change the rest of us can believe in.

Utilizing Coalitions

Two groups that act as facilitators of political activism include Americans for Prosperity and FreedomWorks. These groups often come under fire from the Left for being Astroturf, even though their constituency wouldn't be convinced to show up at a rally for a few bucks. Phil Kerpen, Americans for Prosperity's policy director, claims "Organizations like Americans for Prosperity give people an opportunity to come together and can help with logistics of permitting, and AV equipment, and such. We can give people some basic information about the issues, which we encourage them to verify for themselves. But they are real people and they show up to events to make their voices heard."[17]

In practice, these groups don't give marching orders to push a radical partisan agenda. In sharp contrast to both the principles and practices of the Left's activism, they reject a top-down model. Instead, they act as catalysts for grassroots activists, connecting far-flung concerned citizens throughout the country through online networks. They give activists the information and tools they need to be effective.

Brendan Steinhauser says, "FreedomWorks provides the grassroots training, ideas, strategies, and tactics that local activists use to become better advocates for their cause. Top-down models will never be as successful as bottom-up models. We focus on ways to empower local grassroots leaders with the tools that they can use to organize their own communities and network with other groups to build coalitions that fight for lower taxes, less government, and more freedom."

These organizations' philosophies of facilitation versus a command-and-control approach ring true with our experience planning rallies. In the case of Chicago, the failure of a top-down model is how the planning landed in my lap. I was given complete control of an event with no location, no A/V equipment—nothing. FreedomWorks helped secure insurance for the permit no questions asked, no strings attached. I had complete control over the agenda, speakers, and planning for the event. At a moment's notice, Americans for Prosperity—Illinois agreed to send a speaker, as did the state think tank, the Illinois Policy Institute. All of these organizations pitched in to make the event a success, without any demands on content or messaging or branding of the event.

The coalition building and coordination of this movement can serve as a model for future policy battles down the road.

Coordination not Competition

In 1998, Hillary Clinton dubbed the center-right movement the "vast right-wing conspiracy." In a September 2009 MSNBC interview, the phrase was revived as her husband Bill Clinton used it to describe widespread opposition to President Obama.[18] The dozens of groups and hundreds of think tanks that make up this alleged network are vast, but hardly coordinated enough to warrant the label "conspiracy." There is always room for better coordination. One thing the tea parties brought to light was how petty turf battles can really suck the wind out of an otherwise powerful movement. Like any office scenario within an organization, groups working together, even toward a common goal, hit friction of varying degrees. Personalities get in the way of otherwise easily achieved goals. These mentalities must be avoided and rejected whenever they rear up. Coordination among groups—as seen in the tea parties—is a great example of the power of driven, like-minded people working toward a unified goal.

At the very outset of the tea party movement, individuals began asserting themselves as "official organizers" setting up *the* official web sites and organizations for the tea parties. The consequences of this type of thinking only hinder the movement, thus this mentality must be rejected at every turn. If there is a niche, a real market for something new to be done, by all means do it.

Reinventing the wheel and attempting top-down control of a grassroots movement are unproductive and against the very principles of a movement that values individual liberty and personal responsibility.

Promoting Principles over Personalities

There's no shortage of good reasons to shy away from tapping politicians as speakers or as leaders of the tea party movement. Politicians, even if you found the purest of the pure, are polarizing figures. We know that people typically vote the way they did in their first election. When you choose a politician as a lead figure, you run the risk of instantly alienating about 50 percent of your audience. Take the global warming movement. Al Gore is ostensibly the head of the movement, the lead alarmist, crying out for drastic change. As his message has gotten to more people, however, the issue has gone from an obscure, scientific theory to a deeply polarizing issue that both sides argue with religious fervor. Besides the junk science and disregard for sound economics,[19] the global warming camp's critical flaw, and likely downfall, is ironically linked to its biggest, most well-known proponent: Al Gore. Boring old Al Gore. Al Gore, the *Democrat*. Al Gore, the guy who "invented the Internet" is now inventing stories about floods and famine.

The last thing a genuine, philosophically pure movement like that of the tea party needs is to be usurped by a polarizing political figure. On an e-mail exchange I was copied on between some young conservative journalists, it was suggested that Sarah Palin would be a natural spokesperson for the movement. I almost fell out of my chair. It had been days since she announced that she would not only opt out of running for reelection as governor of Alaska, but would soon step down from office all together. Sarah Palin has her merits—both personal and political. But why the tea party movement? The movement is not about personalities but about principles. That said, the Sarah Palin temptation is understandable. Why not have a young up and comer or a conservative rock star speak for or even lead a movement? Someone without a bad past, someone who is a good speaker and sticks to his or her guns! Two words: Mark Sanford.

At the 2008 Conservative Political Action Conference where I began my foray into tea party rabble rousing, South Carolina Governor Mark Sanford gave a long, heartfelt speech on constitutionalism and returning to our nation's founding principles in which he quoted extensively from the Constitution itself—without notes. It was hard to leave that room not thinking *this* man should be president. This man can be what the

GOP needs to regain the trust of the United States. Within months of the event, though, it was revealed that Gov. Sanford had been engaging in a foreign affair of the extramartial type.[20] Imagine if this man had become the face of the GOP in 2012, proudly proclaiming a new era of fiscal responsibility? The repercussions for not only the GOP but for the ideals Sanford espoused would have been devastating.

It behooves the counterradical *not* to put all of his eggs in one basket, not to hitch a movement's wagon to the brightest rising star. Obama and Palin were turned into icons to rally their respective bases. This can be effective in the short-term, but it's a cheap trick. When one casts a mere human as the personification of all one believes, you subject yourself to inevitable disappointment and your movement to certain demise.

Counterradicals must reject the hero-worshipping of politicians and instead embrace the *ideals* for which they stand, embracing politicians as necessary evils—imperfect vehicles for these ideals, constantly insisting on consistency and honesty from them not only in words but action. Accentuating the ideas, not the persons, ensures that they stray minimally from the path we've set them to walk upon, and it inoculates the movement from which they are born against taking the heat for their every misstep.

A general paradigm shift in how we view politicians in our country would be helpful. We need to stop treating elected officials like rock stars for photo ops and more like employees who need to be managed with a heavy hand. And sometimes that hand needs to be unforgiving. As employees we receive annual performance reviews and merit increases. Most politicians are up for election every four years or longer. The only feedback they get other than at election time is through political contributions—with most of the monies coming from wealthy self-interested groups or corporations. The only way we, the people, have to influence them is by standing up and speaking out.

Keeping Your Cool in a Fiery Debate

It goes without saying that civil conduct is a prerequisite for any town hall protest or tea party rally. Passions often flare on these heated topics, so a reminder is in order.

More often than not, as was seen in recent town hall meetings, tempers flare on the other side—often culminating in outright yelling and violence. This is not surprising as the Left is often in the position of defending a job or handout that really shouldn't exist. They often don't think through the real consequences of their policies, as they believe their very actions as progressives are noble in and of themselves. They often do not and cannot judge policy on its true merits. Confronting this is quite frustrating, but keeping it civil is the key to success. Record everything, take pictures. A level-headed constituent juxtaposed with a shrieking politician backed into a proverbial corner or union thugs pushing senior citizens around will do wonders for the movement on YouTube.

Using Social Networking

While it seems goofy and foreign to many readers and participants in this movement, the power of social networking cannot be underestimated. Only with tools like Twitter, Facebook, and e-mail were the tea parties as wildly successful as they were.

There simply is no better way to get information to more people more efficiently than through these tools on the Internet. Conservatives already dominate Twitter, a burgeoning microblogging utility.[21] I had 40- and 50-year olds telling me that they barely navigated e-mail but made themselves open Facebook accounts to be plugged into the tea parties. Counterradicals of every age group must embrace this technology and make it their own.

Don't take my word for it. Eric Qualman is author of the book *Socialnomics: How Social Media Transforms the Way We Live and Do Business* (Wiley, 2009). Qualman makes the case for why businesses should adapt social networking for marketing and advertising, but the case rings true, if not truer, for political movements. Take these stats he features:

- By 2010 Gen Y will outnumber baby boomers; 96 percent of them have joined a social network.[22]
- One out of eight couples married in the United States last year met via social media.[23]
- Years to reach 50 million users: radio (38 years), TV (13 years), Internet (4 years), iPod (3 years). Facebook added 100 million

users in less than 9 months.[24] iPhone applications hit 1 billion in 9 months.[25]

- The fastest growing segment on Facebook is 55- to 65-year-old females.[26]
- The second largest search engine in the world is YouTube.[27]

Looking beyond the Rallies

Action cannot stop at rallies, because (like small children) politicians have a short attention span. You can't count on the media to pretend to cover rallies fairly for long, if at all. Remember, too, that rallies are not ends in themselves, but means of asserting voice with a specific purpose: publicity, solidarity, and pressure in the name of tangible results. There are, of course, other effective means of influencing politicians and outcomes.

Fortunately, the American Founders didn't know that cable news and Twitter were in the stars, and they carved out the right to directly, actively contact, educate, and lobby Congress:

- Call (or even visit) your elected officials. A few calls to a district office from constituents on a specific issue can easily push an elected official over the fence one way or another.
- Write letters to the editor. You can help combat media bias and the other side of things often not reported by writing concise responses to even the most outrageously liberal columns and Op-Eds.
- Vote, as Chicago's Richard J. Daley said, "early and often." Don't just yell at the TV on Sunday mornings and go to a tea party—get out there and help the right candidates and get to the voting booth.
- Join a grassroots group that facilitates things like tea parties and calling and letter writing campaigns.
- Contribute to organizations that educate and lobby Congress on the issues important to you.

Taking Consistent, Principled Action

Keep politicians accountable once they are in power. Many on the right apologized for the Bush administration's ventures into big government.

One think tank even actively defended TARP. Journalism's credibility has deteriorated. Whether because of cost-cutting or liberal bias, the media seems to devote more time to giving free publicity than to investigative reporting (and when journalists do investigate it's often of a salacious nature, preferably targeting conservative politicians—liberals give sexual conduct a free pass unless the practitioner is Republican). So, too, will the conservative movement lose credibility if the think tanks and the grassroots base aren't consistent and principled, demanding the same from the politicians in power—both those they voted for and those they did not.

Maintaining Accountability and Transparency

We must demand accountability from politicians. The counterradical must reject vague platitudes of tough legislative battles and reaching across the aisle and instead demand results. What taxes were cut, what bad legislation was killed, what good legislation passed. We are electing these people to go to bat for us; the score at the end of the game matters.

Demand transparency as well. Simply demanding that public records be public is a phenomenally important step in demanding good, accountable government. This information—save top secret military information—can and must be public, particularly online where it is easy to access and review. Just as a corporate board or investors get financial reports at corporations and nonprofits, so, too, should tax-payers see what they are investing in so that they may make the most informed decisions.

Earmarks, wasteful government spending, and a lack of transparency and oversight in government are the tools through which the Left has won. They are the shadows and corners in which tyrants thrive. It is absolutely amazing what good things transparency can do, and how hard those on the Left fight it at every turn.

Why do politicians oppose transparency? They will often cite that it is too costly. This is a favorite trick of unions regarding the transparency of where member dues are funneled.

For one, the Left fears transparency could result in killing its policy proposals. President Obama stated that in order to pass universal health care, it had to happen quickly. This is because when legislation that is overly complex pops up, people start to ask questions. The more people look at it, the less they like it. Politicians are often so quick to pass legislation that they don't even read the bills they are voting for. This is criminal. President Obama campaigned on the promise of not signing any nonemergent bill into law without having it posted on the Internet for at least five days of public review. Once in office, he broke this pledge as well as the pledge to have health care reform debated openly on CSPAN.[28]

Second, the Left fears that taxpayers will see waste, fraud, and abuse. In Illinois, Commissioner Tony Peraica, a constant champion of transparency and reform, posted all Cook County employee salaries online, searchable by name and salary range.[29] Believe it or not, there are five people making over $400,000 dollars from taxpayers. What good does this do? For one, it is the right thing to do. These people are getting paid by the public, thus their salaries and benefits should be public knowledge. The citizens are the shareholders and board of directors. There are wider benefits to transparency as the *Chicago Sun-Times'* Stephen Warmbir notes. Employees at the state and local level know exactly how little some of their colleagues work and exactly what kind of funny business they may be up to:

> Those hard-working county employees see what goes on, see what those rascals get paid, and sometimes, they pick up the phone. . . .
> . . . Those are the folks who help start federal investigations, help put stories in the newspaper, and once in a great while, actually help make a difference.[30]

Taking It to the States

The tea parties and similar nationally publicized rallies were mostly focused on the federal government, and with good reason. Sometimes, taking on issues in a state seems as daunting as taking on the federal government. Real, high-profile victories were made at the federal level following the tea parties. However, to enact and sustain real change, pressure needs to be kept at state and local levels of government. As the federal government expands in size and scope, it increasingly affects the everyday lives of citizens throughout the country.

The Right is local in spirit but regretfully often top-down in practice. Conservatives and libertarians embrace individualism—personal responsibility and independent thinking and action, but often overly emphasize a powerful presidency (Reagan, Bush). Too often we look to journalists and talking heads inside the Beltway as leaders, not local businessmen and local and state elected officials closer to real America. Liberals are the opposite. They preach a top-down approach of governance but have mastered local, person-by-person organizing. The counterradical must think locally in both theory and practice. While the Beltway issues are attention grabbers, the local issues affect everyone every day.

One of the key factors in the tea parties' success was local organization. At the end of the day, the rallies happened on the ground city-by-city, town-by-town, and decisions had to be made at that level. Even the command-and-control types recognized this in the days leading up to the tax day tea parties. In the same sense, votes happen person-by-person, booth-by-booth—*not* from Beltway dinners and panels, not from a command-and-control state- or nation-wide organization.

In addition to the numerous grassroots facilitators out there, each and every state is home to a center-right think tank that engages in public policy analysis and, in many cases, activism. To find the free-market, state-based think tank in your state, visit the State Policy Network at spn.org.

No state is too difficult to make headway. Take Illinois, ranked fairly high by most metrics[31] in corruption, not to mention the long-standing "Crook County" moniker for Chicago's Cook County. The recent political nonsense and criminal activity surrounding disgraced Gov. Rod Blagojevich[32] and his appointment of Roland Burris to Barack Obama's Senate seat,[33] made the chance for real reform or transparency of any kind seems daunting to say the least.

Believe it or not, Illinois is home to a very active and very effective free-market think tank: the Illinois Policy Institute (IPI). IPI's CEO John Tillman spoke at the Chicago tax day tea party. As he explains:

> Even though Illinois is largely known for its political scandals and machine politics, it's also a place where great progress is being made for liberty. The tea party protests are one element of that progress. At the tea party event in Chicago, I spoke with citizens from a wide

range of backgrounds who wanted to stand up against mounting state spending and debt, rising taxes, and unaccountable government both at the state and federal level. What's clear is they understand how policy changes lives for better or worse. Tea party participants—Republicans, Democrats, Independents, Libertarians, Greens—came by the thousands to events throughout the country to demand accountability from their representatives in government. They're making a real difference.

Tillman and his staff are making a difference in Illinois. Like other state-focused think tanks, IPI reviews, critiques, and proposes public policy. In addition to that, it has instituted a Liberty Leaders program to actively engage its membership—concerned citizens of Illinois.

The program seeks to create a network of spokespeople for liberty by providing citizens with knowledge of free-market policies and the tools to get them turned into law. The new program has already brought about tangible victories for Illinois. Nancy Thorner of Lake Bluff was tapped to publish numerous letters to the editor with proposals on solving Illinois's budget problems. Thorner stated, "The Institute is not only getting information on health care and tax policy to me and other Liberty Leaders, but also the politicians, and that's what really counts." Through participation in the tax day tea party protests and town hall meetings, IPI played a major role in stopping a proposed statewide tax increase in the 2009 regular session of the General Assembly. "The April 15 tea parties were absolutely essential to stopping a massive income tax increase in Illinois," said IPI Executive Vice President Kristina Rasmussen. "At the beginning of 2009, almost all of the political players in Springfield expected a tax increase to pass. Just a month and a half after the tax day tea parties, the income tax hike failed in the Illinois House, with many Democrats joining all Republicans in voting no. Thanks to the momentum created by Liberty Leaders in tea parties and town hall meetings, the tax hike has yet to pass."

The activism on the local level is equally impressive. Brian Costin runs the Schaumburg Freedom Coalition in Schaumburg, Illinois, a suburb of Chicago. Says Costin:

Starting the Schaumburg Freedom Coalition was a leap of faith. Coming from Cook "Crook" County I didn't know if I could compete with the entrenched political machine and achieve wins for good governance and fiscal responsibility. What I realized is that it doesn't take a lot of money to have a positive effect on my community. In the first year of our organization I was able to achieve major victories in increasing government transparency and eliminating red light cameras from our community.

What started with one person, one blog, and an idea has grown rapidly to an organization with hundreds of members, a recognized political force in the community, and the start of a robust campaign to lower sales taxes [Schaumburg's 12 percent restaurant tax is the highest in U.S. history] and eliminate corporate welfare.

Sometimes our voices can get lost on the national stage but on the local level the ability to make positive changes for our community is easier. The Schaumburg Freedom Coalition ties in with the broader tea party movement by taking the global issue of fiscal responsibility and tax limitation and acting on it locally. As the saying goes "all politics is local." Organizing and growing grassroot groups from the local level up will give our movement more influence and power to promote fiscal responsibility and low taxes on the state and federal level."[34]

This one-man taxpayer advocacy shop has already made waves in its short existence. Costin and his group have been vocal opponents of red light cameras in the town, criticizing them as mere revenue boosters that may actually endanger drivers.[35] Costin actively pushes for government transparency at the local level, particularly pertaining to the town's convention center boondoggle that has cost taxpayers more than $20 million, with a larger bill to come, all in the name of corporate welfare.[36]

Examples abound from elsewhere in the country. The Sam Adams Alliance seeks to empower individual activists, particularly in the new media realm. The group's annual awards banquet, The Sammies, features and rewards individual freedom fighters. The 2009 Sammies featured awards ranging from bloggers who helped defeat tax hikes to two activists who created original videos educating the public on the state of Virginia's backward liquor laws.

The lesson? Everyday people can make a difference on the state and local levels; they do so every day. The resources are out there for those willing to step up.

The Right Ideals and the Right People

All the ideals and ideas mean nothing if there aren't good people in the movement pushing them and in office upholding them.

What matters is that these *ideals* of the movement remain in the forefront of every politician's mind. Elected officials of every stripe—Democrat, Republican, Libertarian, and Independent—know that millions of Americans are fed up with big spending and reckless government. Many anticipate the 2010 election cycle will see big spending, big-government Democrats and Republicans thrown out on the street. This is good. What this movement has shown is that Americans cannot trust the traditional labels of Democrat and Republican. You can't trust what politicians *say*, so we need to look at what they *do*. When they stray, we need to find them another line of work.

Thus, we must make sure that in addition to getting out there to a tea party and calling your congressmen, you're stumping for the right candidate. That's another challenge we face: good candidates.

Protests and letter and call campaigns should serve as a check on our elected officials—reminders of who they work for and what they were elected to do. The ideal situation is that these tools are used as reminders for politicians when they appear to stray from the path we elected them to take not heavy-handed arm-twisting once they've already gone off the reservation.

Thus it is crucial to make sure the best people possible get into office in the first place. There's no question the GOP has lost the mantle of fiscal responsibility and small government. The brand is tarnished, but not irreversibly so. It may or may not recapture its former standing. The GOP is the most likely breeding ground for the fiscally responsible constitutionalists the tea party movement—and America—craves.

That said, the GOP may or may not play a role in rebuilding America's faith in small government and fiscal responsibility. Retreads and scandal-plagued governors are not the catalysts for change. They largely failed to capitalize on the tea party uprising. To have done so, they needed to speak to the ideals of fiscal responsibility and limited government the nation is crying out for. They need to have clear leaders, not idols, but leaders getting out and selling these ideas in the context of facing current problems. Conservatives and libertarians aren't look-ing for *new* ideals, but new ways of applying founding principles to the challenges our nation faces today and will face in the future.

While no candidate can nor will nor should be all things to all people, the GOP especially must come up with better candidates. While no candidate can be all things to all people, one can get a heck of a lot closer to that ideal than John McCain, for example. We must keep the pressure on politicians in office and make sure the right ones get into office.

The need for good politicians to step up to the plate cannot be under-estimated. Those drawn to politics naturally are often inherently flawed leaders. The movement needs to be conducive to getting philosophi-cally sound and principled candidates in power because that is where the rubber meets the road when it comes to the ideals the liberty movement espouses. This means spreading the wisdom of citizen-politicians and encouraging people to participate in public service as a part of their career.

The tea parties already brought out a number of principled, natural leaders. Remember Megan Barth, the enthusiastic volunteer from Cal-ifornia? As Megan reports, following her impassioned speech at her tax day tea party, she was approached to run for office:

> The tea party movement gave me an outlet to be heard and stand for what I believe in. The principles of limited government, fiscal responsibility, fair taxation, and our Constitution, drew me to the movement. Upon organizing a few rallies and talking to the crowds that gathered, I had many people approach me and encourage me to run for office. I have been inspired to enter into politics, not only as an observer, or an activist, but as a candidate. I intend to run for mayor of my city.

Barth isn't the only example. As Politico.com reported, Tom Cox of Arkansas decided to run for the Senate.[37] "Cox, who plans to run in the Republican primary, is the first leader of the grassroots antitax movement to run for federal office. He is seeking the Senate seat held by Democratic Sen. Blanche Lincoln."

Keith Sipmann of Phoenix, Arizona, also found a political calling as he got involved in the movement. A bank underwriter and father of three, Sipmann describes himself a "concerned patriot":

> I got involved in this grassroots movement because I was concerned as to where this nation was headed. We are on a slippery slope to socialism. I felt that Americans have become too complacent and tolerant of the actions of their government.... The government continued (and still does continue) to spend hand over fist, taking a bigger and bigger slice of our money and our children's and grandchildren's future earnings.
>
> I scoured the Internet using social networking sites and called all like-minded Arizona locals to band together to protest against this government's overspending and lack of financial control. Americans of all political affiliations are getting very tired of the irresponsible behavior of our government's economic policies....
>
> Since the tea party, I have become more involved in the political arena by becoming a precinct committeeman and starting my own organization and blog that is dedicated to educating the American people about the issues and the actions/inactions of our government.

We need more active, concerned patriots like Keith, Tom, and Megan.

In Conclusion

There is only one crucial ingredient to stopping today's radical policies: you. It may sound corny or trite, but if there is one thing this movement has shown, it is that anyone, *anyone*, can step up to the plate and make a difference.

Whether it is helping out with a rally or a letter writing campaign, consistently going to the voting both, or attempting to be one of those names on the ballot—you cannot underestimate the large impact of millions of small contributions to this fight.

It is easy to give into giving up. The political reality of our times can be frustrating. The temptation to throw in the towel and call it a day is real and understandable. The political pendulum will often swing through the election cycles. In the long term, however, we can and will win this fight on the strength of our ideas.

The tea party movement saw hundreds of thousands of Americans get involved in the political process in ways they never have before. This is an incredible thing, but it needs to last beyond rallies and the immediate policy battles of today. This revived enthusiasm for taking an interest in policy that affects our lives and for seizing the reins of our democracy and holding tight must continue so that we may pass those reins on to future generations for the inevitable policy battles to come.

NOTES

Bailout Nation: A Spending Timeline

1. Mark Pittman and Bob Ivry, "Financial Rescue Nears GDP as Pledges Top $12.8 Trillion," Bloomberg.com, www.bloomberg.com/apps/news?pid/20601087&sid/armOzfkwtCA4 (accessed October 2009).

2. Catherine Dodge and Dawn Kopecki, "U.S. Rescue May Reach $23.7 Trillion, Barofsky Says," Bloomberg.com, July 2009, www.bloomberg.com/apps/news?pid=20601087&sid=aY0tX8UysIaM.

3. TreasuryDirect.gov "Total Public Debt," www.treasurydirect.gov/NP/BPD Login?application=np. See also: USDebtClock.com and National Debt Clock, www.brillig.com/debt_clock (accessed October 8, 2009).

4. Institute for Truth in Accounting, "Estimate of Financial Condition," October 30, 2009, http://truthin2008.org/content/?articlesource=439. See also: U.S. Department of the Treasury, "Financial Statements of the United States Government for the Years Ended September 30, 2008, and September 30, 2007," http://fms.treas.gov/fr/08frusg/08stmt.pdf and "2009 Medicare Trustees Report," www.cms.hhs.gov/reportstrustfunds/downloads/tr2009.pdf.

5. Ibid. See also: 2009 Social Security Trustees Report, www.ssa.gov/OACT/TR/2009/.

6. Institute for Truth in Accounting: Our National Debt. www.truthin2008.org/content/?articlesource/432.

7. Jeanne Sahadi, "47% Will Pay No Federal Income Tax," CNNMoney.com, October, 2009, http://money.cnn.com/2009/09/30/pf/taxes/who_pays_taxes/index.htm.

8. Victoria McGrane, "Senate Urged to Raise $12T Debt Cap," Politco.com, September, 2009, www.politico.com/news/stories/0909/26996.htm.

Chapter 1   The Tea Parties

1. Megan McArdle, "Home Sweet Home," *The Atlantic*, http://meganmcardle.theatlantic.com/archives/2009/02/home_sweet_home_5.php.

2. Tyler Cowan, "What to Think of Obama's Housing Plan," *Marginal Revolution*, www.marginalrevolution.com/marginalrevolution/2009/02/what-to-think-of-obamas-housing-plan.html.

3. "Poll: February 18–22, 2009," *New York Times*, February 2009, http://graphics8.nytimes.com/packages/pdf/politics/20090224_poll.pdf.

4. Patrik Jonsson, "Arguing the Size of the Tea Party Protest: In Any Case, Experts See It as Democracy in Action, and That's a Good Thing," *Christian Science Monitor*, April 2009, www.csmonitor.com/2009/0418/p25s03-usgn.html.

5. Jeff Poor, "ACORN, HuffPo Organizing Efforts to Infiltrate Tax Day Tea Parties: FNC's Cavuto says efforts underway to make protests appear as 'fringe-group efforts' and in some cases as 'racist undertakings,'" Business and Media Institute.

6. Americans for Tax Reform. "People Attended Yesterday's Tax Day Tea Parties," www.atr.org/people-attended-yesterdays-tax-tea-parties-a3138.

7. Rasmussen Reports, "51% View Tea Parties Favorably, Political Class Strongly Disagrees," www.rasmussenreports.com/public_content/politics/general_politics/april_2009/51_view_tea_parties_favorably_political_class_strongly_disagrees.

Chapter 2   How We Got Here

1. Mary Kate Cary, "Is Barack Obama The Next Ronald Reagan?" *U.S. News & World Report* (April 3, 2009), www.usnews.com/blogs/mary-kate-cary/2009/04/03/is-barack-obama-the-next-ronald-reagan.html (accessed October 21, 2009).

2. Alfred S. Regnery, Upstream: The Acendance of American Conservativism (New York: Simon & Schuster, Inc., 2008), 285.

3. Robert Ajemian, "Where Is the Real George Bush?," *Time* (January 26, 1987), www.time.com/time/magazine/article/0,9171,963342-2,00.html (accessed August 16, 2009).

4. Theda Skocpol, *Boomerang: Healthcare Reform and the Turn against Government* (New York: W W Norton & Company, Inc., 1997), 178.

5. "The Year Everyone You Liked Quit," *Newsweek*, December 25, 1995, www.newsweek.com/id/104404 (accessed August 19, 2009).

6. David Brady, Daniel M. Butler, and Jeremy C. Pope, "The Midterm Revolution that Wasn't," *Hoover Digest* 1 (2007), www.hoover.org/publications/digest/6731081.html (accessed August 19, 2009).

7. Robert D. Novak, *The Prince of Darkness: 50 Years Reporting in Washington* (New York: Random House, Inc., 2007).

8. Karen Tumulty, *Time*, June 26, 1995.

9. Jonathan Rauch, "Is There an Excuse for George Nethercutt?" *Reason Magazine*, August 12, 2000, www.reason.com/news/show/34556.html (accessed August 20, 2009).

10. Jonathan Rauch, "Thompson: Washington Changed Us," CNNPolitics.com. http://politicalticker.blogs.cnn.com/2007/06/05/thompson-washington-changed-us (accessed August 20, 2009).

11. Peter J. Wallison, "The True Origins of this Financial Crisis," *The American Spectator*, February 2009, http://spectator.org/archives/2009/02/06/the-true-origins-of-this-finan (accessed August 20, 2009).

12. Mary Daly, "Obama Revs Up at U. Missouri," CBSNews.com, www.cbsnews.com/stories/2008/11/01/politics/uwire/main4562676.shtml (accessed August 20, 2009).

13. Peggy Noonan, "'You Are Terrifying Us': Voters Send a Message to Washington, and Get an Ugly Response," The *Wall Street Journal*, August 6, 2009, http://sbk.online.wsj.com/article/SB10001424052970204908604574334623330098540.html (accessed August 20, 2009).

14. Fred Thompson, "Ron Paul Tops McCain in Cash on Hand," ABC News. http://blogs.abcnews.com/politicalradar/2007/07/ron-paul-tops-m.html (accessed August 20, 2009).

15. James Kirchick, "The Angry White Man: The Bigoted Past of Ron Paul," *The New Republic*, www.tnr.com/politics/story.html?id=e2f15397-a3c7-4720-ac15-4532a7da84ca (accessed August 20, 2009).

16. Alex Koppelman, "My Convention Is Bigger than Your Convention," Salon, www.salon.com/news/feature/2008/09/03/ron_paul/ (accessed August 20, 2009).

17. Susan Davis, "Ron Paul—Finally—Gets His Due," *Wall Street Journal*, January 5, 2009, http://blogs.wsj.com/washwire/2009/01/05/ron-paul-finally-gets-his-due/ (accessed August 20, 2009).

Chapter 3 The Whistling Teapot

1. Jonathan Weisman, "Economic Slump Underlines Concerns about McCain Advisers," *Washington Post*, April 2, 2008. www.washingtonpost.com/wp-dyn/content/article/2008/04/01/AR2008040102860_pf.html.

2. Gerald Prante, "More Bad Ideas for Housing Tax Credits," *Fiscal Facts*, no. 122, April 3, 2008, www.taxfoundation.org/news/show/23073.html.

3. Lawrence H. White, *Cato Journal,* Vol. 29, no. 1 (Winter 2009), www.cato.org/pubs/journal/cj29n1/cj29n1-9.pdf.

4. Congressional Budget Office, "Federal Subsidies and the Housing GSEs," www.cbo.gov/doc.cfm?index=2841&type=0&sequence=3.

5. Alan Greenspan, "Testimony of Chairman Alan Greenspan on Government-Sponsored Enterprises," The Committee on Banking, Housing, and Urban Affairs, U.S. Senate, February 24, 2004, www.federalreserve.gov/boarddocs/testimony/2004/20040224/default.htm.

6. Dan Mitchell, "What to Do with Fannie and Freddie?" *Los Angeles Times*, October 16, 2008. www.cato.org/pub_display.php?pub_id=9724.

7. CNN.com, "Timeline: Banking Crisis," October 16, 2008, http://edition.cnn.com/2008/BUSINESS/09/30/us.bailout.timeline/index.html#cnnSTCText.

8. Congressional Oversight Panel for the Troubled Asset Relief Program; September Oversight Report: "The Use of TARP Funds in Support and Re-organization of the Domestic Automotive Industry," September 9, 2009, http://cop.senate.gov/documents/cop-090909-report.pdf.

9. Neal Barofsky, "Statement of Neal Barofsky Special Inspector General Troubled Asset Relief Program," House Committee on Oversight and Government Reforms, July 21, 2009, http://oversight.house.gov/documents/20090720173415.pdf.

10. Mark Pittman and Bob Ivry, "Financial Rescue Nears GDP as Pledges Top $12.8 Trillion," March 31, 2009, www.bloomberg.com/apps/news?pid=20601087&sid=armOzfkwtCA4&refer=home.

Chapter 4   The Political Class Reacts

1. Glenn Beck, "You Might Be an Extremist if . . ." FOX News, www.foxnews.com/story/0,2933,516898,00.html.

2. David Corn, "George Bush Won't Be Reading This," LAWeekly.com, October 2003,.laweekly.com/2003-10-30/news/george-won-t-be-reading-this.

3. Hamid Debashi, "Katie Couric's Sarah Palin Moment?," CNN.com, October 1, 2009, http://edition.cnn.com/2009/WORLD/meast/10/01/dabashi.couric.ahmadinejad/.

4. Rasmussen Reports characterizes the Political Class as those that (1) trust the federal government over the American people, (2) reject the notion that the federal government itself is a special interest group, and (3) reject the idea the government works with businesses and special interest groups in ways that

hurt consumers and investors. www.rasmussenreports.com/public_content/ politics/ideology/55_of_americans_are_populist_7_support_the_political_class.

5. Rasmussen Reports, "51% View Tea Parties Favorably, Political Class Strongly Disagrees," www.rasmussenreports.com/public_content/politics/ general_politics/april_2009/51_view_tea_parties_favorably_political_class_ strongly_disagrees.

6. The White House, "Briefing by White House Press Secretary Robert Gibbs, 2/20/2009," www.whitehouse.gov/the_press_office/Briefing-by-White-House-Press-Secretary-Robert-Gibbs-2-20-2009/.

7. Robert Holmes, "Who's to Blame for the Economy? Homeowners," TheStreet.com, www.thestreet.com/story/10470251/1/whos-to-blame-for-the-economy-homeowners.html.

8. Federation of American Scientists, "U.S. Department of Homeland Security's Rightwing Extremism: Current Economic and Political Climate Fueling Resurgence in Radicalization and Recruitment," www.fas.org/irp/eprint/ rightwing.pdf.

9. Stephen Gordon, "Homeland Security Document Targets Most Conservatives and Libertarians in the Country," The Liberty Papers, www .thelibertypapers.org/2009/04/12/homeland-security-document-targets-most-conservatives-and-libertarians-in-the-country/.

10. UCB Libraries. "Freedom of Information Act (FOIA)," http://ucblibraries .colorado.edu/govpubs/us/foia.htm.

11. AARC Public Library Contents. "Volume 6: Federal Bureau of Investigation," www.calvin.edu/library/knightcite/index.php.

12. Cornell University Law School. "U.S. Code Collection: 552a. Records Maintained on Individuals," www.law.cornell.edu/uscode/5/usc_sec_05_ 00000552—a000-.html.

13. FOX News. "White House Move to Collect 'Fishy' Info May Be Illegal, Critics Say," www.foxnews.com/politics/2009/08/07/white-house-collect-fishy-info-health-reform-illegal-critics-say/.

14. Matthew Benson, "Governor Vetoes Bill on Lifelong Weapons Permits," *Arizona Republic*, www.azcentral.com/arizonarepublic/local/articles/ 0528vetoes0528.html.

15. Paul Krugman, "Green Shoots and Glimmers," *New York Times*, April 16, 2009, www.nytimes.com/2009/04/17/opinion/17krugman.html.

16. Our Voice: The American Legion. "DHS Apologizes for Language in Report," http://ourvoice.legion.org/story/1543/dhs-apologizes-language-report.

17. Joshua R. Miller, "Napolitano Apologizes for Offending Veterans after DHS Eyes Them for 'Rightwing Extremism,'" FOX News, www.foxnews.com/

politics/first100days/2009/04/16/napolitano-apologizes-offending-veterans-
dhs-eyes-rightwing-extremism/.

18. Code Pink, "Larry Summers Protest: Activists Jump on Stage During Speech,"
www.codepinkalert.org/article.php?id=4821.

19. Community Law Center, "Bill Could Help Baltimore Homeowners
Avoid Foreclosure," www.communitylaw.org/about/news-press/2009/Bill%
20could%20help%20Baltimore%20h...pdf.

20. Lisa Gersing, and Ian Katz, "Protesters Enter Bear Stearns Lobby, Demand Meeting with Dimon," Bloomberg.com, www.bloomberg.com/apps/
news?pid=20601087&sid=akGvUo2phD9Y&refer=home.

21. Sam Jones, Jenny Percival, and Paul Lewis, "G20 Protests: Riot Police Clash with Demonstrators," guaridan.co.uk, www.guardian.co.uk/world/
2009/apr/01/g20-summit-protests.

22. Joshua R. Miller, "Napolitano Apologizes for Offending Veterans after DHS
Eyes Them for 'Rightwing Extremism,'" FOX News, www.foxnews.com/
politics/first100days/2009/04/16/napolitano-apologizes-offending-veterans-
dhs-eyes-rightwing-extremism/.

23. Federation of American Scientists, "U.S. Department of Homeland Security's Rightwing Extremism: Current Economic and Political Climate Fueling Resurgence in Radicalization and Recruitment," www.fas.org/irp/eprint/
rightwing.pdf.

24. ABC News, "Japan Says Sea Shepherd Protesters Threw Acid," www.abc
.net.au/news/stories/2008/03/03/2178466.htm.

25. YouTube, "Violent Extremists Sea Shepherd Ram into Whalers," www
.youtube.com/watch?v=vIYdmM6eBQY.

26. Josh Loposer, "First Casualty of the Whale Wars?" Green Daily, www
.greendaily.com/2009/01/07/first-casualty-of-the-whale-wars/.

27. Paul Watson, "The Beginning of the End for Life as We Know It on Planet
Earth? There Is a Biocentric Solution," Sea Shepherd Conservation Society,
www.seashepherd.org/news-and-media/editorial-070504-1.html.

Dan Gainor, "Eco-Extremist Wants World Population to Drop below 1 Billion: Sea Shepherd Founder Says Mankind Is a 'Virus' and We Need to
'Re-Wild the Planet,'" Business and Media Institute, http://businessandmedia
.org/articles/2007/20070506180903.aspx.

28. Animal Planet: Whale Wars, http://animal.discovery.com/tv/whale-wars/.

29. David Noss, "Md. Guard Issues Warning to Staff about Local TEA Party
Protestors," Southern Maryland Online, http://somd.com/news/headlines/
2009/9833.shtml.

30. Ibid.

Stephen Gordon, "MD and AL: Two Tea Party Items of Interest," The Liberty Papers, www.thelibertypapers.org/2009/04/16/md-and-al-two-tea-party-items-of-interest/.

31. Brian Cross, Anna Schecter, and Megan Churchmach, "Fear for Obama's Safety Grows as Hate Groups Thrive on Racial Backlash: Violent Signs, Gun, Standoff Latest in Emerging Anger Towards the President," ABC News, http://abcnews.go.com/Blotter/story?id=8324481&page=1.

32. KTVU San Francisco, ktvu.com, April 15, 2009, www.youtube.com/watch?v=geL8smut0tQ.

33. Christy Hoppe and Robert T. Garrett, "Texas Gov. Rick Perry Rejects Stimulus Money for Jobless Claims," *Dallas Morning News*, March 13, 2009, www.dallasnews.com/sharedcontent/dws/bus/stories/031309dntexperrystimulus.2b47185d.html.

34. CNN. CNN newsroom transcript, April 15, 2009, http://transcripts.cnn.com/TRANSCRIPTS/0904/15/cnr.06.html.

35. Jim VanDehi and Chris Cillizza, "A New Alliance of Democrats Spreads Funding," *Washington Post*, July 16, 2006, www.washingtonpost.com/wp-dyn/content/article/2006/07/16/AR2006071600882_pf.html.

36. Joe Nocera, "Self-Made Philanthropists," *New York Times*, March 2008, www.nytimes.com/2008/03/09/magazine/09Sandlers-t.html.

37. Money Week, "George Soros: Selfish Speculator or Market Prophet?" www.moneyweek.com/news-and-charts/george-soros-selfish-speculator-or-market-prophet-42117.aspx.

38. Andrew S. Ross, "Herb Sandler Takes on SNL after Snark Attack," *San Francisco Chronicle*, www.sfgate.com/cgi-bin/article.cgi?f=/c/a/2008/10/06/BUL713C93P.DTL.

39. Stanley Kurtz, "Inside Obama's Acorn: By their Fruits Ye Shall Know Them," National Review Online, http://article.nationalreview.com/?q=NDZiMjkwMDczZWI5ODdjOWYxZTIzZGIyNzEyMjE0ODI=&w=MA.

40. Howard Wolinsky, "The Secret Side of David Axelrod: The Obama Campaign's Chief Strategist Is a Master of 'Astroturfing' and Has a Second Firm that Shapes Public Opinion for Corporations," *BusinessWeek*, March 14, 2008, www.businessweek.com/bwdaily/dnflash/content/mar2008/db20080314_121054.htm.

41. Timothy J. Burger, "Obama Campaign Ad Firms Signed on to Push Health-Care Overhaul," Bloomberg.com, www.bloomberg.com/apps/news?pid=20601087&sid=aV3dLt6wmZH4.

42. Garance Franke-Ruta, "Obama Town Hall Questioners Were Campaign Backers," *Washington Post*, March 27, 2009, http://voices.washingtonpost.com/44/2009/03/27/obama_town_hall_questioners_we.html.

43. Jesse Lee, "Retrospective in Missouri," The White House—The Blog, www
.whitehouse.gov/blog/09/04/29/Retrospective-in-Missouri/.

44. Paul Krugman, "Federal Spending Mythology," *New York Times*, February
2, 2008, http://krugman.blogs.nytimes.com/2008/02/02/federal-spending-
mythology/.

45. Veronique de Rugy, "Spending under President George W. Bush," Merca-
tus Center at George Mason University, www.mercatus.org/PublicationDetails
.aspx?id=26426.

46. Lee, "Retrospective in Missouri."

47. Mike Allen, "Obama Vows to Cut Huge Deficit in Half," Politico.com, www
.politico.com/news/stories/0209/19124.html.

48. The Heritage Foundation, "Bush Deficit vs. Obama Deficit in Pictures," http://blog.heritage.org/2009/03/24/bush-deficit-vs-obama-deficit-
in-pictures/.

49. Lee, "Retrospective in Missouri."

50. Dan McLaughlin, "The Health Care Cost Saving Myth," CBS News, www
.cbsnews.com/stories/2009/08/21/opinion/main5257556.shtml.

51. Lee, "Retrospective in Missouri."

52. Mark Silva, "Obama Broadens Bush's Faith-Based Programs," *Los Angeles
Times*, February 6, 2009, http://articles.latimes.com/2009/feb/06/nation/na-
faith6?pg=1.

53. Nancy Kruh, "Balance of Opinion: Obama and Iranian Protests," *Dallas
Morning News*, June 18, 2009, www.dallasnews.com/sharedcontent/dws/dn/
opinion/viewpoints/stories/DN-balance_19edi.State.Edition1.2160492.html.

54. Ralph Z. Hallow, "Steele: GOP Needs 'Hip-Hop' Makeover," *Washington
Times*, February 19, 2009, www.washingtontimes.com/news/2009/feb/19/
steele-gop-needs-hip-hop-makeover/.

55. Ben Smith, "Steele 'Choice' Gaffe Sparks GOP Revolt." *Politico*, www
.politico.com/news/stories/0309/19956.html.

56. Rachel Weiner, "Chicago Tea Party Rejects Michael Steele." *The Huffington Post*, www.huffingtonpost.com/2009/04/09/chicago-tea-party-rejects_
n_185026.html.

57. Paul Bedard, "GOP Chairman Michael Steele Denies Tea Party Claim," *U.S.
News & World Report*, April 10, 2009, www.usnews.com/blogs/washington-
whispers/2009/04/10/gop-chairman-michael-steele-denies-tea-party-claim
.html.

58. Andy Barr, "GOP Govs Plan Tea Party Sequel," *Politico*, www.politico.com/
news/stories/0509/22436.html.

59. MSNBC *Hardball with Chris Matthews,* April 15, 2009.

Chapter 5   The Media Strikes Back

1. Chris Ariens, "Susan Roesgen Out at CNN," Media Bistro, July 16, 2009, www.mediabistro.com/tvnewser/cnn/susan_roesgen_out_at_cnn_121788.asp (accessed October 22, 2009).

2. Paul Krugman, "Tea Parties Forever," *New York Times*, April 2009, www.nytimes.com/2009/04/13/opinion/13krugman.html.

3. MSNBC, "'Meet the Press' transcript for August 16, 2009," www.msnbc.msn.com/id/32420049/ns/meet_the_press/page/2/.

4. "Obama's 95% Illusion: It Depends on What the Meaning of 'Tax Cut' Is," *Wall Street Journal,* October 13, 2008, section A, 18, http://online.wsj.com/article/SB122385651698727257.html.

5. Sandra Fabry, "Obama Breaks Tax Pledge, Signs SCHIP," The Heartland Institute's *Budget & Tax News*, April 2009, www.heartland.org/publications/budget%20tax/article/24817/Obama_Breaks_Tax_Pledge_Signs_SCHIP.html.

6. William Snyder, "SCHIP Is for Children in Name Only," The Heartland Institute's *Heartland Perspective*, September 2007, www.heartland.org/full/22009/SCHIP_Is_for_Children_in_Name_Only.html.

7. Michelle C. Bucci and William W. Beach, "22 Million New Smokers Needed: Funding SCHIP Expansion with a Tobacco Tax," The Heritage Foundation, July 11, 2007, www.heritage.org/research/healthcare/wm1548.cfm.

8. George Stephanopoulos, "Geithner Won't Rule Out New Taxes for Middle Class," ABC News, http://blogs.abcnews.com/george/2009/08/geithner-wont-rule-out-new-taxes-for-middle-class.html.

9. CNN. *Anderson Cooper 360 Degrees*, April 14, 2009, http://transcripts.cnn.com/TRANSCRIPTS/0904/14/acd.01.html.

10. Federation of American Scientists, "U.S. Department of Homeland Security's Rightwing Extremism: Current Economic and Political Climate Fueling Resurgence in Radicalization and Recruitment," www.fas.org/irp/eprint/rightwing.pdf.

11. Sandra Fabry, "Obama Breaks Tax Pledge, Signs SCHIP," www.heartland.org/policybot/results/24817/Obama_Breaks_Tax_Pledge_Signs_SCHIP.html.

12. Declan McCullagh, "Obama Admin: Cap-and-Trade Could Cost Families $1,761 a Year," CBSNews.com, September 2009, www.cbsnews.com/blogs/2009/09/15/taking_liberties/entry5314040.shtml.

13. Steve Stanek, "Feds Play Down Carbon Cap-and-Trade," The Heartland Institute's *Budget & Tax News*, April 1, 2009, www.heartland.org/policybot/results/24819/Feds_Play_Down_Carbon_CapandTrade.html.

14. "Medial Temporal Lobe (The Limbic System)," http://thalamus.wustl.edu/course/limbic.html.

15. Medline Plus, "Medical Encyclopedia: Limbic System," www.nlm.nih.gov/medlineplus/ency/imagepages/19244.htm.

16. B. Rensch, "The Intelligence of Elephants," *Scientific American*, 1957, 196, 44–49, Cambridge: Harvard University Press.

17. Drew Western, et al., "Neural Bases of Motivated Reasoning: An fMRI Study of Emotional Constraints on Partisan Political Judgment in the 2004 U.S. Presidential Election," *Journal of Cognitive Neuroscience*, Vol. 18, (Nov. 11, 2004), MIT Press.

18. MSNBC, "Political Bias Affects Brain Activity, Study Finds Democrats and Republicans Both Adept at Ignoring Facts, Brain Scans Show," www.msnbc.msn.com/id/11009379/.

19. *Wired*. "Dems, GOP: Who's Got the Brains?" www.wired.com/politics/security/news/2004/10/65521.

20. Andrew Breitbart, "BREITBART: I am Kenneth Gladney," *Washington Times*, August 10, 2009, www.washingtontimes.com/news/2009/aug/10/i-am-kenneth-gladney/print/.

21. Patrik Jonsson, "Arguing the Size of the 'Tea Party' Protests," *Christian Science Monitor,* April 18, 2009, www.csmonitor.com/2009/0418/p25s03-usgn.html.

22. Americans for Tax Reform, "People Attended Yesterdays Tax Day Tea Parties," www.atr.org/people-attended-yesterdays-tax-tea-parties-a3138.

23. Nate Silver, "Tea Party Nonpartisan Attendance Estimates: Now 300,000+," FiveThirtyEight. www.fivethirtyeight.com/2009/04/tea-party-nonpartisan-attendance.html.

24. Rasmussen Reports, "51% View Tea Parties Favorably, Political Class Strongly Disagrees," www.rasmussenreports.com/public_content/politics/general_politics/april_2009/51_view_tea_parties_favorably_political_class_strongly_disagrees.

25. "*American Idol* Attracts More than 32 Million Viewers," FOX News, www.foxnews.com/story/0,2933,248786,00.html.

Chapter 6   Radical Ideas

1. Mary Daly, "The Maneater," University Wire (Oct. 31, 2008), University of Missouri.

2. Gerald F. Seib, "In Crisis, Opportunity for Obama," *Wall Street Journal,* November 21, 2008, http://online.wsj.com/article/SB122721278056345271.html.

3. Pete Harrison, "Never Waste a Good Crisis, Clinton Says on Climate," Reuters India, http://in.reuters.com/article/environmentNews/idINTRE5251VN20090306.

4. The White House, "Press Briefing by Press Secretary Robert Gibbs," www
.whitehouse.gov/the_press_office/Briefing-by-White-House-Press-Secretary-
Robert-Gibbs-3-9-09/.

5. Center for Fiscal Accountability, "Cost of Government Day 1977-2009,"
www.fiscalaccountability.org/index.php?content=cog09-3#.

6. MSNBC, "Biden Calls Paying Higher Taxes a Patriotic Act: 'We Want
to Take Money and Put It Back in the Pocket of Middle-Class People,'"
www.msnbc.msn.com/id/26771716/.

7. Money Blue Book, "2009 Federal Income Tax Brackets (Official IRS
Tax Rates)," www.moneybluebook.com/2009-federal-income-tax-brackets-
official-irs-tax-rates/.

8. Sudeep Reedy, "TurboTax Responds to Treasury Nominee's Disclosure," *Wall Street Journal,* January 21, 2009, http://blogs.wsj.com/washwire/
2009/01/21/turbotax-responds-to-treasury-nominees-disclosure/.

9. George Stephanopoulos, "Geithner Won't Rule Out New Taxes for Middle Class," ABC News, http://blogs.abcnews.com/george/2009/08/geithner-
wont-rule-out-new-taxes-for-middle-class.html.

10. Erik Sofge, "Why Shovel-Ready Infrastructure Is Wrong (Right
Now)," *Popular Mechanics,* February 5, 2009, www.popularmechanics.com/
technology/industry/4302578.html.

11. Ibid.

12. Brian Faler, "Much of Stimulus Won't Be Spent Before 2011, CBO
Says," Bloomberg, www.bloomberg.com/apps/news?pid=20601087&sid=
aJAoR5GECKWo.

13. Dan Gainor, "It's Not an Auto Bailout, It's a Union Payoff," CNS News,
www.cnsnews.com/Public/Content/article.aspx?Rsrcid=39484.

14. Andy Barr, "McCain Decries Bailout Earmarks," Politico, www.politico
.com/news/stories/1008/14214.html.

15. Matt Kelley and John Fritze, "Governors Reject Stimulus Money for
Unemployment," *USA Today,* March 15, 2009, www.usatoday.com/news/
nation/2009-03-15-unemployment_N.htm.

16. MSNBC. "Inspector Questions Airport Stimulus Projects: 50 Airport Projects
Didn't Meet Grant Criteria, Government Watchdog Says," www.msnbc
.msn.com/id/32365788/ns/politics-white_house/.

17. Jonathan Weisman and Christopher Conkey, "GOP Faults Some Stimulus Projects," *Wall Street Journal,* June 16, 2009, http://online.wsj.com/
article/SB124510694878716707.html.

18. Senator Tom Coburn M.D., "100 Stimulus Projects: A Second Opinion,"
United States Senate 111th Congress, www.google.com/url?sa=t&source=

web&ct=res&cd=1&url=http%3A%2F%2Fcoburn.senate.gov%2Fpublic%
2Findex.cfm%3FFuseAction%3DFiles.View%26FileStore_id%3D59af3ebd-
7bf9-4933-8279-8091b533464f&ei=N-KRSqi.

19. Ambar Espinoza, "Delayed Bus Order Forces Layoffs at New Flyer," MPR
    News Q, http://minnesota.publicradio.org/display/web/2009/08/20/new-
    flyer-jobs/.

20. David Wessel, "Stimulus: Some Facts," *Wall Street Journal*, August 21, 2009,
    http://blogs.wsj.com/economics/2009/08/21/stimulus-some-facts/.

21. Geoff Earle, "Sex-Study 'Stimulus,'" Sept. 2, 2009, www.nypost.com/
    seven/08242009/news/nationalnews/sex_study_stimulus_186153.htm.

22. Louise Radnofsky, "GSA Posts $18 Million Contract to Improve Recov-
    ery.gov," *Wall Street Journal,* August 3, 2009, http://blogs.wsj.com/washwire/
    2009/08/03/gsa-posts-18-million-contract-to-improve-recoverygov/.

23. David Freddoso, "Is $18M Too Much for a Web Site?" *Washington Exam-
    iner*, July 9, 2009, www.washingtonexaminer.com/opinion/blogs/beltway-
    confidential/A-gold-plated-Recovery-20-50395992.html.

24. Ibid.

25. Ned Potter, "Obama's 'Transparent' Stimulus Plan: Is It? Recovery.gov, Stim-
    ulus Web Site, Redesigned—But Description Is Blacked Out," ABC News,
    http://abcnews.go.com/Technology/story?id=8242044&page=1.

26. Rick Klein, "$18M Being Spent to Redesign Recovery.gov Web Site,"
    ABC News. http://blogs.abcnews.com/thenote/2009/07/18m-being-spent-
    to-redesign-recoverygov-web-site.html.

27. David Freddoso, "Updated: Hoyer-Linked Firm Wins $18M Recovery.gov
    Contract," *Washington Examiner*, July 9, 2009, www.washingtonexaminer
    .com/opinion/blogs/beltway-confidential/Hoyer-linked-firm-will-do-
    Recoveryorg-redesign-50353982.html.

28. Howie Carr, "This Is Not Your Father's Welfare State," *Boston Herald*,
    May 7, 2009, http://bostonherald.com/news/columnists/view.bg?articleid=
    1170618.

29. Davis Migoya, "Poor in Colorado May Get Free Phones: TracFone Wireless
    Wants to Give Cellphones to Coloradans Who Receive Public Assistance,"
    Denver Post, July 16, 2009, www.denverpost.com/ci_12838433.

30. Recovery.gov. "Where Is Your Money Going—Tabular View," www.recovery
    .gov/?q=node/88 (accessed August 9, 2009).

31. Pedro Nicolaci da Costa, "Biden Says Some Waste Inevitable Part of Stim-
    ulus," Reuters, www.reuters.com/article/politicsNews/idUSTRE5516HE
    20090602.

32. Jennifer Liberto, "TARP Cop: Get Tough on Banks." CNN Money, http://
    money.cnn.com/2009/07/20/news/economy/TARP_report/?postversion=
    2009072018.

33. Greg Morcroft, "Fraudsters Eye Huge Stimulus Pie, Consultant Says Companies Will Face Extra Requirements to Prevent Problems," *Wall Street Journal: Market Watch*, www.marketwatch.com/story/stimulus-fraud-could-hit-50-billion.

34. Grant McCool and Martha Graybow, "FBI Targets Fraud in TARP, Stimulus Fund," Reuters, www.reuters.com/article/ousiv/idUSTRE5515MF 20090602.

35. Joe Edwards, "Tenn. Man Sentenced in Bank Bailout Fraud Case," AP, http://abcnews.go.com/Business/wireStory?id=8271034.

36. Federal Bureau of Investigation, "Mortgage Fraud," www.fbi.gov/hq/mortgage_fraud.htm.

37. Damien Cave and James Glanz, "Agents Raid Bank and Lender in Florida," *New York Times*, August 3, 2009, www.nytimes.com/2009/08/04/business/04florida.html?_r=1&scp=2&sq=bailout%20fraud&st=cse.

38. Ralph Vartabedian, "Click Here to Find Out More! TARP Case Leads to Search of Bank and Lender's Florida Offices," *Los Angeles Times*, August 4, 2009, www.latimes.com/business/la-fi-tarp4-2009aug04,0,1591069.story.

39. Chris Isidore, and Julianne Pepitone, "BB&T Buys Colonial Bank; 4 Other Banks Fail," CNN Money, http://money.cnn.com/2009/08/14/news/companies/colonial_bancgroup/?postversion=2009081500.

40. Devlin Barrett, "FBI May Shift Counterterror Agents to Anti-Fraud," FOX News, www.foxnews.com/wires/2009Feb11/0,4670,BailoutFraud,00.html.

41. Stephen Ohlemacher, "Government Sent 3,900 Economic Stimulus Checks to Prison Inmates, 2,200 Got to Keep Them." *Los Angeles Times*, 26 August 2009. www.kxnet.com/getForumPost.asp?ArticleId=427174.

42. Ibid.

43. Richard S. Chang, "The Final Numbers on 'Clunkers'," *New York Times*, August 26, 2009, http://wheels.blogs.nytimes.com/2009/08/26/the-final-numbers-on-clunkers/.

44. CARS: Official Information, www.cars.gov/official-information.

45. "Does Cash for Clunkers Help the Environment? It's Debatable," FOX News, www.foxnews.com/politics/2009/08/04/clunkers-programs-environmental-impact-debate/.

46. Jennifer Robison, "Political Climate for Energy Policies Cools," *Las Vegas Review-Journal*, August 9, 2009 www.lvrj.com/news/52828402.html.

47. CARS: Official Information. www.cars.gov/official-information.

48. Michael Gerrard, "Cash-for-Clunkers Program a Missed Opportunity to Reduce Greenhouse Gases," Columbia Law School, www.law.columbia.edu/media_inquiries/news_events/2009/july2009/clunkers.

49. Edmunds, "Cash for Clunkers—Eligible New Cars," www.edmunds.com/cash-for-clunkers/new-car-candidates.html#h.

50. Dianne Feinstein and Susan Collins, "Handouts for Hummers: We're Astonished How Quickly Lobbyists Fouled Up a Good Idea," *Wall Street Journal*, June 11, 2009, http://online.wsj.com/article/SB124467696781404127.html.

51. Open Congress, "H.R.2346: Making Supplemental Appropriations for the Fiscal Year Ending September 30, 2009, and for Other Purposes," www.opencongress.org/roll_call/show/5736.

52. Richard S. Chang, "The Final Numbers on 'Clunkers'," *New York Times*, August 26, 2009. http://wheels.blogs.nytimes.com/2009/08/26/the-final-numbers-on-clunkers/.

53. Angela Greiling Keane and Mark Drajem, "'Cash-for-Clunkers' Prospects Bolstered by Feinstein," Bloomberg, www.bloomberg.com/apps/news?pid=20601103&sid=aB9Penvo0Hho.

54. Chris Shunk, "Chrysler Announces 'Double CA$H for Your Old Car,' Promotion," www.autoblog.com/2009/07/22/chrysler-announces-double-ca-h-for-your-old-car-promotion/.

55. Manu Raju and Mike Allen, "'Cash for Clunkers' Going Broke," *Pittsburgh Post-Gazette*, August 1, 2009, www.post-gazette.com/pg/09213/987909-473.stm.

56. Timothy P. Carney, "Special Interests Cash in on Clunker Boondoggle," *Washington Examiner*, August 5, 2009, www.washingtonexaminer.com/politics/Special-interests-cash-in-on-clunker-boondoggle-52473487.html.

57. Matthew Bandyk, "Maybe Cash For Clunkers Helped the Economy after All?" *U.S. News & World Report*, August 25, 2009, www.usnews.com/blogs/capital-commerce/2009/08/25/maybe-cash-for-clunkers-helped-the-economy-after-all.html.

58. Michael Felberbaum, "As Resellable Guzzlers Are Crushed, Used-Car Dealerships Feel the Pain," *Boston Globe*, August 14, 2009, www.boston.com/business/articles/2009/08/14/as_resellable_guzzlers_are_crushed_used_car_dealerships_feel_the_pain/.

59. Simone Baribeau, "Warning over U.S. Cash-for-Clunkers Scheme," *Financial Times*, www.ft.com/cms/s/940088ae-8830-11de-82e4-00144feabdc0, Authorised=false.html?_i_location=http%3A%2F%2Frl>www.ft.com%2Fcms%2Fs%2F0%2F940088ae-8830-11de-82e4-00144feabdc0.html%3Fnclick_check%3D1&_i_r.

60. Ken Thomas, "AP sources: Gov't to Suspend 'Cash for Clunkers,'" Breitbart, www.breitbart.com/article.php?id=D99P2U9G1&show_article=1.

61. Jim Puzzanghera and Martin Zimmerman, "Senate OKs More Cash for 'Clunkers,'" *Los Angeles Times*, August 7, 2009, www.latimes.com/business/la-fi-clunkers7-2009aug07,0,6297192.story.

62. Gary Dymski, "LI Salvage-Yard Owners Criticize Clunker Program," *Newsday*, August 13, 2009, www.newsday.com/business/li-salvage-yard-owners-criticize-clunker-program-1.1368432.

63. Dan Strumph, "NY Dealers Pull Out of Clunkers Program." Breitbart, www.breitbart.com/article.php?id=D9A63RC81&show_article=1.

64. Peter Valdes-Dapena, "Clunkers: Toyota Passes GM as Top Seller," CNNMoney.com, August 2009, http://money.cnn.com/2009/08/17/autos/clunker_toyota_tops/index.htm.

65. Josh Mitchell, "Toyota's Corolla Top-Selling Vehicle in U.S. 'Clunkers' Program," *Wall Street Journal*, August 21, 2009, http://online.wsj.com/article/BT-CO-20090821-711151.html.

66. Angela Greiling Keane and Holly Rosenkrantz, "Four of Top 'Clunkers' Model Purchases Are Foreign," Bloomberg, www.bloomberg.com/apps/news?pid=20601087&sid=am1mj6R6tAcg.

67. Martin Feldstein, "Give Unions Bitter Pill to Cure Big 3," *New York Post*, November 21, 2008, www.nypost.com/seven/11212008/news/columnists/give_unions_bitter_pill_to_cure_big_3_140051.htm.

68. Kelsey Mays, "The Cars.com American-Made Index," Cars.com, www.cars.com/go/advice/Story.jsp?section=top&subject=ami&story=amMade0707&referer=&aff=national.

69. Neil E. Boudette and Matthew Dolan, "Race Is on to File Clunker Deals," *Wall Street Journal*, August 24, 2009, http://online.wsj.com/article/SB125107384711152373.html.

70. "Cash for Clunkers Sells 700,000 New Vehicles," *London Free Press*, August 27, 2009, http://lfpress.ca/newsstand/Business/2009/08/27/10630026-sun.html.

71. CARS web site, www.cars.gov/.

72. "Cash from Clunkers: Let's Have a $4,500 Subsidy for Everything," *Wall Street Journal*, August 2, 2009, http://online.wsj.com/article/SB10001424052970204313604574326531645819464.html.

73. Ibid.

74. Ibid.

75. Brian Hartman, "'Cash for Refrigerators': Like Clunkers, but for Appliances," ABC News, http://abcnews.go.com/Technology/JustOneThing/story?id=8374739.

76. Shawn Neisteadt, "Some Surprised by 'Clunker' Tax," Keloland Television, www.keloland.com/NewsDetail6162.cfm?Id=0,89084.

77. Don, Jorgensen, "Dealers Still Waiting for Clunker Cash," Keloland Television, www.keloland.com/NewsDetail6162.cfm?Id=89419.

78. "Obama: Stimulus Will Create 4.1 Million Jobs," AP, January 2009, www.msnbc.msn.com/id/28590554/.

79. Bureau of Labor Statistics, "The Employment Situation: January 2009," www.bls.gov/news.release/archives/empsit_02062009.htm.

80. Matt Kelley, "Obama Advisers: 1M Jobs Saved or Created," September 2009, USAToday.com, www.usatoday.com/money/economy/2009-09-10-stimulus-jobs_N.htm.

81. Don Lee and Tiffany Hsu, "Unemployment Rate Hits 9.8 Percent, Highest in 26 Years: More Workers in September Saw Hours Cut Back; Economists Say Near Future Looks Bleak," *Chiago Tribune*, October 3, 2009, www.chicagotribune.com/business/chi-tc-biz-jobs-1002-1003-oct03,0,4896728.story.

82. Bureau of Labor Statistics, "The Employment Situation—September 2009," www.bls.gov/news.release/archives/empsit_10022009.htm.

83. CBS News, "Can Private Security Guards Act as Cops? That's Exactly What They May Soon Be Doing on the Far South Side," http://cbs2chicago.com/local/police.private.security.2.966243.html.

84. "A Good Way to Beat Traffic: Lease Major Toll Roads," *USA Today*, July 4, 2006, www.usatoday.com/news/opinion/editorials/2006-07-04-our-toll-roads_x.htm.

85. Steve Stanek, "Privatized Fire District Keeps Costs Low and Service High," The Heartland Institute's *Budget & Tax News*, April 2006, www.heartland.org/publications/budget%20tax/article/18741/Privatized_Fire_District_Keeps_Costs_Low_and_Service_High.html.

86. August Cole, "Afghanistan Contractors Outnumber Troops: Despite Surge in U.S. Deployments, More Civilians Are Posted in War Zone; Reliance Echoes the Controversy in Iraq," *Wall Street Journal,* August 22, 2009, http://online.wsj.com/article/SB125089638739950599.html.

87. Mackinac Center for Public Policy, "Search Results for 'Michigan Privatization Report,'" www.mackinac.org/features/search/search.aspx?Type=12&MainTitles=True.

88. Daniel J. Mitchell, "The Fallacy that Government Creates Jobs," CATO Institute, www.cato.org/pub_display.php?pub_id=9825.

89. William McGurn, "The Media Fall for Phony 'Jobs' Claims: The Obama Numbers Are Pure Fiction," *Wall Street Journal,* June 10, 2009, http://online.wsj.com/article/SB124451592762396883.html.

90. Ibid.

91. Stuart Epperson, "The Fairness Doctrine: A Brief History and Perspective," Townhall.com, http://townhall.com/columnists/StuartEpperson/2007/08/

23 / the _fairness_doctrine_a_brief_history_and_perspective?page=full&com
ments=trueTown.

92. Gallup, "'Conservatives' Are Single-Largest Ideological Group," www
.gallup.com/poll/120857/Conservatives-Single-Largest-Ideological-Group
.aspx.

93. Brian Maloney, "Liberal Talk Radio: Don't Believe the Hype," World Net
Daily, www.wnd.com/news/article.asp?ARTICLE_ID=42500.

94. Daily Kos, "Reinstitute the Fairness Doctrine," www.dailykos.com/
storyonly/2009/7/29/755540/-Reinstitute-the-Fairness-Doctrine.

95. James Sherk, "Card Check Undermines Workplace Democracy," The Heritage Foundation, www.heritage.org/research/labor/wm1255.cfm.

96. Rush Limbaugh, "A Brief History of the Fairness Doctrine," *Time*, February
20, 2009, www.time.com/time/nation/article/0,8599,1880786,00.html.

97. John Shu, "Fairness Doctrine: New Federal Initiatives Project," The Federalist
Society, www.fed-soc.org/publications/pubID.1327/pub_detail.asp.

98. Ibid.

99. Almanac of Policy Issues, "Cato: McCain-Feingold Violates 1st Amendment,"
www.policyalmanac.org/government/pr/campaign_finance_001.shtml.

100. Rush Limbaugh, "A Brief History of the Fairness Doctrine," *Time*, February
20, 2009, www.time.com/time/nation/article/0,8599,1880786,00.html.

101. Judson Berger, "White House: Obama Opposes 'Fairness Doctrine'
Revival," FOX News, www.foxnews.com/politics/first100days/2009/02/
18/white-house-opposes-fairness-doctrine/?CFID=740261&CFTOKEN=
458172cc4d999463-8CF9307D-1851-8FFD-EC683EB336C71DE7.

102. Peter Drivas, "Obama Hits Fox News: They're 'Entirely Devoted to
Attacking My Administration'—Fox News Responds, The Huffington
Post, www.huffingtonpost.com/2009/06/16/obama-hits-fox-news-theyr_n_
216574.html.

103. "FCC's New Hire Targeted Conservative Radio Stations in Writings,"
FOX News, www.foxnews.com/politics/2009/08/10/pub-fccs-new-hire-
previously-targeted-gop-radio-stations/.

104. The Washington Prowler, "In All Fairness," *American Spectator*, February 16,
2009, http://spectator.org/archives/2009/02/16/in-all-fairness/1.

105. Deborah Solomon, and Damian Paletta, "U.S. Eyes Bank Pay Overhaul," *Wall Street Journal*, May 13, 2009, http://online.wsj.com/article/
SB124215896684211987.html#mod=testMod.

106. Josh Gerstein, "Obama to CEOs: 'Show Some Restraint!'" Politico.com,
www.politico.com/news/stories/0309/20583.html.

107. Michael R. Crittenden, "House Passes Bill to Curb Executive Pay," *Wall Street Journal*, August 1, 2009, http://online.wsj.com/article/ SB124908505587098285.html.

108. Stephanie Condon, "Democrats Scrutinize Health Insurance Executive Pay," CBS News, www.cbsnews.com/blogs/2009/08/19/politics/ politicalhotsheet/entry5253373.shtml.

109. Jonathan Allen, "House Speaker Will Keep Money from 'Villains': Pelosi Called Insurers 'Immoral,' Despite Receiving Funds from Industry," MSNBC, www.msnbc.msn.com/id/32237227/ns/politics-cq_politics/.

110. James M. Taylor, "Falling Temperatures Confound Alarmists," The Heartland Institute's *Environment & Climate News*, September 2009, www.heartland.org/ publications/environment%20climate/article/25791/Falling_Temperatures_ Confound_Alarmists.html.

111. "Roger Revelle & Al Gore: Coleman's Video Report, 3/6/09," Kusi News San Diego, www.kusi.com/weather/colemanscorner/40867912.html.

112. "Ethanol Fuel," The Heartland Institute's *Research & Commentary*, May 2008, www.heartland.org/article/23208/Ethanol_Fuel.html.

113. "Ethanol's Grocery Bill: Two Federal Studies Add Up the Corn Fuel's Exorbitant Cost," *Wall Street Journal*, June 3, 2009, http://online.wsj.com/ article/SB124389966385274413.html.

114. "Scientists: End Biofuel Production to End Food Shortage," FOX News, www.foxnews.com/story/0,2933,353380,00.html.

115. "CAFE Standards Issue Resurfaces on Capitol Hill," The Heartland Institute's *Environment & Climate News*, June 1997, www.heartland.org/publications/ environment%20climate/article/14213/CAFE_Standards_Issue_Resurfaces_ on_Capitol_Hill.html.

116. Alex Johnson, "Shining a Light on Hazards of Fluorescent Bulbs: Energy-Efficient Coils Booming, but Disposal of Mercury Poses Problems," MSNBC, www.msnbc.msn.com/id/23694819/.

117. David Kreutzer, Ph.D, Karen Campbell, Ph.D, William W. Beach, Ben Lieberman, et al., "The Economic Consequences of Waxman-Markey: An Analysis of the American Clean Energy and Security Act of 2009," The Heritage Foundation, www.heritage.org/Research/EnergyandEnvironment/ cda0904.cfm.

118. Kerry Picket, "Obama: Energy Prices Will Skyrocket under My Cap-and-Trade Plan," NewsBusters, http://newsbusters.org/blogs/kerry-picket/2008/11/02/obama-energy-prices-will-skyrocket.

119. Glenn Beck, "Obama Told Us This Was Coming," Free Republic, www.freerepublic.com/focus/news/2303155/posts.

120. Joseph L. Bast, "Why Won't Al Gore Debate?" The Heartland Institute's News Releases, June 2007, www.heartland.org/policybot/results/20873/Why_Wont_Al_Gore_Debate.html.

121. Jeff Poor, "CBS 'Global Warming Special' Host Likened Warming Skeptics to Holocaust Deniers," NewsBusters, http://newsbusters.org/blogs/jeff-poor/2008/01/21/cbs-airs-conspiratorial-global-warming-special-hosted-reporter-who-likene.

122. "NASA Scientist: Put CEOs On Trial for Global-Warming Lies," FOX News, www.foxnews.com/story/0,2933,370521,00.html.

123. Rasmussen Reports, "Only 34% Now Blame Humans for Global Warming," www.rasmussenreports.com/public_content/politics/current_events/environment/only_34_now_blame_humans_for_global_warming.

124. Rasmussen Reports, "56% Don't Want to Pay More to Fight Global Warming," www.rasmussenreports.com/public_content/politics/current_events/environment/56_don_t_want_to_pay_more_to_fight_global_warming.

125. The Pew Research Center, "Economy, Jobs Trump All Other Policy Priorities in 2009," http://people-press.org/report/485/economy-top-policy-priority.

126. Global Warming Petition Project, www.petitionproject.org/.

127. Paul Georgia, "IPCC Report Criticized by One of Its Lead Authors," The Heartland Institute's Environment & Climate News, June 2001, www.heartland.org/policybot/results/1069/IPCC_report_criticized_by_one_of_its_lead_authors.html.

128. Climate Change Reconsidered, www.nipccreport.org/index.html.

129. "Population of Nearly Extinct Mountain Yellow-Legged Frog Discovered," Science Daily, www.sciencedaily.com/releases/2009/07/090726093404.htm.

130. John M. Broder, "Climate Change Seen as Threat to U.S.: Security Issue Could Become Central in Senate Debate over Energy Legislation," MSNBC, www.msnbc.msn.com/id/32344842/ns/technology_and_science-the_new_york_times/.

131. Brody Mullins and T W. Farnam, "Lawmakers' Global-Warming Trip Hit Tourist Hot Spots Penguins, a Rocket-Propelled Airplane (and Tax Dollars) Also Involved," Wall Street Journal, August 8, 2009, http://online.wsj.com/article/SB124967502810515267.html.

132. The Heartland Institute: Global Warming, Was It Ever Really a Crisis? Interviews from the 2009 International Conference on Climate Change (DVD) 2009.

133. Ibid.

134. Jeff Poor, "Report: Gore's Lights Left on for Media-Hyped 'Earth Hour'," NewsBusters, http://newsbusters.org/blogs/jeff-poor/2009/03/29/report-gore-s-lights-left-media-hyped-earth-hour.

135. Jake Tapper, "Al Gore's 'Inconvenient Truth'?—A $30,000 Utility Bill: Think Tank Blasts Gore for Hypocrisy, Defenders Call Report a Last Gasp from Warming Skeptics," ABC News. http://abcnews.go.com/Politics/GlobalWarming/Story?id=2906888&page=1.

136. Pete Schweizer, "Gore Isn't Quite as Green as He's Led the World to Believe," *USA Today*, December 7, 2006, www.usatoday.com/news/opinion/editorials/2006-08-09-gore-green_x.htm.

137. "Obama Getting Heat for Turning Up the Oval Office Thermostat," FOX News, February 3, 2009, www.foxnews.com/politics/2009/02/03/obama-getting-heat-for-turning-up-thermostat/.

138. Sheryl G. Stolberg,. "White House Unbuttons Formal Dress Code," *New York Times*, January 29, 2009, www.nytimes.com/2009/01/29/us/politics/29whitehouse.html.

139. Marshall Leob, "How Charities Are Coping: It's Tough Times in the Business of Giving, Yet Some People Still Dig Deep," *Wall Street Journal,* April 9, 2009.

140. Sandra Miniutti, "Charities Hurt by Madoff Scandal," Charity Navigator, http://blog.charitynavigator.org/2008/12/charities-hurt-by-madoff-scandal.html.

141. Andy Sullivan, "Tax Change Should Not Affect Charities, Obama Says," Reuters, www.reuters.com/article/politicsNews/idUSTRE52O0IV20090325.

142. Mike Dorning, "Obama Defends His Plan to Limit Tax Deductions," *Los Angeles Times*, March 25, 2009, http://articles.latimes.com/2009/mar/25/nation/na-obama-tax25.

143. "Charities Skeptical About Obama's Proposed Tax Change," FOX News, www.foxnews.com/politics/first100days/2009/03/25/obama-urges-charities-worry-proposed-tax-change/.

144. Jim McTague, "Obama's Reagan Fixation Doesn't Add Up," Barron's, http://online.barrons.com/article/SB124908140058798125.html.

145. Suzanne Perry, "Obama's Plan to Reduce Charitable Deductions for the Wealthy Draws Criticism," The Chronicle of Philanthropy, http://philanthropy.com/news/updates/7244/obama-plans-to-reduce-charitable-deduction-for-wealthy-donors.

146. Obama, July 2, Colorado Springs, CO.

147. Shawn McBurney, "Americorps the Pitiful," Citizens Against Government Waste, www.cagw.org/site/PageServer?pagename=reports_americorps.

148. AmeriCorps, "What Is AmeriCorps?" www.americorps.gov/for_individuals/why/index.asp.

149. Ibid.

150. Byron York, "How Republicans Can Crack the AmeriCorps Scandal," *Washington Examiner*, June 18, 2009, www.washingtonexaminer.com/politics/How-Republicans-can-crack-the-AmeriCorps-scandal-48556282.html.

151. Richard Albert, "Czars Run Counter to Barack Obama's Promises," Politico, www.politico.com/news/stories/0709/25129.html.

152. Stephan Dinan and S.A Miller, "Jindal Rejects La.'s Stimulus Share," *Washington Times*, February 21, 2009, www.washingtontimes.com/news/2009/feb/21/lousiana-gov-rejects-states-stimulus-share/.

153. "A bill passed by both houses shall be signed by the presiding officers and delivered to the Governor within three days after passage." La. Const., Article III, §17. "If the Governor does not approve a bill, he may veto it." La. Const., Article III, §18.

154. Article III, §§15, 17 La. Const. Congress does not contemplate a distinction between resolutions and bills. See "Congressional Bills: Glossary: 'Definitions of Types of Legislation' accessed online on March 26, 2009, at http://www.gpoaccess.gov/bills/glossary.html.

155. This would likely be the case in all states. Although I have only certified this fact for all of the twelve state constitutions I have reviewed, this number is substantial enough to indicate that it is true for all states.

156. "No joint, concurrent, or other resolution shall require the signature or other action of the Governor to become effective." Article III, §17, La. Const.

157. See, e.g., the Mississippi constitution, which states "but orders, votes, and resolutions of both houses, affecting the prerogatives and duties thereof, or relating to adjournment, to amendments to the Constitution, to the investigation of public officers, and the like, shall not require the signature of the Governor." Article 4, §60 Miss. Const.

158. Nick Timiraos, "Barney Frank Threatens Return of 'Cramdown' Legislation," *Wall Street Journal*, August 4, 2009, http://blogs.wsj.com/developments/2009/08/04/barney-frank-threatens-return-of-cram-down-legislation/.

159. Renae Merle, "Subprime Lenders Getting U.S. Subsidies, Report Says," *Washington Post*, August 26, 2009, http://www.washingtonpost.com/wp-dyn/content/article/2009/08/25/AR2009082502975.html.

160. Jane J. Kim, "Fiduciary Duty Hits the Street—Sort of," *Wall Street Journal*, August 21, 2009, http://online.wsj.com/article/SB125150143646168267.html?mod=rss_whats_news_us.

161. Sara Hansard, Sara, "IAA Backs Obama on Banning Mandatory Securities Arbitration," *Investment News*, October 1, 2009, www.investmentnews.com/apps/pbcs.dll/article?AID=/20091001/FREE/910019983.

162. "White House Move to Collect 'Fishy' Info May Be Illegal, Critics Say," FOX News, www.foxnews.com/politics/2009/08/07/white-house-collect-fishy-info-health-reform-illegal-critics-say/.

163. Macon Phillips, "Facts Are Stubborn Things," The White House—The Blog, www.whitehouse.gov/blog/facts-are-stubborn-things/.

164. "15 USC Chapter 103—Controlling the Assault of Non-Solicited Pornography and Marketing 01/08/2008," http://uscode.house.gov/download/pls/15C103.txt.

165. Sunlen Miller, and Jake Tapper, "Political Punch," ABC News, http://blogs.abcnews.com/politicalpunch/2009/08/white-house-website-makes-security-changes-amid-email-flap.html.

Chapter 7   Radical Tactics

1. Charli E. Coon, "Why the Government's CAFE Standards for Fuel Efficiency Should Be Repealed, Not Increased," The Heritage Foundation, www.heritage.org/Research/EnergyandEnvironment/BG1458.cfm.

2. Berman and Company, "60 Minutes Video," www.bermanco.com/60min.htm.

3. Peter Slevin, "For Clinton and Obama, a Common Ideological Touchstone," *Washington Post*, March 25 2007, www.washingtonpost.com/wp-dyn/content/article/2007/03/24/AR2007032401152.html.

4. Saul D. Alinsky, *Rules for Radicals: A Pragmatic Primer for Realistic Radicals* (New York: Random House, 1971), xviii, i–xx, passim.

5. Ibid.

6. Ibid.

7. Ibid. 10–11.

8. "Report: Is ACORN Intentionally Structured As a Criminal Enterprise?" July 23, 2009, http://republicans.oversight.house.gov/index.php?option=com_content&view=article&id=3%3Areport-is-acorn-intentionally-structured-as-a-criminal-enterprise&catid=21&Itemid=28.

9. Ibid.

10. Ibid, 74.

11. Ibid.

12. Ibid.

13. Ibid. 7–8.

14. Ibid 13–14.

15. Ibid.

16. Ibid. 8.

17. Ibid. 10.

18. Ibid. 5.

19. Ibid.

20. Fred Brooks, "The Evolution of Community Organizing Campaigns at ACORN 1970-2006," May 24, 2009, www.allacademic.com/meta/p177284_index.html.

21. "NYC Lobbyist Search Results," www.nyc.gov/lobbyistsearch/search?lobbyist=Jon+Kest.

22. YouTube, "ACORN Employee Arrested for Prostitution," www.youtube.com/watch?v=zeiZjDn3VNk.

23. Ibid.

24. Joshua Rhett Miller, "Organizers Give Recipes for Effective Tea Parties," FOX News, www.foxnews.com/politics/2009/04/11/organizers-recipe-effective-tea-parties/.

25. Darrell Issa, "Committee on Oversight and Government Reform: Is ACORN Intentionally Structured As a Criminal Enterprise?" July 23, 2009, http://republicans.oversight.house.gov/index.php?option=com_content&view=article&id=3%3Areport-is-acorn-intentionally-structured-as-a-criminal-enterprise&catid=21&Itemid=28.

26. Andrew Taylor, "Senate Votes to Deny Funds to ACORN," Breitbart, www.breitbart.com/article.php?id=D9ANCH580&show_article=1.

27. Jim Abrams, "House Votes to Deny All Federal Funds for ACORN," Yahoo! News, http://news.yahoo.com/s/ap/20090917/ap_on_go_co/us_congress_acorn.

28. Matthew Jaffe, "IRS, ACORN Sever Ties over Scandal," ABC News, http://abcnews.go.com/Politics/Business/irs-acorn-sever-ties-tax-advice-scandal/story?id=8655380.

29. Carol Horowitz, "Justice Department Inspector General Opens Investigation of ACORN," National Legal and Policy Center, www.nlpc.org/stories/2009/09/25/justice-department-inspector-general-opens-investigation-acorn.

30. Iver Peterson, "Glimpse of 'Real Detroit' Given to 13 Republicans," New York Times, July 13, 1980, http://select.nytimes.com/mem/archive/pdf.

31. Ibid.

32. Council on Environmental Quality, "CEQ Chair," www.whitehouse.gov/administration/eop/ceq/chair/.

33. Apollo Alliance, "Apollo Board Member Van Jones Accepts White House Post," http://apolloalliance.org/what%e2%80%99s-new/apollo-board-member-van-jones-accepts-white-house-post/.

34. Glenn Beck, "Linking Social Justice to 'Green' Jobs." FOX News, www.foxnews.com/story/0,2933,535284,00.html.

35. Apollo Alliance, "About," http://apolloalliance.org/about/.

36. Glenn Beck, "Linking Social Justice to 'Green' Jobs." FOX News, www.foxnews.com/story/0,2933,535284,00.html.

37. YouTube, "Glenn Beck Exposes Color of Change Co-Founder Van Jones," www.youtube.com/watch?v=gOgmwyfKuL8.; *See also* http://latimesblogs.latimes.com/showtracker/2009/08/glenn-beck-ignores-ad-boycott.html.

38. http://issa.house.gov/index.cfm?FuseAction=News.PressReleases&ContentRecord_id=ad0751a3-19b9-b4b1-1247-42fb7b539871, or johnmohara.com/ACORNReport.pdf.

39. Alan Cranston, "Interview with Saul Alinsky," *Playboy Magazine,* 1972, www.progress.org/2003/alinsky4.htm.

40. Ibid.

41. Ibid.

42. "Boehner Releases Analysis Showing ACORN Has Received at Least $31 Million in Federal Funding; Untold Millions More through State & Local Agencies," http://republicanleader.house.gov/News/DocumentSingle.aspx?DocumentID=104821.

43. Open Secrets: Center for Responsive Politics, "Labor: Long-Term Contribution Trends," www.opensecrets.org/industries/indus.php?ind=P.

44. United States Department of Labor, Economic News Release: Union Members Summary, www.bls.gov/news.release/union2.nr0.htm

45. *United States v. Butler*, 297 U.S. 1 (1936).

46. "National Affairs: Barrel No. 2," *Time* magazine, June 23, 1947, www.time.com/time/magazine/article/0,9171,797962,00.html (accessed August 20, 2009).

47. Rasmussen Reports, "Just 9% of Non-Union Workers Want to Join Union," March 16, 2009, www.rasmussenreports.com/public_content/business/jobs_employment/march_2009/just_9_of_non_union_workers_want_to_join_union; accessed August 19, 2009.

48. Robert Gavin, "Union Employees Open to Concessions, but Demand Management Cuts as Well," *Boston Globe*, April 5, 2009, www.boston.com/business/articles/2009/04/05/union_employees_open_to_concessions_but_demand_management_cuts_as_well/.

49. Ronald D. White, "Cargo Letup Weighs on Nonunion Dockworkers," *Los Angeles Times*, January 19, 2009, http://articles.latimes.com/2009/jan/19/business/fi-ports19.

50. Steven Greenhouse, "Investigators Say Elevator Union Members Were Paid Millions for No-Show Jobs," January 5, 2001, www.nytimes.com/2002/01/05/nyregion/investigators-say-elevator-union-members-were-paid-millions-for-no-show-jobs.html?pagewanted=1.

51. Bryce G. Hoffman, "12,000 Paid Not to Work; Big 3 and Suppliers Pay Billions to Keep Downsized UAW Members on Payroll in Decades-Long Deal," *Detroit News*, October 17, 2005.

52. Marcia Gelbart, "Detailed Turf Rules Bring Hope for Convention Center Peace: A Month after Unions Reached a General Agreement on Work Issues, They Now Know Who Delivers Hot Tubs and Who Handles Computers," *Philadelphia Inquirer*; February 8, 2001.

53. Josh Barbanel, "A Hard Lesson in Living With Seniority Rules," *New York Times*, January 19, 1993, www.nytimes.com/1993/01/19/nyregion/a-hard-lesson-in-living-with-seniority-rules.html.

54. Jason Song, "Failure Gets a Pass; Firing Tenured Teachers Can Be a Costly and Tortuous Task," *Los Angeles Times*, May 3, 2009, www.latimes.com/news/local.la-me-teachers3-2009may03,0,679507.story. See also "Accused of Sexual Abuse, but Back in the Classroom," Jason Song, *Los Angeles Times*, May 10, 2009, www.latimes.com/news/local/la-me-teachers10-2009may10,0,1620156,full.story (accessed August 21, 2009).

55. Martha Irving and Robert Tanner, "Thousands of Teachers Cited for Sex Misconduct," *USA Today*, October 20, 2007, www.usatoday.com/news/education/2007-10-20-teachermisconduct_N.htm.

56. AP Staff, "Study: Sex Abuse Prevalent in Schools," FOX News, June 2004, www.foxnews.com/story/0,2933,124269,00.html.

57. Robert Tanner, "Weakened Safeguards Have Allowed Teacher Sexual Misconduct to Flourish," NewsOK.com, October 2007, http://newsok.com/weakened-safeguards-have-allowed-teacher-sexual-misconduct-to-flourish/article/315479.

58. Walter E. Williams, *Do The Right Thing: The People's Economist Speaks* (Hoover Institution Press, 1995), 83, http://books.google.com/books?id=SxGurfTCNZcC&printsec=frontcover&dq=do+the+right+thing#v=onepage&q=&f=false; accessed August 21, 2009.

59. Jim Puzzanghera, "Judge Orders West Coast Ports to Reopen," Knight Ridder/Tribune Information Services, October 9, 2002, www.foxnews.com/story/0,2933,64973,00.html (accessed August 19, 2009).

60. Associated Press, "W. Coast Dockworker Talks Stall," *Desert News* (Salt Lake City), October 2, 2002. See also "Off the Waterfront: News Media Have Abandoned the Labor Beat and Missed a Story of Global Financial Import: The Looming Possibility of a Longshoremen's Strike at West Coast Ports," Matt Smith, *San Francisco Weekly*, June 5, 2002.

61. "Bush Intervenes in West Coast Port Lockout," FOX News, October 7, 2002, www.foxnews.com/story/0,2933,64973,00.html.

62. Steven Greenhouse, "Both Sides See Gains in Deal to End Port Labor Dispute," http://archive.ilwu.org/solidarityday/NYTimes20021125.htm; accessed August 19, 2009.

63. Rasmussen Reports, "Just 9% of Non-Union Workers Want to Join Union," March 16, 2009, www.rasmussenreports.com/public_content/business/jobs_employment/march_2009/just_9_of_non_union_workers_want_to_join_union.

64. "Taft-Hartley Changes: It's a Fight Between Professionals," *Time*, February 8, 1954, www.time.com/time/magazine/article/0,9171,860415,00.html.

65. "NLRB Election Report," National Labor Relations Board, www.nlrb.gov/nlrb/shared_files/brochures/Election%20Reports/ER2009/ERMar2009.pdf.

66. Kathy Robertson, "Laundry, Union Settle, but Sutter Still Suing," *Sacramento Business Journal*, July 15, 2005, www.bizjournals.com/sacramento/stories/2005/07/18/story5.html. See also "Union's "Corporate Campaign Tactics Backfire—Jury Awards $17.3 Million in Defamation Lawsuit against Unite Here," July 28, 2006, www.callaborlaw.com/archives/court-decisions-unions-corporate-campaign-tactics-backfire-jury-awards-173-million-in-defamation-lawsuit-against-unite-here.html.

67. "Sutter Hospitals Band Together and File Lawsuit against Union for False and Defamatory Campaign that Misled and Upset Patients," April 28, 2005, www.sutterhealth.org/about/news/news_lawsuit.html.

68. Kevin Mooney, "Unions Gave ACORN nearly $10 Million," *Washington Examiner*, July 9, 2009, www.washingtonexaminer.com/opinion/blogs/beltway-confidential/Unions-gave-ACORN-nearly-10-million-50390017.html.

69. Kevin Mooney and Barbara Hollingsworth, "ACORN's 'Muscle for Money' Does the Bidding of SEIU," *San Francisco Examiner*, July 7, 2009, www.sfexaminer.com/opinion/ACORNs-Muscle-for-Money-does-the-bidding-of-SEIU-50091427.html.

70. Carol Horowitz, "SEIU Hires Union-Busting Security Firm to Aid in California Trusteeship; Company Sues for Back Payment," National Legal and Policy

Center, May 13, 2009, www.nlpc.org/stories/2009/05/13/seiu-hires-union-busting-security-firm-aid-california-trusteeship-company-sues-ba.

71. Jane Roberts, "Overnite Kicks Teamsters Out—Decertification Vote Follows Violent Strike," The Commercial Appeal, July 22, 2003. See also www.employmentblawg.com/2003/overnite-teamsters-nlrb-settlement-reveals-teamsters-ugly-underbelly.

72. See Iron Workers AFL-CIO Local 40 (Filer number 037-089) Form LM-2 Labor Organization Annual Financial Report for Fiscal Year 2005, which lists a disbursement of $52,879 to Premium Cadillac, New Rochelle, N.Y. Form LM-2 Annual Financial Report, www.unionreports.gov.

73. Jeff Shields, "U.S. Sues Resort Union; Diplomat Built With Pension Fund Millions; At Issue: Research, Family Connections," Sun-Sentinel, September 13, 2002.

74. "The Impact of Regulatory Costs on Small Firms," Small Business Administration, Office of Advocacy, September 2005, www.sba.gov/advo/research/rs264tot.pdf.

75. "SEC Moves to Reduce Sarbanes-Oxley Costs," New York Times, May 23, 2007, at www.nytimes.com/2007/05/23/business/worldbusiness/23iht-regs.4.5843700.html. See also C-Span Congressional Chronicles, Text from the Congressional Record, www.c-spanarchives.org/congress/?q=node/77531&id=8123884.

76. Bob Unruh, "Teachers' Free Speech Trumps Union Politics: Supreme Court Calls Claim Labor Has 'Right' to Financing 'Immaterial,'" WorldNetDaily.com, June 14, 2007, www.wnd.com/news/article.asp?ARTICLE_ID=56178.

77. See National Education Association's (Filer Number 000-342) Form LM-2 Labor Organization Annual Financial Report for Fiscal year 2001, www.unionreports.gov.

78. Michael Mishak, "Unplugged: The SEIU Chief on the Labor Movement and the Card Check," Las Vegas Sun, May 10, 2009, www.lasvegassun.com/news/2009/may/10/stern-unplugged-seiu-chief-labor-movement-and-card/.

79. Dan Morain and Evelyn Larrubia, "Hilda Solis' Belief in Unions Runs Deep," Los Angeles Times, January 9, 2009, http://articles.latimes.com/2009/jan/09/local/me-solis9.

80. Don Todd, "Obama De-funding the Union Corruption Busters," Americans for Limited Government, http://blog.getliberty.org/default.asp?Display=1195. Todd served as Deputy Assistant Secretary for OLMS from 2001-2009.

81. Melanie Trottman, "Labor Department to Tighten Scrutiny," *Wall Street Journal*, August 9, 2009, http://online.wsj.com/article/SB125064127552641791.html. See also www.washingtonexaminer.com/opinion/blogs/beltway-confidential / Obama - Labor - Department - to - review - union - transparency - regulations-51417792.html.

82. "Trial Lawyer Bonanza," *Wall Street Journal*, January 9, 2009, http://online.wsj.com/article/SB123146294351966567.html. "For Labor, Small Shifts, Big Wishes," Melanie Trottman, *Wall Street Journal*, August 8, 2009, http://online.wsj.com/article/SB124968706032115785.html?mod=googlenews_wsj.

Chapter 8   The Teapot Boils Over

1. John Breshnahan, "Congressional Jets May Be Scrapped," Politico.com, August 2009, www.politico.com/news/stories/0809/26000.html.

2. Mark Silva, "Obama: Healthcare Reform by Year's End," *Chicago Tribune*, May 13, 2009, www.swamppolitics.com/news/politics/blog/2009/05/obama_healthcare_reform_by_yea.html.

3. Glenn Thrush, "Memo: No Health Vote before Recess Update," Politico, www.politico.com/blogs/glennthrush/0709/Memo_No_health_vote_before_recess.html.

4. "Health Care Costs: A Primer," The Henry J. Kaiser Family Foundation, http://kff.org/insurance/upload/7670_02.pdf.

5. 2007 U.S. Census, www.census.gov.

6. "Obama: 'If You Like Your Doctor, You Can Keep Your Doctor,'" *Wall Street Journal*, June 15, 2009, http://blogs.wsj.com/washwire/2009/06/15/obama-if-you-like-your-doctor-you-can-keep-your-doctor/.

7. YouTube, "Shock Uncovered: Obama in His Own Words Saying His Health Care Plan will Eliminate Private Insurance," www.youtube.com/watch?v=p-bY92mcOdk.

8. George Will, "We Don't Need Radical Health Care Reform," RealClearPolitics, www.realclearpolitics.com/articles/2009/06/21/taking_a_razor_to_the_presidents_plan_97094.html.

9. Rich Lowry, "Success of Medicare Part D is a Bitter Pill for Democrats," RealClearPolitics, www.realclearpolitics.com/articles/2007/01/success_of_medicare_part_d_is.html.

10. 2007 WSJ/Harris Interactive poll.

11. Congressional Budget Office, www.cbo.gov, Preliminary Analysis

12. 2009 Medicare Trustees Report available at www.cms.hhs.gov/ReportsTrust Funds/downloads/tr2009.pdf.

13. Ibid.

14. Gerald F. Anderson and Jean-Pierre Poullier, "Health Spending, Access, and Outcomes: Trends in Industrialized Countries," *Health Affairs*, Vol. 8, No. 3, 1999, 178-192.

15. "The 2007 Commonwealth Fund International Health Policy Survey: Data Sheeted Questionnaire," www.commonwealthfund.org/~/media/Files/Surveys/2007/2007%20International%20Health%20Policy%20Survey%20in%20Seven%20Countries/28662_DSQ_Final_070607%20pdf.pdf.

16. Fraser Institute. "Waiting Your Turn: Hospital Waiting Lists in Canada," www.fraserinstitute.org/commerce.web/product_files/WaitingYourTurn2008.pdf.

17. Clifford Krauss, "As Canada's Slow-Motion Public Health System Falters, Private Medical Care Is Surging," *New York Times*, February 26, 2006. www.nytimes.com/2006/02/26/international/americas/26canada.html?ex=1184644800&en=44cca772dc339429&ei=5070.

18. "Health Care Costs: A Primer," The Henry J. Kaiser Family Foundation, http://kff.org/insurance/upload/7670_02.pdf.

19. The White House: Office of the Press Secretary, "Remarks by the President to a Joint Session of Congress On Health Care," www.whitehouse.gov/the_press_office/Remarks-by-the-President-to-a-Joint-Session-of-Congress-on-Health-Care/.

20. United States Senate Committee on Finance, "The America's Healthy Future Act and Related Links," http://finance.senate.gov/sitepages/Americas_Healthy_Future_Act.html.

21. Mike Allen, "White House Disables E-tip Box," Politico, www.politico.com/news/stories/0809/26188.html.

22. "White House Move to Collect 'Fishy' Info May Be Illegal, Critics Say," FOX News, www.foxnews.com/politics/2009/08/07/white-house-collect-fishy-info-health-reform-illegal-critics-say/.

23. Alex Isenstadt, "Town Halls Gone Wild," Politico, www.politico.com/news/stories/0709/25646.html.

24. Anne Flaherty, "E-Mails from Public Overload House Web Site," My Way, http://apnews.myway.com/article/20090813/D9A25N781.html.

25. Ibid.

26. "Sen. Specter Shouted Down Over Health Care," RealClearPolitics, www.realclearpolitics.com/video/2009/08/11/sen_specter_shouted_down_over_health_care.html.

27. "Crowd Explodes When Arlen Specter Urges That We "Do This Fast,'" YouTube, www.youtube.com/watch?v=J-Bpshk5nX0.

28. "Town Hall To Claire McCaskill: We Don't Trust You," YouTube, www.youtube.com/watch?v=PDPpGJDelHI.

29. Michelle Malkin, "Little Girl at Obama Town Hall Has Not-So-Random Political Connections," http://michellemalkin.com/2009/08/11/little-girl-at-obama-town-hall-has-not-so-random-political-connections/.

30. James Joyner, "Presidential Press Conferences, RIP?" Outside the Beltway, www.outsidethebeltway.com/archives/presidential_press_conferences_rip/.

31. "Obama's Press List: Membership Shall Have Its Privileges," *Wall Street Journal*, February 11, 2009, sec. A16, http://online.wsj.com/article/SB123431418276770899.html.

32. Peggy Noonan, "Pull the Plug on ObamaCare: It's the Best Cure for What Ails the Obama Presidency," *Wall Street Journal*, August 20, 2009. http://online.wsj.com/article_email/SB1000142405297020488440457436297 1349563340-lMyQjAxMDA5MDIwMDEyNDAyWj.html.

33. "'06 Flashback: Pelosi Tells Anti-War Protesters 'I'm a Fan of Disruptors,'" Breitbart TV, www.breitbart.tv/06-flashback-pelosi-tells-anti-war-protesters-im-a-fan-of-disruptors/.

34. "In a Tight Spot, Pelosi Calls Health Care Critics 'Un-American,'" FOX News, www.foxnews.com/politics/2009/08/10/tight-spot-pelosi-calls-health-care-critics-american/.

35. Nancy Pelosi and Steny Hoyer, "Forum-Pelosi-Mug-10 'Un-American' Attacks Can't Derail Health Care Debate," *USA Today*, http://blogs.usatoday.com/oped/2009/08/unamerican-attacks-cant-derail-health-care-debate-.html.

36. "White House Disputes Pelosi Contention that Town Hall Protests Are 'Un-American,'" ABC News, http://blogs.abcnews.com/politicalpunch/2009/08/white-house-disputes-pelosi-contention-that-town-hall-protests-are-un-american.html.

37. "Day's End Roundup," The Hill, http://briefingroom.thehill.com/2009/08/13/reid-protesters-are-evil-mongers/.

38. Jake Wagman, "Citing Safety Concerns, U. City Cancels McCaskills Event," STL Today, www.stltoday.com/blogzone/political-fix/political-fix/2009/08/citing-safety-concerns-u-city-cancels-mccaskills-event/.

39. Melissa Bean, "Chamber Breakfast with Congresswoman Melissa Bean," www.chambermaster.com/directory/jsp/events/EventPage.jsp?ccid=82&eventid=1038.

40. "Score One for Sarah: Where Are Hodes, Shea-Porter?," *Union Leader*, www.unionleader.com/article.aspx?headline=Score+one+for+Sarah:+Where+are+Hodes,+Shea-Porter%3F&articleId=4095b948-c026-404a-bbf9-fb940fa35103.

41. "Rep. Sheila Jackson Lee Talks on the Phone as a Woman Asks a Question at a Town Hall Event," YouTube, www.youtube.com/watch?v=-L3FnWNkIzU.

42. Ashley Hasley III, "Primary-Care Doctor Shortage May Undermine Reform Efforts: No Quick Fix as Demand Already Exceeds Supply," *Washington Post*, www.washingtonpost.com/wp-dyn/content/article/2009/06/19/AR2009061903583.html.

43. Ibid.

44. Amanda Carpenter, "Georgia Democrat Yells at Local Doctor over Health Care," *Washington Times*, August 8, 2009, www.washingtontimes.com/weblogs/back-story/2009/aug/08/georgia-democrat-rages-against-local-doctor-over-h/.

45. Mark Tapscott, "Dean Says Obamacare Authors Don't Want to Challenge Trial Lawyers," *Washington Examiner*, August 26, 2009, www.washingtonexaminer.com/opinion/blogs/beltway-confidential/Dean-says-Obamacare-authors-dont-want-to-challenge-trial-lawyers-55140567.html.

46. "The Case for Medical Liability Reform," American Medical Association, www.ama-assn.org/ama1/pub/upload/mm/-1/case-for-mlr.pdf.

47. Ibid.

48. Ibid.

49. "Medical Liability Reform—Now!" American Medical Association, www.ama-assn.org/ama1/pub/upload/mm/-1/mlrnow.pdf.

50. "Remarks by the President to a Joint Session of Congress on Health Care," The White House: Office of the Press Secretary, www.whitehouse.gov/the_press_office/Remarks-by-the-President-to-a-Joint-Session-of-Congress-on-Health-Care/.

51. Dave Freddoso, "U.S. Chamber Speaks Out on Malpractice Reform 'Demonstration Projects,'" *Washington Examiner*, September 17, 2009. www.washingtonexaminer.com/opinion/blogs/beltway-confidential/US-Chamber-speaks-out-on-malpractice-reform-demonstration-projects-59671337.html.

52. "Broad Health Coalition Disappointed in Baucus Bill: Urges Senate to Take Real Action on Medical Liability Reform," HCLA, www.hcla.org/pressreleases/HCLA%20Baucus%20Release%20final.pdf.

53. Open Secrets: Center for Responsive Politics, www.opensecrets.org.

54. 2006 report from Health Care America.

55. "Lawyers/Law Firms: Long-Term Contribution Trends," Open Secrets: Center for Responsive Politics, www.opensecrets.org/industries/indus.php?ind=K01.

56. Carrie Budoff Brown, "White House to Democrats: 'Punch Back Twice as Hard,'" Politico. www.politico.com/news/stories/0809/25891.html.

57. Ibid.

58. Lydia Saad, "Cost Is Foremost Healthcare Issue for Americans," Gallup, www.gallup.com/poll/123149/Cost-Is-Foremost-Healthcare-Issue-for-Americans.aspx.

59. Michael Kinsley, "Change We'd Rather Do Without," *Washington Post*, August 28, 2009, www.washingtonpost.com/wp-dyn/content/article/2009/08/27/AR2009082703254.html?nav=rss_opinion/columns.

60. Charles Mahtesian, "Charlie Cook: Dem Situation Has 'Slipped Completely Out of Control,'" Politico, www.politico.com/blogs/scorecard/0809/Charlie_Cook_Dem_situation_has_slipped_completely_out_of_control.html.

61. "Obama Slams TV over Health Care 'Ruckus,'" Breitbart, www.breitbart.com/article.php?id=CNG.228e42c5948115405d6f3ec5d1ad6b50.1a1&show_article=1.

62. Jon Ward, "WH Calls Health Care Anger 'Manufactured,'" *Washington Times*, August 4, 2009. www.washingtontimes.com/news/2009/aug/04/white-house-dismisses-health-care-protests/.

63. "Barbara Boxer Objects to Health Care Protesters' 'Attire,'" YouTube, www.youtube.com/watch?v=ZV84OBtGpSQ.

64. Peggy Noonan, "'You Are Terrifying Us': Voters Send a Message to Washington, and Get an Ugly Eesponse," *Wall Street Journal,* August 6, 2009, http://sbk.online.wsj.com/article/SB10001424052970204908604574334623330098540.html.

65. Caleb Howe, "Let's Talk Astroturf," Red State, www.redstate.com/absentee/2009/08/09/lets-talk-astroturf/.

66. Howard Wolinsky, "The Secret Side of David Axelrod: The Obama Campaign's Chief Strategist Is a Master of 'Astroturfing' and Has a Second Firm that Shapes Public Opinion for Corporations," *Business Week*, March 14, 2008, www.businessweek.com/bwdaily/dnflash/content/mar2008/db20080314_121054.htm.

67. "Obama Supporters Plan Pro-Health Overhaul Push," Associated Press, www.google.com/hostednews/ap/article/ALeqM5jlMpJGn28kqCcgU-aGcYE_ZHW-ywD9AA5U3G3.

68. Ibid.

69. Michelle Malkin, "Sebelius Calls Her SEIU "Brothers and Sisters" to Battle; Dennis Rivera Decries 'Terrorist Tactics,'" http://michellemalkin.com/2009/08/07/sebelius-calls-her-seiu-brothers-and-sisters-to-battle/.

70. Leah Thorson, "Six People, Including P-D Reporter, Arrested at Carnahan Meeting," St. Louis Today, www.stltoday.com/stltoday/news/stories.nsf/laworder/story/0470FEB3219207458625760B001142AC?OpenDocument.

71. Seton Motley, "Violence at Townhall against a Conservative; Six Arrested, Including a Reporter," NewsBusters, http://newsbusters.org/blogs/setonmotley/2009/08/07/violence-townhall-against-conservative-six-arrested-including-reporter.

72. Michelle Malkin, *Culture of Corruption*, 220.

73. L. Toni Lewis, MD, SEUI, www.seiu.org/2009/08/stop-the-violence-at-health-care-town-halls.php.

74. Sam Stein, "Unions to Take on Conservative Groups Health Care Town Halls," Huffington Post, www.huffingtonpost.com/2009/08/06/unions-to-take-on-conserv_n_252720.html.

75. Ibid.

76. Medicare web site, www.medicare.gov.

77. Ibid.

78. "AARP, Losing Members over Health Care, Faces Challenge from Grassroots Senior Advocacy Group," FOX News, www.foxnews.com/politics/2009/08/18/aarp-losing-members-health-care-faces-challenge-grassroots-senior-advocacy/.

79. David A. Patten, "AARP: No Mr. President, We Don't Support Your Healthcare Plan," Newsmax, www.newsmax.com/headlines/obama_aarp_healthcare/2009/08/12/246978.html.

80. Rachelm Martin and Jake Tapper, "President Obama's 'Senior' Moment?" ABC News, http://blogs.abcnews.com/politicalpunch/2009/08/president-obamas-senior-moment.html.

81. "AARP Loses Members over Health Care Stance," *USA Today*, August 18, 2009, www.usatoday.com/news/washington/2009-08-17-aarp-health-overhaul_N.htm.

82. Mary Anne Lonze, "Why I Cancelled My AARP Membership," American Thinker, www.americanthinker.com/2009/08/why_i_cancelled_aarp_membershi.html.

83. John Mackey, "The Whole Foods Alternative to ObamaCare," *Wall Street Journal,* August 11, 2009, http://online.wsj.com/article/SB10001424052970204251404574342170072865070.html.

84. Ibid.

85. Kevin Sack, "A Shoppers' Rebellion at Whole Foods," *New York Times*, August 22, 2009, http://prescriptions.blogs.nytimes.com/2009/08/22/a-shoppers-rebellion-at-whole-foods/.

86. Emily Friedman, "Health Care Stirs Up Whole Foods CEO John Mackey, Customers Boycott Organic Grocery Store," ABC News, http://abcnews.go.com/Business/Story?id=8322658&page=1.

87. Calvin Hennick, "Local Protests over Whole Foods CEO's Opinion Piece," *Boston Globe*, August 21, 2009. www.boston.com/business/ticker/2009/08/local_protests.html.

88. John Mackey, "The Whole Foods Alternative to ObamaCare," *Wall Street Journal*, August 11, 2009. http://online.wsj.com/article/SB100014240 52970204251404574342170072865070.html.

89. Ibid.

90. "Our Core Values," Whole Foods Market, www.wholefoodsmarket.com/company/corevalues.php.

91. Ibid.

92. John Mackey, "The Whole Foods Alternative to ObamaCare," *Wall Street Journal*, August 11, 2009, http://online.wsj.com/article/SB10001424052970204251404574342170072865070.html.

93. "Fannie Med? Why a 'Public Option' Is Hazardous to Your Health," The Cato Institute, Policy Analysis No. 642, August 6, 2009

94. U. S. Sen. Kent Conrad, "Bridging the Divide with a Cooperative Health Care Proposal," http://conrad.senate.gov/pressroom/record.cfm?id=315210&.

95. "Fannie Med: The Bipartisan Senate Negotiators Are Leaning toward Proposing a Health-Care Fannie Mae," *Wall Street Journal,* July 30, 2009, http://online.wsj.com/article/SB100014240529702046190045743184 7422 4065070.html.

96. H.R. 3200, 111th Congress, First Session.

97. Monica Gabriel and Marie Magleby, "Democratic Leader Laughs at Idea that House Members Would Actually Read Health-Care Bill before Voting On It," CNS News, www.cnsnews.com/public/content/article.aspx?RsrcID=50677.

98. Jane Adamy and Jonathan Weisman, "Health-Care Anger Has Deeper Roots," *Wall Street Journal*, September 1, 2009, http://online.wsj.com/article/SB125176363081674373.html.

99. Ibid.

100. Ibid.

Chapter 9   The Tea Party Manifesto

1. Saul D. Alinsky, Rules for Radicals: A Pragmatic Primer for Realistic Radicals (New York: Random House, 1971) 10.

2. Rasmussen Reports, "51% View Tea Parties Favorably, Political Class Strongly Disagrees," www.rasmussenreports.com/public_content/politics/general_politics/april_2009/51_view_tea_parties_favorably_political_class_strongly_disagrees.

3. Caleb Howe, "Let's Talk Astroturf," Red State, www.redstate.com/absentee/2009/08/09/lets-talk-astroturf/.

4. "Concord Area Early Bus N.H. to D.C.—Ride and Rally for Health Care Reform (Change that Works—New Hampshire)," SEIU, http://action.seiu.org/page/event/detail/w7f.

5. Author's personal e-mail.

6. Griff Jenkins and Eric Shaw, "Thousands of Anti-Tax 'Tea Party' Protesters Turn Out in U.S. Cities," FOX News, www.foxnews.com/politics/2009/04/15/anti-tax-tea-party-protests-expected/.

7. Aaron Cooper, Jim Acosta, Ashley Fantz, and Jason Hanna, "Nationwide 'Tea Party' Protests Blast Spending," CNN, http://edition.cnn.com/2009/POLITICS/04/15/tea.parties/index.html.

8. Author's personal e-mail.

9. Grover Norquist, Leave Us Alone, (William Morrow, 2008), 3.

10. "People Attended Yesterdays Tax Day Tea Parties," Americans for Tax Reform, www.atr.org/people-attended-yesterdays-tax-tea-parties-a3138.

11. Michael Janofsky, "Federal Parks Chief Calls 'Million Man' Count Low," New York Times, October 21, 1995, www.nytimes.com/1995/10/21/us/federal-parks-chief-calls-million-man-count-low.html?sec=&spon=&pagewanted=1.

12. Naftali Bendavid, "They Don't Make Populism in the U.S. Like They Used To," Wall Street Journal, April 17, 2009, http://online.wsj.com/article_email/SB123992058646826949-lMyQjAxMDI5MzE5NzkxMjcwWj.html.

13. Alinsky, 17–18.

14. Alinsky, 25.

15. IRS, "Estate and Gift Taxes," www.irs.gov/businesses/small/article/0,,id=98968,00.html.

16. Ibid.

17. "State Regulations," DMV.org, www.dmv.org/ma-massachusetts/state-regulations.php#Selling_a_Used_Car.

18. Shannon McCaffrey, "GOP Hopes to Build Momentum behind 'Tea Parties'," guaridan.co.uk, www.guardian.co.uk/world/feedarticle/8458173.

19. Ibid.

20. Aaron Cooper, Jim Acosta, Ashley Fantz, and Jason Hanna, "Nationwide 'Tea Party' Protests Blast Spending," CNN.

21. Alexis de Tocqueville, The Old Regime and the Revolution, ed. Francois Furet (University of Chicago Press, 1998), 105.

22. "Harvard Student Takes on Barney Frank Over Economy," RealClearPolitics, www.realclearpolitics.com/video/2009/04/07/harvard_student_takes_on_barney_frank_over_economy.html.

23. Jeff Poor, "Media Mum on Barney Frank's Fannie Mae Love Connection," Business and Media Institute, www.businessandmedia.org/articles/2008/20080924145932.aspx.

24. Bill Sammon, "Lawmaker Accused of Fannie Mae Conflict of Interest," FOX News, www.foxnews.com/story/0,2933,432501,00.html.

25. Peter S. Canellos, Boston Globe, November 22, 1991, City Edition, 73.

26. Gordon McKibben, Op-Ed, Boston Globe, August 5, 1991, City Edition, 11.

27. Lindsay Renick Mayer, "Update: Fannie Mae and Freddie Mac Invest in Lawmakers," Open Secrets: Center for Responsive Politics. www.opensecrets.org/news/2008/09/update-fannie-mae-and-freddie.html.

28. "Fannie, Freddie Asked to Relax Condo Loan Rules: Report," Reuters, www.reuters.com/article/GCA-Housing/idUSTRE55L39120090622.

29. Thomas Sowell, "Random Thoughts for February 2008," Capitalism Magazine, www.capmag.com/article.asp?ID=5417.

30. Alinsky, 10–11.

31. Alinsky, 18–19.

32. Huma Kahn and Michelle McPhee, "Obama Defends Criticism of Cambridge Police in Arrest of Gates," ABC News, http://abcnews.go.com/Politics/story?id=8153681.

33. James Ridgeway, "Obama Talked Big on Katrina, Did Little," Mother Jones, www.motherjones.com/mojo/2009/08/obama-talked-big-katrina-did-little.

34. Hillary Chabot, "Free Cars for Poor Fuel Road Rage," Boston Herald, May 7, 2009, http://news.bostonherald.com/news/regional/view/2009_05_07_Free_cars_for_poor_fuel_road_rage/srvc=home&position=also.

35. Charles Cooper, "Perspective: Should You Have a Right to Broadband?" CNET, http://news.cnet.com/Should-you-have-a-right-to-broadband/2010-1071_3-5905711.html.

36. Michelle Malkin, "Malkin: And the Winner Is—Peggy the Moocher," Washington Times, November 8, 2008. http://washingtontimes.com/news/2008/nov/08/and-the-winner-is—peggy-the-moocher/.

37. "Investigation of Failure of the SEC to Uncover Bernard Madoff's Ponzi Scheme," United States Securities and Exchange Commission, www.sec.gov/spotlight/secpostmadoffreforms/oig-509-exec-summary.pdf.

Chapter 10   Rules for Counterradicals

1. Kevin Bohn, "Blue Dog: 'Excellent Idea' to Start over on Health Care Reform," CNN Politics, http://politicalticker.blogs.cnn.com/2009/08/17/blue-dog-excellent-idea-to-start-over-on-health-care/.

2. "Federal Budget, Taxes, Economic Policy," PollingReport.com, www.pollingreport.com/budget.htm.

3. "Congress and the Public," Gallup, www.gallup.com/poll/1600/Congress-Public.aspx.

4. "Presidential Approval Ratings—Barack Obama," Gallup, www.gallup.com/poll/116479/Barack-Obama-Presidential-Job-Approval.aspx.

5. Rasmussen Reports, "Daily Presidential Tracking Poll," www.rasmussenreports.com/public_content/politics/obama_administration/daily_presidential_tracking_poll.

6. "America's Best Days," August 26, 2009, www.rasmussenreports.com/public_content/politics/mood_of_america/america_s_best_days, "53% Now Oppose Congressional Health Care Reform," July 22, 2009, www.rasmussenreports.com/public_content/politics/current_events/healthcare/july_2009/53_now_oppose_congressional_health_care_reform.

7. John Fritze, "Poll: Deficit More Worrisome than Health Care," USA Today, August 5, 2009, http://blogs.usatoday.com/onpolitics/2009/08/poll-deficit-more-worrisome-than-health-care.html.

8. Gary Langer, "Poll: Obama's Approval Slips on Stimulus, Deficit and Health Care," ABC News, http://abcnews.go.com/PollingUnit/story?id=8112395&page=1.

9. Mike Allen, "White House Disables E-Tip Box," August 17. 2009, www.politico.com/news/stories/0809/26188.html.

10. Joe Markman, "Crowd Estimates Vary Wildly for Capitol March," LA Times, September 2009, www.latimes.com/news/nationworld/nation/la-na-crowd15-2009sep15,0,1062512.story.

11. Author e-mail.

12. George Russell, "A Gulf in Giving: Oil-Rich States Starve the World Food Program," FOX News, www.foxnews.com/story/0,2933,354677,00.html.

13. Sean Stannard-Stockton, "How Much Did Americans Really Give in 2008?" Tactical Philanthropy Advisors, http://tacticalphilanthropy.com/2009/06/how-much-did-americans-really-give-in-2008.

14. George Will, "Conservatives More Liberal Givers," Real Clear Politics, www .realclearpolitics.com/articles/2008/03/conservatives_more_liberal_giv.html.

15. Stephan Dinan and David R. Sands, "Charity Tax Limits Upset Many." *Washington Times*, February 27, 2009, www.washingtontimes.com/news/ 2009/feb/27/charity-tax-challenged-by-political-friends/.

16. Sean Flynn, "Perverse Incentives," *Forbes*, February 19, 2009, www.forbes .com/2009/02/19/incentives-compensation-bonuses-leadership_perverted_ incentives.html.

17. Author's personal e-mail.

18. "Bill Clinton on the Vast Right-Wing Conspiracy, Redux," WashingtonPost.com, September 29, 2009, http://voices.washingtonpost.com/ 44/2009/09/28/bill_clinton_on_the_vast_right.html?wprss=44.

19. Steven Milloy, "Junk Science: Hot Air Study Melts Global Warming Theory," FoxNews.Com, May 27, 2007, www.foxnews.com/story/ 0,2933,275267,00.html. See Also: Global Warming Petition Project, www .petitionproject.org/.

Paul Georgia, "IPCC Report Criticized by One of Its Lead Authors," The Heartland Institute's *Environment & Climate News*, June 2001, www .heartland.org/policybot/results/1069/IPCC_report_criticized_by_one_of_its_ lead_authors.html.

Climate Change Reconsidered, http://www.nipccreport.org/index.html.

www.junkscience.com.

David Kreutzer, Ph.D, Karen Campbell, Ph.D, William W. Beach, Ben Lieberman, et al., "The Economic Consequences of Waxman-Markey: An Analysis of the American Clean Energy and Security Act of 2009," The Heritage Foundation, www.heritage.org/Research/EnergyandEnvironment/ cda0904.cfm.

20. Andy Barr, "South Carolina Gov. Mark Sanford Admits Affair," Politico, www.politico.com/news/stories/0609/24146.html.

21. Eric Kuhn, "Liberal Bloggers Admit Conservatives Have Upper Hand on Twitter," CNN Politics, http://politicalticker.blogs.cnn.com/2009/08/21/liberal-bloggers-admit-conservatives-have-upper-hand-on-twitter/.

22. Tally Weiss, "Kids Are Heavy Social Network Users, They Don't Say No to Relevant Marketing Efforts: Online Surveys and Tips for Marketers," TrendsSpotting, www.trendsspotting.com/blog/?p=165.

23. Gary Stein, "SES Chicago 2006—Day 1—Advertising in Social Media," Online Marketing Managment Strategy, www.daviddalka.com/createvalue/ 2006/12/04/ses-chicago-2006-day-1-advertising-in-social-media/.

24. Stan Schroeder, "Facebook: From 100 to 200 Million Users in 8 Months," Mashable: The Social Media Guide, http://mashable.com/2009/04/08/facebook-from-100-to-200-million-users-in-8-months/.

25. "Thanks a billion. Over 1 Billion Downloads in Just Nine Months," Apple, www.apple.com/itunes/billion-app-countdown/.

26. Justin Smith, "Fastest Growing Demographic on Facebook: Women Over 55," Inside Network, www.insidefacebook.com/2009/02/02/fastest-growing-demographic-on-facebook-women-over-55/.

27. Joshua Hill, "YouTube Surpasses Yahoo! as World's #2 Search Engine," TD Daily, www.tgdaily.com/content/view/39777/113/.

28. "Promise Broken Rulings on the Obameter," PolitiFact, www.politifact.com/truth-o-meter/promises/rulings/promise-broken/.

29. Cook Employees, "Welcome to CookEmployees.com," www.cookemployees.com/.

30. Steven Warmbir, "Nice Work, Commissioner Peraica," *Chicago Sun Times*, August 13, 2009, http://blogs.suntimes.com/backtalk/2009/08/nice_work_commissioner_peraica.html.

31. Bill Marsh, "Illinois Is Trying. It Really Is. But the Most Corrupt State Is Actually..." *New York Times*, December 13, 2008. www.nytimes.com/2008/12/14/weekinreview/14marsh.html.

32. Ray Long and Rick Pearson, "Impeached Illinois Gov. Rod Blagojevich Has Been Removed from Office," *Chicago Tribune*, January 30, 2009, www.chicagotribune.com/news/local/chi-blagojevich-impeachment-removal,0,5791846.story.

33. Ray Long and Rob Pearson, "Roland Burris, Rod Blagojevich," *Chicago Tribune*, December 30, 2008, www.chicagotribune.com/news/politics/chi-roland-burris-081230-ht,0,2291658.story.

34. Author correspondence.

35. Mike Krauser, "Citizens Want to Give Red Light to Red Light Cameras," WBBM News Radio 780, www.wbbm780.com/Citizens-want-to-give-red-light-to-red-light-camer/5008168.

36. Brian Costin, "Time for Property Tax Transparency in Schaumburg," Schaumburg Freedom Coalition, www.schaumburgfreedom.com/features/time-property-tax-transparency-schaumburg/.

37. Andy Barr, "Tea Party Leader to Run for Senate," Politico, www.politico.com/news/stories/0609/23775.html.

ABOUT THE AUTHOR

John M. O'Hara is external relations manager at The Heartland Institute, a national free-market think tank based in Chicago, Illinois. Previously, O'Hara served as a political appointee under U.S. Secretary of Labor Elaine L. Chao in the administration of George W. Bush. Prior to that, O'Hara was a Collegiate Network journalism fellow at the *American Spectator*. He has been active in political campaigns at the state and federal level, including one presidential campaign.

He has appeared on a number of local and national radio and television programs including *The Dennis Miller Show*, FOX News Channel's *Your World with Neil Cavuto* and *America's Newsroom*, FOX Business Network's *Happy Hour* and *Cavuto*, as well as MSNBC's *Hardball with Chris Matthews*.

O'Hara graduated from Kenyon College with a B.A. in philosophy and a concentration in the Integrated Program in Humane Studies. He studied ancient philosophy and ethics at King's College, University of London, and he was managing editor of the *Kenyon Observer*.

Originally from Needham, Massachusetts, O'Hara resides in Chicago, Illinois.

For more about the author, visit JohnMOHara.com.

INDEX

AARP, 197
ACORN (Association of Community
    Organizers), 81, 129, 144–151, 167–168,
    205–206
Adamy, Janet, 201
AFL-CIO, 196
Air America, 83, 119
Albert, Richard, 132
Alinsky, Saul, 143–144, 150–151, 204, 212,
    223–226
Americans for Prosperity, 205, 245–246
AmeriCorps, 129–130
Angelica Textile Services, 167
Apollo Appliance, 149
Armey, Dick, 29, 80–81
ASK Public Strategies, 63, 194–195
Astroturf:
    defined, 14
    Left and, 62–63, 81, 194–195, 205–206
    Left's accusations about tea parties, 62,
        80–81, 204–205
Axelrod, David, 63–64, 125, 194–195
Ayers, Bill, 144

Bailouts. *See also* Stimulus bill; Troubled Asset
    Relief Program (TARP)
    fiscal irresponsibility, 104–110
    government "spin" on, 52–54

spending timeline, xiii–xxi
tea party rejection of, 217–218, 240–241
Barbour, Haley, 69–70
Barnicle, Mike, 70
Barofsky, Neil, 49, 109
Barrett, Gresham, 68
Barth, Megan, 11, 206, 209–210, 257
Bass, Sidney, 148, 149
Bastiat, Frédéric, 113
Baucus, Max, 117, 183–184, 192
Bea, Robert, 104
Beck, Glenn, 19, 149
Biden, Joe, 103–104, 108, 228
Bishop, Tim, 186
Blagojevich, Rod, 150, 253
Blinder, Alan, 110
Boomerang (Skocpol), 29
Boston Tea Party, xxiii–xxiv
Boxer, Barbara, 194
Brady, David, 30
Breitbart, Andrew, 92, 146
Brown, Campbell, 97
*Buck Wild: How Republicans Broke the Bank and
    Became the Party of Big Government*
    (Slivinski), 24
Burnett, Doug, 206
Burris, Roland, 253
Burton, Bill, 189

Bush, George H. W., 27–28
Bush, George W., 3, 22–23, 33–34, 77, 236

Cap and trade, 122–125
Car Allowance Rebate System (CARS),
    110–115
Card check, 165–168
Cardin, Ben, 48
Carnahan, Russ, 195
Carney, Tim, 112–113
Cash for clunkers, 110–115
Cato Institute, 199
Census, ACORN and, 147–148
Chao, Elaine L., 171–172
Charitable contributions, 125–127, 240–241
Chicago, Illinois:
    reform and, 252, 253–254
    tea parties and, 15–19
Clinton, Bill, 129, 222, 236, 246
Clinton, Hillary, 29, 100–101, 143, 144, 222,
    246
CNN, 76–79, 87–88, 94–97, 209
Coburn, Jon, 105
Coleman, Norm, 120
Collins, Kathleen, 163
Collins, Susan, 112
Community Reinvestment Act (CRA),
    42–43
Compensation limits, 121–122
Condon, Stephanie, 121–122
Conrad, Kent, 199–200
Conservatism, 24
Conservative Political Action Conference
    (CPAC), 5, 24, 247–248
Contract with America, 28–33, 36, 100
Cook, Charlie, 193
Cooper, Anderson, 87–88, 97
Costin, Brian, 16, 17–18, 253–254
Counterradicals, tips for, 235–259
    accountability and transparency, 250–252
    coalitions and cooperation, 245–250
    elected office, 256–258
    facts and positive options, 238–242
    rally organization, 242–245, 250
    state activism, 252–255
Cox, Ana Marie, 83–85
Cox, Christopher, 31
Cox, Tom, 257
Cranston, Alan, 150–151

Crossland-Macha, Virginia, 210
Czars, 131–132

Dean, Howard, 191
Declaration of Independence, 141–142, 232
Dobbs, Lou, 68
Dodd, Chris, 222

Elected office, tea party participants and,
    256–258
Election of 1994, 28–33, 36, 100
Election of 2000, 33, 36
Election of 2006, 35
Election of 2008, 5, 23–24, 36–38, 100, 240
Emanuel, Rahm, 35, 100–101, 222
Entitlement ethic, rejection of, 229–231
Expansion of government, 100–101, 117–139
    cap and trade, 122–125
    compensation limits, 121–122
    czars, 131–132
    Fairness Doctrine, 118–121
    financial crisis, 39–40
    free speech, 137
    health care reform, 137–138
    regulations, 137
    stimulus bill, 133–136
    taxes and charitable contributions, 125–127
    tea party movement's views of, 206–215
    volunteer corps, 127–131

Fairness Doctrine, 118–121
Fannie Mae, 2, 44–46, 47, 65, 149, 220–222,
    231
Federalism. See also Founding principles
    czars and, 132
    stimulus bill and, 133–135
Feinstein, Dianne, 112
Financial crisis:
    bailouts and, xiii–xxi, 47–50
    expansion of government and, 39–40
    housing and, 36, 42–46, 219–222
    origins of, 35–36, 41–47
Finegan, Ben and Bree, 216
Fiscal irresponsibility, 101–117
    bailouts, 104–110
    cash for clunkers, 110–115
    income redistribution, 101–104
    job savings, 115–117
    tea party rejection of, 217–218, 240–241

Fletcher, Dan, 120–121
Flynn, Sean Masaki, 241–242
Founding principles. *See also* Federalism
    drift away from, 21–22
    tea parties and, 39–40, 207–208,
       229–232
Fowler, Mark, 118
Frank, Barney, 135–136, 220–222
Fraud:
    ACORN and voter registrations,
       145–146
    in stimulus spending, 108–110
Freddie Mac, 2, 44–46, 47, 65, 149, 220–222,
    231
Fredosso, David, 106
FreedomWorks, 80–81, 205–206, 237,
    245–246
Free-market capitalism, recent skepticism
    regarding, 2–4
Free speech, 137
Freire, J. P., 4, 6–7, 9, 10, 12

Garofalo, Janeane, 67, 89–93
Garrett, Major, 101
Gates, Henry Louis, Jr., 228
Geithner, Timothy, 87, 136
Gergen, David, 87–88
Gerrard, Michael, 112
Gibbs, Robert, 51–54, 101, 185, 194
Giles, Hannah, 146, 148
Gingrich, Newt, 9, 28–32
Giuliani, Rudy, 23, 28
Gladney, Kenneth, 92
Global warming, 111, 122–125
Gore, Al, 33, 65, 79, 122–125, 247
Government-sponsored enterprises (GSEs).
    See Fannie Mae; Freddie Mac
Greenspan, Alan, 45
Groves, Robert, 147

Hannity, Sean, 19, 97
Health care reform, Clinton administration
    plans for, 29, 182–183
Health care reform, Obama administration
    plans for, 81, 175–201, 251–252
    expansion of government and,
       137–138
    free-market proposals for, 176–177,
       181–182, 197–199

    government reactions to public questions
       about, 184–196
    single-payer government proposals,
       177–181, 182–184, 196–197, 199–201
Hedge funds, regulation of, 238–239
Hill, Dr. Brian, 190–191
Hillman, Lisa, 126
Hoenig, Jonathan, 238–239
Hoffa, Jimmy, 157
Holder, Eric, 228
Hollinger, Joe, 206
Homeland Security, Department of, 54–61
Housing policies, financial crisis and, 36,
    42–46, 219–222
Hoyer, Steny, 106, 189
Huffington Post, 196

Illinois, activism in, 253–254
Income redistribution, 101–104, 217–218
Interest rates, financial crisis and, 43–44
International Longshore and Warehouse
    Union (ILWU), 163–165
Irvine, Martha, 162

Javaid, Mohammed, 106
Jindal, Bobby, 39, 134
Job "saving," 115–117
Jones, Van, 149
Joseph, Peggy, 230

Kasich, John, 32
Kerpen, Phil, 205–206, 245
Kerry, John, 120
Kest, Jon, 147
Kest, Steven, 147
Kinsley, Michael, 193
Kristol, William, 29
Krugman, Paul, 58, 65, 79–81

LaHood, Ray, 110–111, 114
Lassiter, Mark, 110
Lehr, Jay, 124
Lewis, John L., 165
Liberal groups, financial supporters of,
    62–63
Libertarians, 34, 38
Liberty Leaders, 254
Liggett, Heather, 210

Lindsey, Gary C., 162
Lindzen, Dr. Richard, 125
Litan, Robert, 42–43
Livingston, Bob, 31–32
Lockhart, James, 136
Lund, John, 172

Mackey, John, 197–199
Maddow, Rachel, 25, 67, 82–85, 97
Malkin, Michele, 11, 196
Markamn, Joe, 238
Maughan, Chad, 162
McCaffrey, Shannon, 216
McCain, John, 23, 33, 37, 85, 100, 240
McCaskill, Claire, 187
McClellan, John L., 157
McGurn, William, 117
McInturff, William, 201
McTague, Jim, 126
Media, 73–98
  coverage of Republican Party, 73–74,
    79–80
  coverage of tax day tea parties, 18–19,
    75–81
  coverage of Washington DC tea party, 12,
    74–75
  Fairness Doctrine and, 118–121
  liberal bias of, 73–74
  racism slurs about tea parties, 84, 88–89
  sexual slurs about tea parties, 82–88
  tips for working with, 243–244
  viewership numbers, 94–98
Medicare/Medicaid, 65, 66, 177, 178,
    179–181, 184, 197
Mediocrity ethic, rejection of, 231–233,
    241–242
Mehlman, Ken, 34
Miller, Dennis, 76
Mises, Ludwig von, 41
Mitchell, Dan, 45–46
Moran, Jim, 191
Moses, Herb, 221
MSNBC, 82–87, 91, 95–97
Muggeridge, Malcolm, 3

Napolitano, Andrew, 185
Napolitano, Janet, 57, 59, 60
Nethercutt, George, 32
Nickel, Jean, 209

Nixon, Richard, 132, 185
Nonpartisanship, of tea party movement,
    16–17, 208–210
Noonan, Peggy, 37, 188, 194
Norquist, Grover, 208
Novak, Robert, 27, 32

Obama, Barack:
  Alinsky and, 143, 144
  approval ratings of, 236, 237
  background of, 227–228
  class warfare and, 225–226
  as community organizer, 63, 67, 81, 129
  contributions to, 222
  economic policies of, 101–117
  election of 2008 and, 23–24, 36–37
  expansion of government and, 4, 39
  health care reform and, 178–179, 182–183,
    192, 193, 251–252
  job "saving" and, 115–117
  media coverage of, 78
  reactions to tea parties, 51–54, 64–68
  taxes and, 86–87, 89
  transformation of U.S., 100–101
Odom, Eric, 15, 16–17, 69
Office of Labor-Management Standards
    (OLMS), 171–173
Oistad, Leon, 149
O'Keefe, James, 146, 148
Olbermann, Keith, 67, 88–93, 97
O'Reilly, Bill, 97, 220–221

Palin, Sarah, 247
Parable of the Broken Window, 113
Parris, Alan, 106
Parris, John, 106
Partisanship, tea party movement's avoidance
    of, 16–17, 208–210
Paul, Ron, 38, 68, 100
Pelosi, Nancy, 51, 62, 120, 122, 189
Pence, Mike, 70–71, 120
Peraica, Tony, 252
Perry, Rick, 39
Personal responsibility, 219–223
Phillips, Macon, 184
Physicians, health care reform and, 190–191
Political class, reactions to tea parties:
  government agencies, 54–61
  left-leaning, 51, 62–64